Thousands of working-class women joined the Labour Party and Co-operative Movement in the two decades after women won the right to vote in 1918. This book is about their struggle to find a place in the male world of organized labour politics. In the twenties, labour women challenged male leaders to give them separate, but equal status. When male leaders rejected this, labour women abandoned their claim for 'women power' for the sake of unity in the struggle against unemployment and fascism. For most labour women, dedication to the class cause far outweighed their desire for power. This class loyalty also influenced their relations with the middle-class feminists in the post-suffrage years. Despite common reform agendas, labour women rejected a working alliance with feminists on the grounds that 'leisured' women could have no understanding of the problems of the poor.

Using oral and questionnaire testimony, *Labour Women* offers a group portrait of grass-roots activists from the interwar period (men as well as women), examining their early family lives, schooling and work experience for clues to gender differences in their political ideas. It contrasts labour women's failure to win policy-making power in the national organizations with their considerable achievements in community politics, poor law administration and municipal government.

LABOUR WOMEN

LABOUR WOMEN

Women in British Working-Class Politics 1918–1939

PAMELA M. GRAVES

CAMBRIDGE
UNIVERSITY PRESS

Published by the Press Syndicate of the University of Cambridge
The Pitt Building, Trumpington Street, Cambridge CB2 IRP
40 West 20th Street, New York, NY 10011–4211, USA
10 Stamford Road, Oakleigh, Melbourne 3166, Australia

© Cambridge University Press 1994

First published 1994

Printed in Great Britain at the University Press, Cambridge

A catalogue record for this book is available from the British Library

Library of Congress cataloguing in publication data

Graves, Pamela M.
    Labour women: women in British working-class politics, 1918–1939
    Pamela M. Graves.
        p.   cm.
    Includes bibliographical references and index.
    ISBN 0 521 41247 1
    1.   Working class women – Great Britain – Political activity – 20th
century. 2.   Labour Party (Great Britain) – History – 20th century.
3. Great Britain – Politics and government – 20th century.   I. Title.
HQ1236.5.G7G73   1994
305.42'0941 – dc20   93-15079 CIP

ISBN 0 521 41247 1 hardback
ISBN 0 521 45919 2 paperback

TAG

To all the women who have given years of service in the cause of working-class politics — not with thanks but in recognition

Contents

Illustrations

xi

Acknowledgements

The idea for this study came from some brief comments Sally Alexander made in History Workshop in the spring of 1982. She drew attention to the large numbers of women who joined Women's Co-operative Guild branches and Labour Party women's sections in Britain after the first female suffrage grant of 1918. She went on to point out how little we know about them and to speculate that labour women activists may have had 'a different relationship to socialist or labour politics than men'. Her comments stimulated my interest in the first generation of organized labour women and made me eager to give them the opportunity to add their voices to the historical record.

I owe my method of research to Jill Liddington and the late Jill Norris. Liddington and Norris provided the model when they set out to bring to light the forgotten working-class radical suffragists in late nineteenth-century Lancashire cotton towns. They combined interviews with the suffragists' surviving relatives and supporting evidence from local newspaper reports and public records. I reasoned that my task would be easier because I was dealing with a later generation and could interview my subjects directly. As well as suggesting a method of research, Liddington and Norris' work offered insight into one of the themes of the book – how organized working-class women worked as political activists with 'one hand tied behind them'. The handicap was both practical and cultural. They had to fit their politics around the heavy demands of being working-class wage-workers, housewives and mothers, and they had to act within the constraints of a culture which questioned their right to participate in political life at all. I wanted to see if labour women faced the same barriers in the interwar years and how far they were able to overcome them.

I want to acknowledge an intellectual debt to Edward and

Dorothy Thompson. When I returned to the classroom after a fifteen year absence, the man who walked into the Cathedral of Learning in Pittsburgh to talk about hunters in Windsor Forest was Edward Thompson. His classes were my first academic experience of the history of working people and class struggle and they came to me with all the force of a revelation. I attribute to him the principles that I have tried to use in writing this book: respect for the values and choices made by people of earlier generations and recognition that non-elites, including working-class women, were not passive victims of circumstance, but active agents in the making of their own history. I owe a similar debt to Dorothy Thompson who guided me through my MA research paper on Victorian domestic servants and found time to offer suggestions on this manuscript.

At the University of Pittsburgh Maurine Greenwald has given generously of her time, insight into women's history and personal support. She encouraged me to keep to a timetable which enabled me to finish first the dissertation, then the book. Joe White contributed inspiration and guidance drawn from his years of research and teaching in the field of British social democratic politics. Seymour Drescher pointed out murky areas of the text. Steve Sapolski passed on information about relevant secondary literature from his own wide-ranging historical interests and extensive reading. I am grateful to them all.

My warmest thanks go to friends and relatives in England who made it possible for me to conduct some of my research from across the Atlantic. I want to mention two in particular. My friend Winifred Blay, a Labour Party activist herself, put me in touch with many of the respondents for the study from the Liverpool area and elsewhere, and my cousin, Margot Howard, did the same for the Midlands region around Birmingham and Warwick. They put advertisements in local papers and public libraries on my behalf and helped support the Royal Mail with the volume of their letters and enclosures sent to Pittsburgh. I could not have managed without them. I must add a thank-you to two local history groups – sadly no longer funded – the People's History of Tottenham and the Bradford History Recording Unit, who provided transcripts of taped interviews they had made with labour activists in the late seventies. John Rowley, a local historian from Wolverhampton did the same. Stephen Bird, the Labour Party archivist and a host of librarians and local Labour Party men and women also helped me with my research.

I want to thank my husband, Michael and my children, Nancy, Katy, William and Rachel, who did far more than suffer my preoccupation. The book was a rite of passage for us all. Apart from going back to university, it was my first major independent project as a wife and mother. I learnt to relax my vigilance over my children's lives and they became supportive adults in their relations with me. I guarded the book jealously as a symbol of my independent life for most of the period of writing but just before publication, I decided to ask my husband to give it a 'layman's' opinion. I wanted to be sure that the text was accessible to people other than academic historians. He performed his task admirably, pointing out sections where the argument seemed illogical or obtuse, and expressing enthusiastic admiration for the women activists who are the subjects of the study. His only criticism was that my judicious tone sometimes failed to emphasize strongly enough the remarkable contribution they had made.

I hope this is not the case because my final acknowledgement goes to my respondents, the women and men who were active in working-class politics in the twenties and thirties. They answered my questionnaires and some invited me into their homes to conduct interviews. They were all, without exception, courteous and helpful, often providing me with additional information in follow-up letters and other material sent at their own expense. It is hard to single out individuals but I must mention Nina Drongin from Chatham who taught me a great deal about women's work in the Communist Party and the Women's Co-operative Guild and offered me hospitality on several occasions. These respondents provided the major motivating force for the book. Whenever my enthusiasm ebbed, I would listen to a taped interview, read a letter or questionaire and know at once what I was writing for and about. I hope I have done them justice and made sure that their contribution to British social democracy is recognized.

Abbreviations

ALRA	Abortion Law Reform Association
CPGB	Communist Party of Great Britain
CLP	Constituency Labour Party
CU	Co-operative Union
CWS	Co-operative Wholesale Society
DLP	District Labour Party
ILP	Independent Labour Party
ILO	International Labour Organization
LCC	London County Council
NAC	National Administrative Council (ILP)
NCL	National Consumers' League (USA)
NCLC	National Council of Labour Colleges
NCLW	National Conference of Labour Women
NCW	National Council of Women
NEC	National Executive Committee (Labour Party)
NUDAW	National Union of Distributive and Allied Workers
NUSEC	National Union of Societies for Equal Citizenship
NUWM	National Unemployed Workers' Movement
NUWSS	National Union of Women's Suffrage Societies
NWP	National Women's Party (USA)
ODC	Open Door Council
PAC	Public Assistance Committee
RWG	Railway Women's Guild
SJC	Standing Joint Committee of Industrial Women's Organizations
TUC	Trades Union Congress
WBCG	Workers' Birth Control Group
WCA	Women Citizens Association
WCG	Women's Co-operative Guild
WEA	Workers' Education Association

WLA	Women's Liberal Association
WLF	Women's Liberal Federation
WLL	Women's Labour League
WNC	War Emergency Workers' National Committee
WS	Women's Section
WTUL	Women's Trade Union League

Introduction

An equivalent to the nineteen-twenties music hall quip: 'What did you do in the war, Daddy?' might have been: 'What did you do when you got the vote, Mummy?' Thousands of working-class mothers could have replied that they had joined up right away. In the decade following the first female suffrage grant of 1918, working-class women surged into the Labour Party and the Co-operative Movement as if they had been waiting for the doors to open.[1] By 1922, after only four years recruitment, one hundred thousand women had joined the women's sections of local Labour parties and another thirty-five thousand, the Women's Co-operative Guild. Most of the new members were married women with household and family responsibilities. Their mass mobilization surprised even the men of their own movement and confounded those who argued that working-class housewives were not amenable to political organization.

A sense of optimism and evangelical fervour pervaded the British labour movement in the years immediately following the First World War. In such an atmosphere, new women members were not inclined to question the sincerity of the Labour Party's commitment to 'the equality of the sexes.' They expected to join the fight for class justice on equal terms with their male comrades. Some had higher expectations. They were convinced that as women, they would transform the movement, replacing male politics-as-usual with 'something greater and more uplifting for the whole of humanity.'[2] But as the decade progressed, it became clear that they lacked the necessary power to achieve an equal partnership, let alone a feminine transformation. Throughout the interwar period, with the exception of a few 'notables', women remained outside positions of policy-making power in both the Labour Party and the Co-operative Movement. They had only token representation on the national executive committees. No more than a handful were elected as delegates to annual conferences where male trade unionists and co-operators continued to decide on matters of policy. Only nine women became Labour Members of Parliament in the twenty-year period between the wars.[3]

Women's absence from the national power structures no doubt explains why historians have overlooked their mass mobilization and ignored any contribution they may have made to interwar social democracy. Even the histories of the Labour Party and the Co-operative Movement have little to say about women's political activities once they had won the vote.[4] The thousands of women members, it seems, disappeared without a trace into national organizations run by men. The silence implies that labour women were either so similar to their male comrades in their political ideas and activities that they merged unnoticed into their ranks or so different that they were unable to find an accepted place in the mainstream movement.

This book is intended to rescue the interwar generation of labour women from historical anonymity and discover how their mobilization affected the development of British social democracy in its formative years. Since women were not well represented in the national leadership and the traditional arenas of power politics, the book explores their contribution from a number of different perspectives. At the national level, women's membership made gender an issue in the Labour Party and Co-operative Movement, stimulating protracted debates between women and the male leadership over policy concerns and power. A parallel conflict developed between labour women and middle-class feminists in which class and political differences were at issue. The book argues that by challenging both the patriarchal party and organized feminists, labour women helped define the agendas and set the parameters of interwar working-class politics.

A second area of focus is local labour politics and municipal government. Labour Party histories have generally ignored the local constitutencies outside the context of elections and have treated local government as a separate and peripheral area of party politics. A study of labour women inevitably puts the emphasis on local organizations because most women made their political contribution close to home. Local conditions varied widely, but a strong case can be made that in the interwar years, vigorous constituency organization and the strong reform record of Labour councillors did more than the party's brief and unsatisfactory periods in power to win a solid core of working-class support for Labour. This study argues that labour women were an integral part of this grass-roots achievement.

The book places labour women's political activities in a broader context than internal party affairs, one that includes their working-class families and neighbourhoods and a range of issues of concern to working people in the turbulent interwar years, from birth control and married women's right to work, to unemployment and the Means Test. Labour organization records all too often give the impression of self-sufficient male clubs remote from the changing needs and aspirations of their working-class members. Labour women's position outside the closed ranks of power enabled them to avoid some of this isolation. They were highly responsive to rising levels of distress among working-class families, changing their policies and tactics to meet what they saw as the most urgent problems. Their reform agendas recognized a growing working-class acceptance of state responsibility for social welfare in the years after the First World War. Above all, their speeches and policy decisions were a barometer of shifting opinions on women's place as workers and citizens in interwar British society.

METHOD

The guiding principle of the study was to allow the working -class women who were active in interwar labour politics to speak for themselves. Fifty talked or wrote about their experiences in interviews and questionnaires while others spoke through contemporary letters and speeches. To put women's views into a comparative perspective, the same number of male activists from this period provided similar information. All the respondents described their early lives, how they came to be interested in labour politics, their reform priorities and what they felt they had accomplished. They came from many different towns and cities across England with concentrations in the textile areas of Lancashire and Yorkshire, the docklands of Liverpool and North Kent, and the North London area around Tottenham.[5]

Despite their regional and occupational diversity, the respondents had a wide area of common experience. They were overwhelmingly working class at a time of considerable homogeneity in working-class culture. A majority came from families where one or both parents had an interest in socialism and they had been comrades in the rank-

and-file of the interwar political labour movement. Most had devoted a lifetime to the cause, maintaining their dedication through years of mundane political work and the fading hope of living to see the co-operative commonwealth. Their testimony transformed faceless statistics and generalities into individual personalities and served as a point of reference for national organization and government records, local minutes and newspaper reports.

At least seventy per cent of the activists were members of the Labour Party which is the primary focus of the study. Another twenty per cent were co-operators and the work includes frequent references to the Women's Co-operative Guild, the Co-operative Union – the governing body of the movement – and the Co-operative Party formed in 1918. About ten per cent of men and women belonged to the small Independent Labour Party and the even smaller Communist Party of Great Britain. Until the mid-twenties, labour activists made little distinction between these organizations, seeing them as different branches of the socialist family. Joint membership in two or more was common until the Labour Party banned communists from its ranks in 1925 and the ILP disaffiliated from the Labour Party in 1932. Even then, the Women's Co-operative Guild continued to allow communist members. Because of this fluid membership, the term 'labour women' as it is used in the text, applies to women in any branch of organized labour politics. When only women in the Labour Party are meant, 'Labour' is capitalized.

The chapters are arranged more or less chronologically. The first covers the immediate post-suffrage years when labour women negotiated the terms of women's membership in the Labour Party and Co-operative Movement. The second offers a comparative biographical profile of the first generation of labour women activists and their male comrades. The two central chapters trace the gender struggles over power and policy in the Labour Party after 1921 and the parallel class tensions between labour women and middle-class feminists. Chapter 5 contrasts women's lack of success at the national level with their considerable achievements in local politics and government. The last chapter analyses the reasons for labour women's abrupt change of strategy in the thirties which moved them towards closer integration of the male-dominated movement and ended their struggle to secure gender equality in working-class politics.

CHAPTER I

' The doors are open' — women's entry into labour politics, 1918–1921

The timing of women's formal admission into the Labour Party and the Co-operative Movement could hardly have been more promising. The years from 1917 to 1920 were a rare period of unity, strength and optimism in the British labour movement. The First World War helped unite a disparate working class behind a shared resentment of profiteers and the class 'inequality of sacrifice'. Trade union membership for men and women was at an all-time high as the unions resumed their prewar militancy in a barrage of strikes.[1] In politics, the Labour Party was rapidly displacing the divided Liberals as *the* working-class party and the main opposition to the Conservatives. If only at the rhetorical level, the links between socialism and feminism were closer than they would be for another half century. All this, and the socialist victory in Russia, convinced British social democrats that the time was ripe for fundamental social and political change which would include new opportunities for women.

Women helped their own cause by participating to an unprecedented degree in labour's postwar resurgence. Until the war, working-class women were essentially outside the body politic and on the fringes of the labour movement. The wartime state drew them in by making them vital to the war effort as a replacement labour force and as consumers.[2] It exposed many more of them to class confrontations with bosses, landlords, food profiteers and government bureaucrats. For a growing number of working-class women, these new experiences were a source of self-confidence and political awareness. They, in turn, encouraged their fellow workers and neighbours into the streets in numerous public protests ranging from industrial and rent strikes to peace marches and right-to-work demonstrations.[3]

The first suffrage grant to women in 1918 recognized their new status in the public life of the nation. It was the vote, not the war or

women's militancy, that persuaded the male leaders in the Labour
Party and the Co-operative Union to open their doors to women
members. The Labour Party rewrote its constitution in 1918 to
provide, 'special facilities to the prospective women electors to join
our ranks'.[4] The labour press exploded with pamphlets and articles
designed to woo the new women voters. Labour's leaders promised
women an equal partnership in the party and support for their full
political and economic emancipation.[5] Working-class women, most
of them housewives, responded to these promises with enthusiasm.
Between 1918 and 1920 they joined the Labour Party in their
thousands, helping to create the local network of constituency
parties. Lily Watson of North Shields spoke for many when she gave
her reason for joining in 1920: 'The Labour Party, I believe, stands
for the comradeship of the sexes.'[6]

In such an atmosphere of optimism and unprecedented attention
to their sex, the members of the prewar labour women's organizations, the Women's Labour League and the Women's Co-operative
Guild could be excused for thinking that women were about to take
their place as equals in labour politics. From a subordinate position
outside the movement they expected to move to the very centre of
labour's political activity to stand shoulder to shoulder with men. Yet
when the negotiations with the Labour Party and the Co-operative
Union were over, they found that their position fell far short of
equality, however defined. They were neither integrated and equal
nor separate-but-equal. Decision-making power remained firmly in
the hands of those who already held it, the trade union majority in
the Labour Party and male co-operators. Women's Labour League
and Guild members had accepted conditions that virtually ensured
the continuation of a marginal position in national labour politics for
themselves and future generations of women.

The formal relations between men and women in labour politics
thus began with a wide gap between rhetoric and reality, expectation
and outcome. There were many reasons for the failure of the 1918
merger to live up to the equality hyperbole surrounding it, but three
in particular merit attention. The first was the influence on the
negotiators of a prewar and wartime legacy of largely separate
organization for women in a movement dominated by men. The
second was the tendency for both sexes to overestimate the electoral
impact of the women's vote. Thirdly, League women in particular,
discovered their gender interests in conflict with their strong sense of

class loyalty. They divided over whether they wanted full integration or separate gender status in the Labour Party and were so eager to show their solidarity with labour's postwar struggles that they hesitated to insist on constitutional provisions that would allow for gender equality.

THE LEGACY

The optimism generated by labour's resurgence and the female franchise persuaded Labour Party and Co-operative men to open their doors to women members, but when it came to negotiating the terms, both sides took as a frame of reference their experience in prewar and wartime labour politics. The history on which they both drew was one of separate organization, a marked imbalance of power in favour of men and differences in political priorities and strategies that on more than one occasion had erupted into open conflict.

Before 1918, women were not so much late-comers as uninvited guests in mainstream labour politics. Conditions of membership kept the Co-operative Movement and the Labour Party overwhelmingly male. Male heads of households held the family membership in the local co-operative societies and membership in the Labour Party was only possible through an affiliated trade union or socialist society. Both organizations spoke primarily for the interests of workers in craft and industrial unions in which women, even textile workers, had only minimal representation.[7] The Independent Labour Party (ILP) was the exception in welcoming women into its ranks but it was a comparatively small, regional organization with a reputation for attracting 'intellectuals' which intimidated many working-class women.

With such limited access to the men's organizations, the women who were eager to join their husbands or brothers in the struggle to improve the conditions of their class, had little choice but to form separate organizations. Neither the Co-operative Union nor the Labour Party showed any interest in sponsoring a women's side to their movement, so the would-be activists had to look elsewhere for guidance. They found it among educated middle-class women who were already active in their local communities as women's trade union organizers, suffragists, poor law guardians or temperance advocates. At the turn of the century, many of these reformers were socialists, committed to improving conditions at work and at home for their working-class sisters.[8] They endorsed working women's claim for 'women's voices to be heard' in the local co-operatives which they supported as family shoppers and in the Labour Party where they could press for social reforms in the interests of all working-class women and their children.

The prewar Guild and the League shared the same socialist goals as the male-dominated movement but they developed a distinct political philosophy, agendas and strategies. In a culture and a movement that put politics firmly in the male sphere, labour women sought to justify their 'intrusion' in terms of their own traditional sphere of influence – the home and family. Guild and League leaders argued that women's experience as working-class wives and mothers qualified them to make a unique contribution to working-class politics. The Guild's General Secretary, Margaret Llewelyn Davies, claimed that just by shopping in the co-operative store, women were helping to build the co-operative commonwealth. 'Every bar of soap, every pair of boots bought ... is helping to break down capitalism and to destroy autocracy and profit-making in industry.'[9] Marion Phillips of the League explained that although men and women in the Labour Party had essentially the same interests, women could offer greater insight into social problems that concerned 'home life, the nurture of the young, the care of the sick and weakly, the planning of the dwelling itself'.[10] Pioneer working-class members were reassured to discover that their skills as care-givers and household managers were also valuable political skills which they could use to help their neighbours and themselves.

The decision, part tactical necessity and part choice, to emphasize women's 'special contribution' to working-class politics meant that Guild and League agendas concentrated on women-centred social reforms. Margaret Llewelyn Davies envisioned the Guild as a form of trade union for married women who shared the bond of wage-spending rather than wage-earning. Just as trade unions were concerned with the rights of workers and their conditions of work, so the Guild would struggle to secure for married women the right to a safe maternity, protection for the health and welfare of their children, an affordable and accessible divorce and security in widowhood and old age.[11] After 1904, she added suffrage, arguing that the vote would give working-class women the power they needed to achieve their reform programme. The League adopted a very similar agenda. Describing the achievements of 1913, the Annual Conference Report noted: 'We may say that much of the attention given in late years to the condition of children is our work. We have ... directed attention to the need of feeding in the schools ... We have spoken and agitated about the medical needs of children.'[12]

The experience of the First World War confirmed Guild and League members in their women-centred approach to labour politics. The war's insatiable demand for cannon fodder focused national attention on those who produced and reared the nation's soldiers, creating a favourable environment in which to push ahead with the campaign to improve maternity and child care services which the Guild had launched in 1913. Labour women found that as representatives of the interests of working-class women, they gained access to national and local wartime committees.[13] The government consulted them on a whole range of issues from separation allowances paid to soldiers' dependents and training schemes for women war workers, to rents, household thrift, food prices and rationing. The War Emergency Workers' National Committee (WNC), an all-inclusive labour/socialist body, worked far more closely with organized labour women than either the Co-operative Movement or the Labour Party, supporting them in their campaigns to increase separation allowances and fight the reinstatement of the Contagious Diseases Act.[14] At the end of the war, the Guild and the League had achieved public recognition and considerable success directly as a result of representing the interests of working-class women.

League and Guild women also developed their own political strategies in the period before 1918. Lacking the support of the male organizations, they found allies among other women's groups. The successful women's trade unions, the National Federation of Women Workers (NFWW) and the Women's Trade Union League (WTUL), as well as the Railway Women's Guild (RWG) were vigorous allies in the campaigns to end women's sweated labour and improve conditions of maternity and child care.[15] During the war, all these organizations joined together to form the Standing Joint Committee of Industrial Women's Organizations (SJC) to ensure that working-class women had fair representation on all government committees of interest to them. In the case of divorce law reform and suffrage, the group of allies expanded to include mostly middle-class women's organizations such as the Women's Liberal Federation and the National Union of Women's Suffrage Societies (NUWSS).[16] Guild and League women were no more able to work through

organized labour than the suffragists, so they followed a similar
strategy and appealed directly to national and local government
agencies – writing letters and petitions, lobbying members of Parliament and local councillors, holding public meetings, marching
and demonstrating.

By 1918, a pattern of political labour organization had developed
in which men and women pursued their common goals along
different, sometimes divergent, paths. Men had no reason to justify
their political activities in gender terms since they were the dominant
group. They assumed that their reform agendas, which in this period
focused on factory and minimum wage legislation, the legal rights of
trade unions, the use of the general strike and nationalisation of
industry, were the essence of labour politics, not primarily male
concerns within a male environment. Where women's political
activities looked outward to the poverty in working-class communities, to other organized women and the state, much of men's
time was spent on internal policy struggles. Male co-operators
concentrated on problems associated with running the co-operative
manufacturing and retail businesses, while the Labour Party devoted
its energies to questions of industrial versus parliamentary action, the
electoral alliance with the Liberals and the perennial tensions
between socialists and trade unionists.

Gender segregation in labour politics before 1918 allowed for some
interaction between the sexes but it tended to be one-sided. Guild
and League women supported their local co-operative societies and
labour organizations by fundraising, organizing social events and
helping with election campaigns. League branch reports contain
many entries like this one from Woolwich in 1912: 'In connection
with the work of the local Labour Party much quiet work has been
done. Four by-elections for Guardians, Borough Council and LCC
[London County Council] have been fought during 1911 and
towards the close of the year twenty three pounds and ten shillings
was paid over to the funds of the Woolwich Labour Party through the
efforts of some of the members of the branch by bazaar work.'[17]
Every year, the Labour Party leader acknowledged this 'quiet work'
in an effusive speech of gratitude. In 1914, Ramsey MacDonald said:
'If the Labour Party lies under a deep debt of gratitude to anyone, it
is to our women workers who have given their best energies to our
party and our movement.'[18]

Labour leaders withdrew the 'debt of gratitude' when labour

women pursued independent policies which appeared to challenge male authority in the movement or in the home. The years before and during the First World War were marked by considerable gender tension over such policies especially among co-operators. Male co-operative leaders opposed the Guild's political programme of social reforms. They argued that political activities distracted members from the true purpose of the movement – the protection of working-class living standards through the dividend. Margaret Llewelyn Davies pointed out that 'citizenship' work enhanced Guild members' ability to understand the social value of retail co-operation. She warned the Co-operative Union Board, that the growing power of the state to enter 'the home, the factory and the store' made it imperative that the Co-operative Movement become involved in national politics. Otherwise the interests of co-operators would be overwhelmed by the political power of the 'profit making sectors of the community'.[19] It did not improve gender relations that she was proved right when the state attempted to tax the co-operative dividend during the war.

Divorce law reform sparked this debate over ends and means in the co-operative movement.[20] The Guild was an enthusiastic advocate of this reform because the existing laws discriminated against working-class women on the basis of both their gender and their class. While a husband could obtain a divorce on evidence of a wife's adultery alone, the wife was obliged to prove cruelty or abandonment in addition to her husband's infidelity. Added to this injustice, the high cost of divorce made it inaccessible to all but the better-off among the working class. Despite a large Roman Catholic membership in some areas, a majority of Guild branches endorsed equality for men and women before the law and sixty per cent called for the more radical measure of divorce by consent.[21]

The members of the Co-operative Union Board objected to the Guild's involvement in divorce law reform. They insisted that divorce was a private and religious matter which had no place in a workers' co-operative movement. Claiming that it would alienate Roman Catholics and split the membership, they ordered the Guild to drop any further action on this contentious issue. The Guild's central committee refused and the following year, 1914, the Board withheld its annual grant and declared that it would not reinstate it unless the Guild agreed to confine its campaigns to issues approved by the Board. The war years were a stalemate as the Guild refused to yield its independence and the Board maintained its ban on financial support.

League leaders, especially Marion Phillips, were far less willing than Margaret Llewelyn Davies to challenge the authority of their parent body, the Labour Party. Their official journal, the *Labour Woman*, avoided criticizing the party and insisted on the myth that League women were valued partners in labour's cause. Nonetheless, their efforts to combine women-centred policies with party loyalty still brought them into conflict with male leaders. In one instance, the League supported the Guild in calling for an amendment to the National Insurance Act of 1911 that would allow maternity benefits to be paid directly to mothers-to-be, rather than their insured husbands. The Labour Party national executive committee members complained that the amendment was a slur on the character of working men since it implied that they would misuse the benefit if it was entrusted to them. Marion Phillips withdrew League support for the amendment at once without consulting the membership.[22] Whatever the outcome of the disagreements between labour men and women, it is clear that the Co-operative Union and the Labour Party assumed the right to control the actions of organized women long before they allowed them to become members.

These prewar conflicts in labour politics were the result of differences between men's and women's policy concerns and power. They were also an indication of tension between the movement's rhetorical commitment to gender equality and cultural values that stressed difference and inequality. The question of women's suffrage brought out this contradiction in a way that left a lasting impression on labour men and women. The issue was one of the most divisive in prewar labour politics and although the split did not fall neatly along gender lines, male and female members recognized the suffrage question as a test of the attitudes of the Labour Party and the entire labour movement, towards women's equality.[23]

Supporters of votes for women within organized labour politics fell into two broad camps – the egalitarians who called for the vote on the same limited terms as men then held it, or might hold it in the future, and the adult suffragists who wanted women to wait until all men had the vote. In 1910, the egalitarians included the Guild, about half of League women, a section of the ILP led by Kier Hardie, labour leaders George Lansbury, Ben Turner, Phillip Snowden and an unknown number of rank-and-file party members. Between

1910 and 1912, opinions changed so that by the later date, the Labour Party, the League and the Guild were united behind adult suffrage. The League /felt that it had scored a significant victory when the Labour Party passed a resolution in 1912 stating that it would oppose any extension of the suffrage that did not include women.

Despite this apparent accord, men and women had different motives for supporting adult suffrage. Labour women recognized very early that they needed the vote to secure their reform measures and give them more power in the wider movement. For the Labour Party's national executive committee, support for adult rather than manhood suffrage was in large measure an electoral calculation influenced not so much by pressure from the League as the prospect of millions of new Labour voters. Votes, not women's rights, were the lure that persuaded the NEC to accept the National Union of Women's Suffrage Societies' offer to raise an Election Fighting Fund to give financial and organizing support to Labour candidates opposing anti-suffrage Liberals.[24]

When deciding on the suffrage issue, Labour Party and ILP leaders had also to take into account the strength of the opposition to women's suffrage within their movement. Much of this opinion was privately expressed at least at the leadership level because of the party's official commitment to women's equality. But Kier Hardie had no illusions about the depth of resentment felt by many labour men over the prospect of women voting. He pointed out: 'The male, even he of the working-class, will not lightly or all at once, part with the authority which has so long been his and admit the wife of his bosom to a political equality with himself.'[25] His friend and comrade Bruce Glasier was a good example of the highly emotional response the issue could invoke. Recalling an ILP executive meeting, he wrote in his diary: 'At last get round to speak with something like scorn of their miserable individualist sexism and virtually tell them that the ILP will not stir a finger more than it has done for all the women suffragettes in creation.'[26] Some rank-and-file labour men evidently shared the view that women's suffrage was a distraction from the real business of socialism. A Bradford ILP man wrote to the *Labour Leader* in April, 1904 to complain that, 'these energetic women seem to aim at shaping the policy of our party so that this question of women's suffrage shall occupy a foremost place therein. This will mean that some of the efforts of our hard workers will have to be turned from other pressing political questions towards realising the vote for women.'[27]

The suffrage issue left deep, but very different impressions on men and women in labour politics. Labour men, especially the leaders, concluded that sexually specific issues, by which they meant women's issues that a significant number of men opposed, were political dynamite. They were much more divisive than ideological disputes between labour men because they threatened the 'natural' order of male control in the home, the workplace and in public life. Party leaders used the term 'sex antagonism' to describe this dangerous state of affairs and it appeared for the first time over the suffrage issue. In the post-suffrage decade, they repeated it as a warning bell whenever women put forward 'controversial' policy issues or demanded more autonomy within the movement.

Organized women learnt quite a different lesson from the suffrage struggle. League leaders heaped praise on the Labour Party for being the only party to give parliamentary support to women's right to citizenship. They seemed to think that the party had responded directly to an appeal by one of their leaders, Margaret Bondfield, asking them to refuse 'to enter their heritage of citizenship and leave out the women'.[28] They interpreted the party's support for adult suffrage and the alliance with the NUWSS as a sign of its firm commitment to women's concerns. Katherine Glasier felt able to say in 1913: 'We know and glory in the fact that we are an integral part of the Labour Party itself, that it is the woman's party as well as the men's and that we have our own special work in it to do.'[29]

The war years did little to diminish the gap in experience and perception between labour men and women. The men's side was deeply divided over support for the war; the ILP opposed it and maintained a pacifist stance; the Labour Party endorsed the war and accepted two positions in the war cabinet. Guild and League women were also officially split, the Guild opposing and the League loyally following the party, but in practice, the women's groups continued to work closely and amicably together.[30] They were able to find common ground in providing help for women in the workforce and at home who were suffering the disruptive effects of war.

Women's wartime labour substitution was another source of tension between men and women in the movement. Among male trade unionists, the war revived old fears that employers – aided this time by the state – would take advantage of women workers, with their tradition of low wages and weak organization, to undermine the structure of skilled wage rates and craft work practices so painstakingly built up over the years. It was primarily with women workers in mind that the Labour Party and the Trades Union Congress (TUC) negotiated the Restoration of Prewar Practices Act to ensure that male workers returning from the war would get their jobs back at prewar rates.[31] While labour men fought to maintain what was in effect the family wage system, Guild and League leaders saw women's wartime wage work as an opportunity to gain some long-term advantages that would improve women's economic status and ultimately raise general working-class living standards. They called for equal pay and a concerted effort to bring women workers into trade unions. The incompatibility of these two points of view put a further strain on gender relations in the political movement.

Like women's suffrage, the question of women's war-time wage labour revealed how far most labour men and women were in 1918 from accepting the idea of equal rights. Few male trade unionists were willing to recognize women's right to work as equal to their own. Labour women themselves were ambivalent on the question. Many would have agreed with Mrs Mitchell, a founding member of the North Tottenham Labour Party who willingly gave up her wartime job as a booking office clerk at Finchley Road station because: 'It seemed only fair that women who had taken men's jobs during the war, should relinquish them when the men came back.'[32] Others, including several of the middle-class leaders, supported Winifred More who wrote to *Labour Woman* about the male attack on women workers at the end of the war. She said: 'The attack is a general one and works out in plain language thus: "that no woman has a right to earn her bread in industry while any man is out of work."' She argued that the only winners in the scramble for bread between working men and women would be the employers. She called for equal pay and trade union organization to bring women to the same bargaining level as men at which point women would only ask for 'a fair field and no favour'.[33]

It would be unreasonable to expect that all the shared enthusiasm for labour's cause and the equality rhetoric that followed the war and the suffrage grant of 1918 could have overcome the weight of this history of gender separation, unequal power and differences in policy and strategy. Even Kier Hardie and Phillip Snowden, labour's strongest advocates of women's suffrage and equal rights, seem to

have had a clear sense of gender difference. Hardie's highest praise
for ILP women like Enid Stacy, Isabella Ford and Katherine Glasier
who worked so hard for the cause was a reference to their 'motherly
sympathies', while Phillip Snowden spoke in terms reminiscent of
Ruskin, of 'the unsexing and condemning to slavery of what should
have been pure and cultured womanhood'.[34] Some of the middle-
class women leaders used similar language. Ethel Snowden, wrote: 'I
have conceived my own reason for wishing to be in politics to be the
reason of most women possessed of the same desire, that we may
protect, nourish and cherish the life which women give.'[35] No
wonder labour men and women found it difficult to translate the
socialist ideal of sexual equality into political reality.

THE VOTE AT LAST!

The first franchise grant to women in February 1918 promised to
change the unequal relations between men and women in organized
labour politics. For many women suffragists the long-awaited female
franchise was anti-climactic. After fifty years of struggle, the
government gave women the vote as a reward for services rendered
during the war, not in recognition of their equal right to citizenship.
Furthermore the grant fell short of labour women's demands for full
adult suffrage by giving the vote to all males over twenty-one, but
only to most women over thirty.[36] Despite the disappointment of a
partial victory, organized labour women remained convinced that
the vote would dramatically improve their political status and benefit
the working-class as a whole. This optimistic outlook was linked to
uncertainty about the long term political impact of the women's vote.
As long as it was 'that great unknown force' it fired the imagination
and the hopes of labour men and women alike.

League and Guild leaders heralded the vote as the beginning of
working-class women's full integration into political life. They
anticipated a significant increase in women's power nationally
and in labour politics. Margaret Llewelyn Davies explained that
Guild women would find that 'they have suddenly become much
more important and that their views and actions will receive
far greater consideration'.[37] Marion Phillips told League women
that the suffrage grant was 'the great charter of liberties, a promise
of further reform and yet in itself having the possibilities of change

of the most far reaching kind'. She then outlined its political implications:

Women step at one stride into the very centre of political interests. They are from the day on which the [Representation of the People] Act became law, imbued with a power and importance that completely changes their place in the world of politics. No candidate and no party can in the future completely ignore their wishes. ... It would be mere foolishness to pretend that the position of women in the Labour Party was the same when they were voteless as now when they may sway the result of an election.[38]

At last, it seemed that labour women would be able to wield the same kind of political leverage within the mainstream movements as their male counterparts. League and Guild leaders assured their members that now that a large majority of working-class housewives had the vote, they could expect the party and the government to pay more attention to women's special interests in education, housing, maternal and child welfare, widows' pensions, rents and food prices. Mrs. Harrison Bell, a prominent ILP woman, explained to war widows that the vote was going to be their weapon for ' a better life and better opportunities' for themselves and their children.[39]

Margaret Davies and Marion Phillips were careful to point out that women were newcomers to citizenship and must be prepared to learn how to use this valuable new tool. But they assured them that after a brief apprenticeship they could expect the power of the franchise to raise their status as working women. In support of their optimism, they pointed to the women-centred legislation that the suffrage grant brought in its wake: in 1918, the Maternity and Child Welfare Act for which the Guild had campaigned since 1913; in 1919, the Sex Disqualification (Removal) Act which ended the legal restrictions on women, married or single, entering the professions or holding public, civil or judicial office; in 1923, the Matrimonial Causes Act which reformed the divorce laws, another Guild campaign, and in 1925 the Widows' Pensions Act. Although it could well be argued that these reforms owed as much to the war as to the suffrage grant, organized women were convinced that they demon-strated the power of the women's vote. They argued that if a Conservative-dominated government was prepared to concede these reforms to the new female electorate, how much more would be achieved once women had helped bring Labour into office.

Rank-and-file activists expressed some of the same optimism about the likely effects of the vote. Lily Watson who joined the Labour Party in 1918 when she herself was still too young to vote, commented in a 1986 interview: 'The women's vote was most important to me. I thought we would change things for good and all'.[40] In 1921 she had written that she believed the vote would give women the chance to be 'a bigger influence in the world than they have ever been.'[41] Local labour women fervently believed that enfranchised women would bring a new humanitarianism and morality into politics. Mrs Fawcett of the National Federation of Women Workers, for example, replying to Arthur Henderson's suggestion at the 1918 Labour Party conference that women should follow the political example of their trade union husbands, retorted: 'She hoped that they would not. She hoped that women would lead them into something more business-like, something bigger and greater and more uplifting for the whole of humanity than the men had done in the past'.[42]

The response of the male side of the movement to the extension of the suffrage reinforced the sense that the vote would usher in a new era for labour women. Although there was little evidence that previous male suffrage grants had resulted in an immediate or significant increase in the political power of the workers, the Labour Party, the ILP and the newly formed Co-operative Party acted initially as though the female franchise would shift the existing balance of political forces in favour of labour. They made strenuous efforts to recruit the newly enfranchised wives of working men and began to develop programmes and services to appeal to the woman voter. The abrupt appearance of positive gender-conscious rhetoric in the mainstream organization records and the labour press from late 1917 when the Representation of the People Act was certain to pass, makes it clear that the suffrage grant and not the war brought about the change of heart.

At the end of 1917, in anticipation of the women's franchise, the party negotiated with the League for a merger and made provisions in its new constitution for women to become individual members of local constituency parties. At the Annual Conference of 1918, Arthur Henderson, after the now obligatory reference to the 'deep debt of gratitude' that the party owed to 'our women workers who ... without vote and without recognition ... have given ungrudging service', welcomed the newly enfranchised women within the fold of the Labour Party as 'equal partners'. He promised that 'working men and working women standing side by side' would 'move forward unitedly' and 'in sympathetic co-operation' towards a bright labour future.[43]

The party's newspaper, *The Daily Herald*, edited by George Lansbury, a long time supporter of women's rights, epitomized the post-suffrage interest in women's political and labour activities. It is not too much to claim that in the four years of postwar reconstruction, labour women as well as women wage workers received more press coverage from the Herald than at any time before or after. There were full reports of the women's conferences, their election successes, the speeches of women leaders and strikes involving women workers. On the picture page at the back of the paper, organized women and their leaders were shown taking part in local and national marches and demonstrations. The paper's 1919 creed seemed to indicate that women had at last become a recognized part of the labour movement: 'We believe in the unity of interest between the workers and the soldiers ... in the unity of interest between men and women and in the unity of interest between nations.'[44]

In a marked departure from earlier practice, the party went on to incorporate the spirit of its equality rhetoric into policy. Its manifesto for the 1918 general election, *Labour and the New Social Order*, included a lengthy set of resolutions submitted by the Standing Joint Committee of Industrial Women's Organizations (SJC) entitled, 'The Complete Emancipation of Women'. Among the economic provisions were the organization in trade unions of women in all trades in which they were employed, a full enquiry into trades and processes previously considered unhealthy or unsuitable for women with a view to their future employment in such trades, and the universal adoption of the principle of equal pay for equal work. In the area of legal rights, the party committed itself to the immediate extension of the suffrage to all women of twenty-one and over, an end to legal restrictions on the entry of women into the professions on the same terms as men and the inclusion of women on all committees and at all conferences, national or local, dealing with subjects 'not of exclusively male interest'.[45] In 1919, the party introduced a 'Women's Emancipation Bill' based on the legal resolutions into Parliament but it was defeated in the Lords and replaced by the government's Sex Disqualification (Removal) Bill which did not include the equal suffrage clause.

While hardly a revolutionary statement, the 'complete emancipation of women' in combination with the 'equal partners' speech represented a much stronger endorsement of women's economic and civil rights than the party had been prepared to give before the suffrage grant. Furthermore, the party backed its words with actions, giving parliamentary support to the women-centred social welfare legislation of the reconstruction period. It introduced a bill for mothers' pensions and another for nursery schools. It passed resolutions in favour of women's right to be magistrates and jurors and in support of equal pay for teachers and civil servants (though not for industrial or commercial workers). In 1919, the party endorsed the candidacies of at least a hundred Labour women for local councils and three times as many for the boards of guardians.[46] At the parliamentary level, the party's record was less reassuring; only four of the seventeen women who stood in 1918 were Labour and in 1921 the party only endorsed five women candidates. However, in the general election of December 1923 which brought labour to power for the first time as a minority party, Margaret Bondfield, Susan Lawrence and Dorothy Jewson became the first women members of Parliament to be elected in their own right.[47]

Internally, the party gave full coverage to the activities of the women's sections and the national women's conferences in its annual reports, noting each year, women's growth in numbers and political consciousness. By 1919, it had appointed five national women organizers and supported the SJC's efforts to get women representatives on various central and local government committees. To attract the new women voters, the labour press published a series of pamphlets including Marion Phillips' *Women and the Labour Party* and Ethel Snowden's *The Real Women's Party* both of which stressed the party's record of support for female suffrage and its commitment to social reforms in the interests of working-class women.

The Co-operative Union underwent a similar change in rhetoric and policy towards its women members in response to female enfranchisement. Its first act following the grant was to restore financial support to the Guild and thus end the four-year effort to curb its independence. Instead of issuing dark warnings about sex antagonism and complaining about the divisiveness of Guild policy as it had done throughout the war years, it began to stress the unity of interest between male and female co-operators. As with the Labour Party, the Union found itself in need of the goodwill and the votes of Guild women. Worried by the government's wartime threats to tax dividends as profits, it had launched the Co-operative Party to protect its interests in Parliament. Guild support would be needed to deliver the votes of women co-operators and help with recruiting, fundraising and canvassing. Mr Allen, the President of the United Board explained: 'Man has to be freed from the intolerable burden of being a producer of profits for others, and for this tremendous effort every democratic force must march side by side in mutual understanding.'[48] The Co-operative Movement, it seemed, was finally acknowledging the importance of the Guild's political work and offering a parliamentary vehicle for their social reform programme. In return, the Guild pledged that its members would 'go out into the highways and byways and show all married women voters that the Co-operative Party is *the* party for housewives and mothers'.[49]

Women had their first opportunity to exercise the right to vote in the 1918 'coupon election'. The results were disappointing for all those in the labour movement who had expected newly enfranchised working-class women to dramatically increase the Labour vote. The party won only fifty-nine seats at least half of which went to the Miners' Federation. Although there were no gender-specific voting statistics, both the Labour Party and the ILP leaders placed the blame for Labour's poor showing on the lack of education and political awareness of the new women voters. However, rather than diminishing the attention that the political movement paid to women, the election results stimulated further efforts to reach them through propaganda that would appeal to their interests as housewives and mothers.

It was a new experience for working-class women, organized and unorganized, to be wooed by the political labour movement. Until they had the vote, they were the ones who had knocked at the doors of the mainstream organizations asking support for their programmes. The same was true in their relation to the government. Before the war, the Guild and the League had lobbied the various central and local government bodies with perseverance and imagination on behalf of working-class women but their prewar legislative achievement seemed small in comparison with the postsuffrage gains. Labour women had every reason to believe that the vote would transform their political lives, ensuring their future equality in the movement and their effectiveness as social reformers in national politics.

JOINING THE LABOUR PARTY

Women's political weakness in the Labour Party and in labour politics generally in the interwar years originated in the merger of the Women's Labour League and the Labour Party and the terms of the 1918 party constitution. Since labour women were in a better bargaining position after the suffrage grant than at any time in their past, it is worth looking closely at how the conditions of the merger were arrived at, who made the decisions that confirmed them, what ideas Labour Party and League leaders brought to the negotiations and whether the rank-and-file accepted the settlement without protest.

For some time before the end of the war, League women had expressed an interest in becoming an integral part of the Labour Party. In 1915, the League executive committee headed by Mary Longman, sent a letter to the Labour Party stating that the League wanted to be 'regarded not merely as one among a number of societies affiliated to local labour parties but as something much more closely connected, a part of the Labour Party itself'.[50] The main purpose of the letter was to ask the party to increase its grant to the League by a hundred per cent but that does not mean that the expressed desire for a merger was merely a stratagem. The League leadership, had always been loyal to the party, following its lead, glossing over or accommodating differences. Local members often developed a close working relationship with local labour organizations, especially at election times.

The Labour Party did not respond to the League's suggestion of a merger until late in 1917. The timing was significant. By the end of the war, it was clear that the party had increased its strength at the expense of the Liberals and was ready for electoral independence. Party leaders recognized the need to build a local party structure based on individual membership similar to that of the other two major parties. Since the majority of new women voters would not have access to party membership through trade unions, their arrival reinforced the necessity for reorganization. The first step was to bring the League into the party to form the core of local organization for labour women.

The members of the Labour Party's NEC framed the 1918 constitution in light of the existing relationship between the sexes and with the firm intention of preventing the emergence in the party of the kind of 'sex antagonism' that the suffrage issue had raised. Structurally, they decided to keep the gender separation that had characterized labour's political organization since the foundation of the League. League branches became the women's sections of the party with an assured representation of one on the executive committees of the local constitutency parties. Women had the option of joining the party as individual members of their sections and/or their local 'mixed' parties. They also secured a guaranteed four seats out of the initial twenty-three on the National Executive Committee as well as a Chief Woman Officer and a Women's Advisory Committee.

The 1918 constitution treated Labour women as a distinct interest group to the extent of recognizing their desire for separate meetings and guaranteeing them minimal representation on local and national party committees. However, in all areas that involved the power to influence policy-making, it assumed that women members were indistinguishable from their male comrades with whom they would have to compete on 'equal' terms. The most obvious example of this was the election of women representatives to the NEC. The women in the sections would not be able to select their own candidates for this all-important committee nor could they vote for them. This would be the responsibility of the delegates to the annual conferences the vast majority of whom were male trade unionists with powerful block votes. Women would have to compete with men in the unions and in the constituency parties to be chosen as delegates to the conferences.[51] Nor did the constitution make any provision for the Women's Advisory Committee to create policy even in relation to women's concerns. Its functions were restricted to providing information and offering recommendations.

When the League executive committee first discussed the terms of the merger in November 1917, members objected to the 'position with regard to the election of women on the NEC', finding it 'undesirable'.[52] They realized that this provision, combined with the minority representation, would make it unlikely that the 'women's point of view' would carry much weight on the NEC. Marion Phillips who had recently been chosen as Chief Woman Officer, took on the role of propagandist for the new constitution. She argued that women had secured a 'fair share of representation' considering their lack of political experience. Once they had 'proved themselves capable of active work in the party,' then their representation would

increase. In any case, as soon as the women in the party approached
the men in numbers and experience, there would no longer be any
need to discriminate between the sexes in any aspect of party
organization including the election of representatives to the NEC.[53]

This argument clearly implied that the provisions made for women
members in the new constitution were temporary and would be
revised as women gained political experience. There is no evidence to
suggest that the male party leaders on the NEC took this view either
then or later, since they repeatedly refused to concede women's
demands for constitutional changes. Marion Phillips' argument also
introduced the idea that the ultimate goal of the merger was to
eliminate gender distinctions as they pertained to women in the party
and there seems little doubt that this was in the minds of the framers
of the constitution. Although there is no record of a response to these
arguments, they apparently satisfied the critics among the members
of the League executive committee since the question of the inequality
of women's representation did not reappear on their agenda until
1921.

The first official opportunity for the rank-and-file to discuss the
Labour Party's new constitution was at the National Women's
Conference held at Nottingham in January 1918 where in addition to
the League, the Women's Co-operative Guild, the Railway Women's
Guild, the ILP and the women's trade unions were all represented.
The question of the election of the women members to the NEC was
not on the agenda but two other issues show the delegates' initial
responses to the merger. They gave firm support to the resolution
from the League executive asking that provision be made for the
holding of an annual conference of labour women's sections. They
were anxious that women in the Labour Party should have 'an
opportunity of expressing collectively, the women's point of view.'[54]

The delegates also wanted the right to select the members of the
party's Women's Advisory Committee. Evidently, they were concerned that the merger would mean a loss of independence and the
chance for them to pursue their women-centred reforms inside the
movement. On the other hand, they unanimously rejected the
Labour Party's proposal of a lower membership fee for women. The
message of the conference seemed to be that Labour women wanted
to be equal to the men in the movement while continuing to represent
the special interests of their sex. No delegate or group of delegates,
however, questioned the general desirability of the merger. After they

had given it their endorsement, Marion Phillips congratulated them on 'the fine spirit in which they had set aside their natural regrets for their old freedom and independence in their enthusiasm for the heavier responsibilities and the more difficult work which the new constitution sets before them'.[55]

Over the next twelve months, with Marion Phillips as its spokesperson, the party set out to dispel the remaining doubts of organized women and sell its new constitution to the working-class woman voter. In a show of goodwill, the NEC was quick to respond to the demands of the Nottingham Conference. The final draft of the constitution, which was placed before a special party conference held in June 1918, allowed for an annual women's conference to be held 'in conjunction with' that of the entire party. Some weeks later, the party agent announced that the Standing Joint Committee of Industrial Women's Organizations (SJC), whose members were chosen by all the industrial and political organizations of working women with a membership of a thousand or more, would act as its Women's Advisory Committee. Neither concession actually changed the gender balance of power under the constitution but Labour women's demands had been promptly met and, it could be argued, they had not asked for any more significant changes to be made.

Party propaganda emphasized the complete equality of men and women in both its national and local councils under the terms of the new constitution. As the editorial in *Labour Woman* explained: 'Under the changed constitution, men and women alike have the opportunity of direct membership of the party. Both will have a share of the representation on the local executives. Both will have the right to have separate meetings of their respective sections and to conduct special work suitable to their interests.'[56] The somewhat ambiguous slogan for the 1918 election proclaimed: 'Labour stands for no sex in politics.' In the party publication, *Women and the Labour Party*, Marion Phillips argued that if there were any departures from the principle of equality between the sexes in the constitution they were in favour of women since their four seats on the NEC and their representation on local party executives were guaranteed. This bias, she explained, was intended to nurture women's contribution during their political maturation.[57] The propaganda seemed to work very well. Apart from the members of the Railway Women's Guild, who refused to give up their independence and resisted all the efforts of Marion Phillips to draw them into the party, the majority of Labour women appeared to accept the provisions made for them in the new constitution without protest. New working-class women members flocked to join the party – by 1921 there were over 70,000 women in the sections from a base of about 5,000 at the end of the war.[58]

The League's generally positive response to the Labour Party's merger proposals was in sharp contrast to the way the Women's Co-operative Guild handled the issue of its future relations with the Co-operative Union. The Co-operative Union was even more anxious than the Labour Party to avoid a repetition of its prewar and wartime experience of gender antagonism and women's independent political activity. In 1919, the Union suggested that the Guild dissolve its organization and merge with the recently formed men's guilds, hinting at future restrictions on Guild independence as the alternative. With the redoubtable Margaret Llewelyn Davies still at its head, the Guild's answer was predictable. As it had done over the issue of divorce law reform, the Guild made a ringing declaration of resistance: 'The Guild has always stood with uniform determination for its own self-government.' Guild leaders argued that the merger with the men's guilds would negate its purpose of 'raising women to their proper status in the movement ... and securing attention for the reforms needed by them as wives, mothers and housewives'.[59] In the face of such an adamant refusal, the Co-operative Union Board backed down and the Guild continued as a separate organization right up to the present.

Why did Guild members react so differently from League women to a similar merger proposal? The Guild had a longer history of separate existence (since 1883 as opposed to 1906) and was numerically a more significant organization than the League in 1918. It had always been much more independent in its relations with the Co-operative Union than the League had been with the Labour Party. In contrast to Marion Phillips and Margaret Bondfield, who went to great lengths to avoid any suggestion of disagreement with the Labour Party, Margaret Llewelyn Davies had been outspoken in her criticism of co-operative policy and leadership. Guild women's hard struggle for acceptance as active co-operators and the Union's attempt to restrict their political activities by withholding financial support, created a reservoir of bad feeling that undoubtedly reinforced the desire to remain independent.

In spite of the change in the Co-operative Union's rhetoric after the suffrage grant, Guild women soon realized that it was offering little in the way of real power. For example, Guild women had high hopes of a significant role in the Co-operative Party since for decades they had been far more involved in national politics than the rest of the Co-operative Movement, yet the party constitution initially made no provision for Guild women's representation on the new party's executive committee. Guild members noted that they were worse off in this regard than women in the Labour Party. After a year's struggle, the Guild managed to win two seats on the party executive but from then on progress in getting a more equal share for women in the movement was so slow as to appear non-existent. In 1920, of the seventy members on the Central Board of the Union, only three were women. After twenty years of Guild pressure, there was still no woman on the Co-operative Newspaper Board and the Co-operative Party had yet to adopt a woman Parliamentary candidate.[60]

While Labour women seemed to have had faith in the sincerity of the Labour Party's claim to support gender equality, Guild women had no such illusions about the Co-operative Union. Here again, the difference in leadership may have been crucial. Margaret Davies appears, in hindsight, to have had a much more realistic sense of the postwar situation of Labour and Co-operative women than Marion Phillips. She wrote: 'It is always said that there is equality for men and women in the movement. Certainly most of the doors are open. But the seats are full and possession is nine-tenths of the law so that in reality the opportunity is not equal and seats are hard to win.'[61]

Another reason for the different choices that Guild and Labour women made in 1918 was the larger percentage of new recruits among the post-suffrage generation of Labour as compared to Guild women. The Guild already had a substantial membership in 1918 which grew steadily in the postwar years, while the thousands of women recruits to the Labour Party quickly outnumbered the small core of League pioneers. Eager to be part of the workers' movement and hearing Marion Phillips urging acceptance of the party's terms, these recruits were less inclined than Guild women to look beyond the equality rhetoric. They were also more ambiguous and less united than Guild women on the question of what form of sexual equality they wanted as members of the class party.

THE DEBATE OVER WOMEN'S PLACE

Labour Party women went on talking about women's place in the party long after they had become members. There was no formal debate on the question as such but discussion on a number of issues revealed that they had not resolved the fundamental issue of whether they were to be integrated and equal or separate-but-equal. Some of them argued that Labour women should accept the challenge of equal status and submerge their concerns as women in the common goals of the party while others maintained that in spite of shared class interests, women had different needs that would not be addressed by the mainstream movement unless they had some measure of separate organization and power. This issue was not resolved in the period of postwar reconstruction and was to reappear later in the twenties.

The first indication of the difference of opinion occurred at the National Women's Conference in 1919 in a discussion about whether or not there ought to be separate women's sections. According to the chairwoman, organizers had found that 'women's sections were not always welcomed, that the men and the women wished to meet together'. She explained that women already had the option of separate or mixed organization in the local constituencies but the subject generated further discussion. Miss E. H. Howse of the Union of Post Office Workers, felt that 'as no difference was made in the trade unions and the TUC between men and women, so she did not agree that any difference should be made by the Labour Party'. With prescience, she argued that the women's sections and the separate women's conference would strengthen the idea that women's concerns were somehow distinct from those of the mainstream party. As a result, they would not be discussed by the party as a whole and would stand little chance of becoming party policy.

Two other delegates disagreed with her. Mrs More from Birkenhead reported that it was mainly the older, more experienced Labour women who did not want sections. Newer members felt more comfortable learning their political skills among other women than in the presence of men. She warned the conference that if sections were abolished, women might turn to the non-partisan, middle-class women's groups which, in her view, were trying to undermine the Labour Party. Miss Wainwright from Leeds thought it was very important for women to have their own sections and conferences, 'so that they could discuss those questions in which they were interested and with which men had no patience'. Marion Phillips closed the discussion by explaining that the issue was one of political expediency. Separate sections had proved the most effective way of rapidly mobilizing the new women voters into the party. In areas where sections existed, the number of women members was much higher than in those areas without them.[62]

It is hard to tell from the available evidence just how rank-and-file activists divided on the issue. Mrs More may have been right in her view that it was a question of age and experience. Certainly long-term activists, especially those who were also in the ILP, were among the group who felt that gender separation encouraged inequality. Hannah Mitchell, for example, poured scorn on the Labour Party's women's sections which she labelled 'a permanent Social Committee, or Official cake-maker to the Labour Party'. She believed in complete equality and found her 'spiritual home' in the ILP with its 'open membership of both sexes'.[63] Two other prewar ILPers, Emma Sproson of Wolverhampton and Jessie Stephen then in Bermondsey, echoed this sentiment. Both believed that women's goal should be equality with the men in the movement. Selina Cooper, on the other hand, thought it was possible and necessary to combine equality within the Labour Party with special provisions for women members.[64]

Among the postwar generation of activists, the majority clearly chose to join women's sections. In the four years after the 1918 suffrage grant, 650 were formed. Section minutes and interview evidence suggest that women enjoyed their own sections and did not see them as barriers to equality at the local level. Mrs Ford of the South Tottenham Labour Party was typical of many in her enthusiasm for her local section: 'We weren't what you call women's libs but we stood our ground for our own section, you see ... We had very nice women's meetings ... well, the women's meetings were entirely separate from the men's, the men had no jurisdiction in our meetings ... and we used to have some very, very interesting meetings.' Asked about the relationship between men and women in the party just after the war, she answered that they had generally worked well together especially during elections. She insisted that 'there has never been any difference between men and women in the Labour Party'.[65]

Mrs Ford did not seem to be aware of, or perhaps did not

remember, the continuing debate over women's position in the Labour Party in the immediate postwar years. At the 1921 National Conference of Labour Women, for example, the Manchester Women's Advisory Committee whose chief spokeswoman was the prewar suffragist and ILPer, Annot Robinson, resurrected some of the doubts Labour Party women had expressed in the early months about their rights under the 1918 constitution. Mrs Robinson proposed asking the party to make two amendments to that constitution. The first called for the direct election of the four women on the NEC by the women's sections and the divisional labour parties instead of by the trade union-dominated national conference. The second proposed to confine the women's conference to delegates from local labour parties and women's sections and to make it a statutory conference of the Labour Party with the power to submit resolutions for discussion and a vote directly to the annual party conference.

The debate over these proposed amendments showed the same division between the gender 'integrationists' and the 'separatists' that was present in the discussion of the need for women's sections. The main argument of the former was that any attempt to separate the sexes in the party would isolate women in a backwater and leave them with no right to speak on the wide range of issues with which the party as a whole was concerned. As Miss Henning of the Post Office workers warned: 'If they insisted on this sectionalising, they would find that claiming given rights for women as such, they [would be] barred out of the most important issues raised because they were held to concern only men.' Mrs Corner asked her fellow delegates if they were prepared to accept the logical consequences of the Manchester resolution, namely that the women representatives on the NEC should confine themselves to women's issues, that women magistrates should hear only cases involving women and that women jurors should only try cases with women plaintiffs or defendants. Mrs Lave of London felt that the majority of women wanted to be in the Labour Party as representatives of all working people not just of their own sex.

In their counter-arguments, those who urged a separate power structure for women drew the attention of the delegates to the very limited representation Labour women enjoyed under the existing 'equal' terms of the constitution. Mrs Sykes of Bradford asked them to 'look how the matter worked out at present. Everywhere there was a preponderance of men over women candidates. At the last general election, the Labour Party took up a miserable half dozen or so. All the rest of the hundreds of Labour candidates were men.' As long as the trade unions chose the women representatives, women who were outside the unions would continue to have no voice in the party. Mrs Mottram declared that there was 'very much dissatisfaction amongst the women's sections' over women's lack of adequate representation in the party. When a vote was taken, rather surprisingly, in view of the strong arguments presented on the other side, it was the 'separatists' who won. The resolution containing the two amendments was passed and Annot Robinson promised to find a way to place it on the agenda of the national party conference to be held the following month.[66]

As they prepared to take their proposals to the Annual Party Conference, Labour women found sympathetic allies among some of their male comrades in the constituency parties. The constitution was then four years old and its effect on the party power structure was clear. Local parties were aware that because of their inability to compete in numbers with the large industrial unions, they were destined always to be outvoted at the annual conferences. They shared the women's view that they were insufficiently represented at the policy-making level in the party and that their contribution was distinctly undervalued. These common concerns produced mutual support at the 1921 conference and an alliance that continued intermittently throughout the twenties.

Annot Robinson based her case for women to elect their own NEC members to the national party conference, on the argument that the new provision was merely a logical extension of the idea already embodied in separate sections that women had distinct interests. She explained that Labour women, 'wanted the right to feel that when the four women were sitting on the Executive, that the women had had a hand in electing them and that they represented the views of the women'. Applying the leverage of the vote, she said that if the party expected to get women's help at election time, they must show that they trusted them with the responsibility of electing their own representatives. She was asking the conference to give women, 'the right to come in and help shape the policy as it affected the women's question'.[67]

Several male delegates from the constituency parties spoke in support of Annot Robinson's direct election amendment. Mr E. Baker of Lambeth North urged its adoption on the grounds that 'in the local constitutencies, they found that it was the women who gave the greatest [financial] support and therefore they ought to have more representation on the Committee [NEC]'. Mr F. H. Edwards from the Bury Labour Party, commented that 'women in the past had very largely been elected to the NEC because they were prominent and respected members of the trade unions but he thought that women with a precise knowledge of women's questions throughout the country should be elected by the women themselves to the NEC'.[68] In contrast, Labour women's own leaders were among those who firmly opposed the amendment. Margaret Bondfield described it as 'a great mistake and very reactionary' on the grounds that it would divide the party along sex lines.[69] She insisted that if Labour women wanted to be taken seriously as equals in the Party, they must not ask for special privileges.

Undaunted, Mrs Robinson proposed the second amendment to allow the women's conference the power to submit resolutions directly to the whole party conference where delegates could discuss and vote on them. She pointed out the futility of women passing resolutions that never appeared on the party's agenda but were buried and forgotten in reports submitted to the NEC. Once again she stressed the 'women's point of view' and the need for it to be translated into policy. Arthur Henderson rejected the amendment reminding the women that the concession of a separate conference had been intended only to give them a chance to discuss issues of importance to them. Mrs Robinson's proposed conference would not be 'subsidiary to their [the party] conference but independent of it' which was 'very dangerous' because it would encourage sectionalism and destroy labour unity.[70]

In her response to Annot Robinson's proposed amendments, Margaret Bondfield stated categorically that the majority of Labour women did not support them. She chose to ignore the majority decision of the women's conference endorsing the proposed constitutional changes and the many resolutions of support sent in by local sections.[71] Her pronouncement failed to make the issue disappear. Labour women remained divided on the central issue of women's place in the party. Although those who favoured separate power for women gave up their attempts to change the 1918 constitution after Annot Robinson's amendments were lost, the question was raised again by the local constituency parties at the Labour Party Annual Conference in 1922 and by a reconstituted group of Labour women in 1926 following their failure to secure party support for birth control.

There were several reasons why Labour Party women did not persevere in their efforts to change those provisions of the 1918 constitution that effectively tied their hands as a distinct group. In spite of their rapid growth, women were still a minority in the party and perhaps overly self-conscious about their lack of political experience. Moreover, the division on the issue of integration or separate gender power seems to have placed many of the educated women leaders and 'career politicians' on the side of integration. Prominent leaders urged the necessity of subordinating women's needs to class and party unity, leaving the less experienced postwar rank-and-file and a handful of feminists to argue the case for preserving a distinct women's presence. It is also likely that many local Labour women, like Mrs Ford, did not clearly perceive that a conflict existed. Above all, however, Labour women were caught up in a period of class struggle and they showed a strong inclination to answer the call for class solidarity rather than continuing the divisive argument over their gender status.

WOMEN AND THE POSTWAR LABOUR INSURGENCY

The willingness of Labour women to accept the terms of the merger with the Labour Party and not press for concessions for women owed much to the environment of working-class solidarity stimulated by the war and the postwar labour insurgency. Few working women were direct participants in the massive industrial strikes among miners, transport workers and railwaymen that characterized this period. Yet the strikes were only the most militant aspect of a more general working-class challenge to the authority of the traditional ruling class after the war. Inspired by a widespread belief in the inevitability of social change as the only just response to the inequality of their sacrifice in that war, numerous working-class women joined male workers in direct political action and in enthusiastic support for the Labour Party.

The labour uprising of 1918–20 was in many ways a continuation of the prewar industrial strife but it was fuelled by war-related grievances affecting women as much as men. Significant numbers of married working-class women had experienced class confrontation at first hand during the war. In large urban areas, they had been involved in street battles with landlords over tenant evictions; as managers of the family budget, they had been most affected by rising prices and the rampant profiteering in food that the government's belated introduction of rationing had done little to curb. Many of those who had been in the wartime work force had been introduced to shop floor confrontations and trade union practices.[72] As munitions workers or recipients of separation allowances and war pensions, they had been in effect employees of the state and had become aware of its power to intervene in many areas of their lives. These experiences undoubtedly raised working-class women's class and political consciousness and made them more receptive to post-suffrage Labour Party propaganda.[73]

Women's wartime militancy continued and even increased in the postwar years contributing to their integration and acceptance in the broader labour movement. Organized women drew the unorganized into a variety of direct political activities. In late 1918 and in February 1919, there were huge marches through London of unemployed women war workers.[74] The labour press reported major strikes among women workers in a number of occupations including laundries and engineering works.[75] In Glasgow and Manchester, working women picketed local companies who were known to have made huge profits from the war.[76] There were large contingents of Guild and Labour women at the 1919 May Day demonstration at the Albert Hall and again at the Hyde Park demonstration against profiteering in September. Labour and Co-operative women took part in nationwide protests against the blockade of central Europe where women and children were dying of starvation. They were also active participants in the 'Hands Off Russia' campaign which brought the entire labour movement together in opposition to war against Russia in 1919 and 1920.

In addition to these direct forms of political activism, organized women took the opportunity provided by the industrial strikes of 1919–20 to send a message to the men that they were working together in a common cause. In 1919, the members of the Leyton Women's Co-operative Guild for example, wrote to the *Daily Herald* to announce that as the wives of trade unionists, they had 'sworn to stand by and support (their) husbands to fight to a finish, let the consequences be what they may. In the past, we working women have been blamed for holding our men back. They cannot blame us this time. Our motto is "Fight to the finish and win the world for the workers."[77] In a similar vein, a miner's wife wrote from South Wales, pointing out the very difficult conditions under which she and other wives worked to run a miner's home on a miner's wage but ending with the exhortation to the miners on strike: 'Strike on, men! Better die a death of starvation out of work than go down the pit on sweating terms.'[78] *Labour Woman* reported the story of Mrs Noble, a railwayman's wife and newly elected Labour councillor from Swindon. During the 1919 railway strike, she refused to take a blackleg train and set out to walk from London to Swindon rather than show disloyalty to the strikers.[79]

How the men in the movement responded to these enthusiastic demonstrations of support is not altogether clear. As might be expected, there were official expressions of gratitude especially from the miners. Mr E. L. Poulton who was the chairman of the Standing Orders Committee said, 'he hoped that the movement would never forget the extraordinary devotion of the women in this matter and the help and encouragement they had given the men to stand boldly against this frontal attack that had been made upon Labour'.[80] However, in general, the industrial side of the movement was preoccupied throughout the reconstruction years with getting male workers back into the jobs that women had taken over during the war and showed none of the willingness to accept them as 'partners' that the political side had felt obliged to do following the suffrage grant.

The area of greatest gender co-operation was undoubtedly in the constituency parties which were formed at the same time as the women's sections in many parts of the country. In these early years, women were sometimes in a majority in the local parties and their willingness to take on what Ellen Wilkinson described as the 'slogging work' for the party, especially in raising money, was much appreciated by local labour organizations struggling to establish constituency parties. There is no evidence that local parties ever tried to exclude women as co-operative societies had done before the war. Indeed, a rough and ready partnership seems to have developed which, although it was based more on a gender division of labour than on true equality proved to be a politically effective working relationship and one that was satisfactory to most of the women members most of the time. One of the reasons for this was that the postwar Labour Party attracted large numbers of married couples. Wives commonly attended the women's sections in the afternoons and constituency party meetings with their husbands in the evenings whenever they could.

The recent testimony of women who became political activists just after the war shows their tremendous enthusiasm for labour politics in these years. Lily Watson from North Shields explained in an essay for a WEA class written in 1921 why she was going to vote labour as soon as she had the vote. She wrote: 'I am convinced that the Labour Party at the present moment is the only progressive party in the country.' She gave no hint of dissatisfaction with the position of women in the party; on the contrary, she argued that Labour was the only one of the political parties that had always advocated the equality of the sexes and which could claim credit for the suffrage grant to women. She thought that the Labour Party would ensure that the majority of people received a fair share of the things they produced, bringing them better homes, food and opportunities.[81]

In those postwar years, the Labour Party seems to have inspired some working-class women with feelings akin to religious fervour. Mrs Ford of Tottenham remembered that just after the war she had described her feelings about the Labour Party and the policies for which it stood to a friend in these terms: 'It's my religion and it's my young man's religion.'[82] Shortly after their marriage in 1918, she and her husband joined the South Tottenham Labour Party together. Another Labour woman, Mrs Jessie Lynch who, with her husband was also a founding member of the South Tottenham party, recalled how they had both been stirred by the socialist ideas in the Labour Party's policy statement of 1918, *Labour and the New Social Order*. They felt as if they were, 'in the grip of a new and impelling faith' and they became, ' in imagination, citizens of a new and better world'. She started the first women's section in Tottenham and by 1921, it had a membership of over 500.[83]

Politically aware working-class women responded energetically to the resurgence of a strong industrial and political labour movement in the years between 1918 and 1921. They were better able to identify with the class grievances and expectations fuelling the resurgence than the prewar generation of working women. Labour organizations, in their turn, showed more willingness than their predecessors to accept women's right to participate in the class struggle, so long as their actions did not undermine male authority. Under the new conditions of the postwar years, most rank-and-file women did not hesitate to identify themselves first and foremost as members of the working-class movement and to give their loyalty to its ascendant political arm, the Labour Party.

The years from 1918 to 1921 were full of promise for those working-class women who were eager to play an active part in mainstream labour politics. The few who wrote about their feelings at the time expressed their enthusiasm for the cause and the sense of exhilaration that came from the opportunity to join the movement alongside the men. Would-be Labour Party activists in particular, spoke of their faith in the party's promise to support the complete equality of the sexes. They looked forward to being partners in the struggle for the co-operative commonwealth which the capitalist war and the Bolshevik revolution had brought so much closer.

The constitutional settlements of 1918 in the Labour Party and the Co-operative Movement contradicted the promises of equality and comradeship between the sexes. They reasserted men's dominance and women's marginality and made these enduring features of interwar labour politics. The party's constitution gave women an 'on paper' equality which barely concealed the reality of their distance from decision-making power. With some minor changes, the League accepted the party's terms. In contrast, the Guild refused the Co-operative Union's less than generous suggestion that it abandon its autonomy and merge with men's guilds. In both cases, the end result was much the same. Labour women remained outside the main arenas of power and authority in British social democratic politics.

With the advantage of hindsight, it is clear that a good opportunity for structuring labour politics to take full advantage of the skills and insights of both men and women was lost in 1918. In the aftermath of the First World War and the suffrage grant, the political labour movement gave strong rhetorical support to gender equality. Unfortunately, neither men nor women leaders had a formula for translating the rhetoric into practical political organization. Labour Party and Co-operative leaders were far from accepting a gender power-sharing arrangement. They appear to have wanted only enough 'sexual equality' to secure the electoral support of working-class women voters. League negotiators in their turn were divided over the issue of whether they wanted equality based on integration or separation. They tended to follow a prewar pattern of accommodation to the male leaders. Margaret Llewelyn Davies was one of the very few labour women's leaders who publicly acknowledged the reality of unequal power in these postwar negotiations. She predicted the long struggle that women would have to persuade men to move over and allow them an equal place in the movement.

Lacking a clear idea of what this place should be, the men and women whose job it was to decide fell back on their past experience. A history of separate organization, different policy concerns and strategies as well as some crucial areas of conflict helped shape the terms of the 1918 settlement. In drawing up their plans for women's membership, male labour and co-operative leaders showed a common determination to avoid an organizational structure that would allow direct competition for power between the sexes. One could say that this was a measure of their reluctance to yield control, but it also had roots in their experience of the divisiveness of the suffrage and divorce law reform campaigns of the prewar period. Male leaders remembered the bitter resentment and antagonism that many of their members expressed over these issues and feared that direct competition between men and women in the movement would only encourage further episodes of 'sex antagonism'. Guild and League women seemed unaware of how much tension their reform policies had created among labour men. They were more inclined to remember that their prewar and wartime political achievements were all derived from their identification with the interests of working-class women and children. They feared that abandoning this special agenda would leave working-class women without a voice in the movement.

The women's vote cast its shadow over the merger in other ways. Without it, there is little doubt that women would have remained outside the mainstream movement. There is no evidence to suggest that the Labour Party or the Co-operative Union had plans to allow women full membership rights until the suffrage grant was a certainty. However, once it was clear that up to five million working-class women would be enfranchised after the war, labour men and women began to build castles in the air. Labour men sought political independence, electoral majorities and parliamentary power; labour women looked forward to much greater leverage within the movement, social welfare legislation to meet the needs of working-class women and eventual inroads into the poverty and deprivation in working-class communities. It took some years for activists of both sexes to realize that they were expecting too much too soon, from working-class women voters who were so new to citizenship. The faith in the power of the vote was especially damaging for Labour Party women, because it encouraged them in the false idea that the inequities of the 1918 settlement would disappear as women's voting strength grew.

Another reason why League leaders settled for less than they hoped for in 1918 was their awareness that entry into the party had raised the issue of conflict between their class and gender loyalties. Guild and League women had always emphasized that their concern for working-class women and children was their special contribution to class politics, not a separate or conflicting interest. Male Labour and Co-operative leaders put forward a different view. Their experience of the suffrage and divorce reform campaigns told them that women's gender concerns could represent a serious threat to party unity. Their constitutional proposals in 1918 pushed home the message that labour women's autonomous pursuit of women-centred concerns was inimical to the best interests of the class party. League leaders like Margaret Bondfield endorsed this view, arguing that women's request for a separate power structure, was in effect a demand for 'special privileges' which the party was fighting against in the society at large.

It is difficult to discover how many local women activists perceived that their special interest in the women of their class was somehow in conflict with their loyalty to the working-class as a whole. There was a certain self-consciousness in their assertions of support for the miners and other male trade unionists during the postwar strikes, as if they were determined not to be accused of holding back the men. Yet there was nothing equivocal about their enthusiastic partici-pation in a range of direct actions of their own to improve the conditions of their class. It must have been a heady experience for working-class housewives to feel this unprecedented degree of involvement in what had once been an overwhelmingly male movement. In such an environment of common struggle, it makes sense that many Labour Party women, new members in particular, were not inclined to challenge the party's constitutional arrange-ments. They showed the same reluctance to pursue women's concerns in the thirties when the labour movement and the working class were again in crisis, this time as a result of economic depression not resurgence. How could they think of themselves when their class and party needed their help?

Was the settlement of 1918 inevitable? Although no set of decisions can ever be considered inevitable, it was certainly the case that the forces against a more equitable gender division of power in the Labour Party and the Co-operative Union weighed heavier in the balance than those that promised equality. Labour men were no different from any other entrenched power group in their reluctance to give up their control of the movement. The vote brought women membership and support for their political and economic rights, but its power was tied to electoral results and so was limited and short-lived. Women's other postwar legislative gains as well as their militancy and high profile in the labour movement rested on the temporary circumstances of economic boom, labour power and widespread expectations of social change. Above all, very few men and women in the workers' movement, no matter how fervently they talked of sexual equality seemed able to move far beyond traditional views of sexual difference when they had to decide what work was appropriate for each sex in the context of class politics.

CHAPTER 2

' *Their devotion was about equal*' – *women and men in interwar working-class politics*

In the two decades following the suffrage grant in 1918, close to a quarter of a million women joined a labour or socialist political organization. At least seventy-five per cent of them went into the Labour Party to become co-founders and builders of Labour's national network of constituency parties. Twenty per cent joined the Women's Co-operative Guild and the rest the ILP and the Communist Party. A majority of the new recruits were working-class housewives, many of them married to men who were also active in the movement. They were the first generation of working-class women to be admitted as citizens into organized labour politics and with one or two exceptions they have remained historically anonymous.

Studies of the Labour Party and the co-operative movement have entirely overlooked the dramatic postwar upsurge in women's membership.[1] The omission implies that the new women members were either indistinguishable from their male comrades or so different from them in interests and activities that they remained effectively outside mainstream labour politics. These assumptions need to be tested by looking closely at who the women activists were and how far they resembled labour men in the experiences and political ideas they brought with them into the movement. It means examining key areas of the lives of interwar labour activists, their family circumstances, education, wage-work, trade union or other associations, to discover the significance of gender difference and how much it affected the way men and women defined their political goals and responsibilities in organized labour politics.

Only a handful of rank and file socialists from this period have written autobiographies or left contemporary records describing their political activities.[2] The group portrait presented here is drawn from questionnaire and interview testimony from fifty women and the same number of men who were active in the interwar Labour

Party, Co-operative Movement, ILP or Communist Party.[3] The respondents talked or wrote about their family backgrounds, where they grew up, their schools and jobs. They recalled what stimulated their initial interest in labour politics, the organizations they joined and the work they did as members. Those who had served in local government explained their social reform priorities in the interwar period and what they felt they had accomplished. Each respondent also gave an opinion about gender relations and the division of responsibility between the sexes in his or her labour organization.

The advantage of having the direct testimony of even so small a number is the opportunity to discover individual experience within the usually undifferentiated mass of the rank and file. Placing just a hundred labour activists in a broader context than party politics, one that includes working-class families and neighbourhoods, schools and workplaces, gives an idea of the diversity as well as the shared interests within labour's interwar membership and constituency. It throws light on the connection between policy decisions made at the national level and those that rank-and-file activists discussed and acted upon in the local parties. However, the question remains, can such a small group be considered representative of the thousands who joined the party in the nineteen twenties and thirties?

In many respects, the self-selected sample shares the characteristics of the larger movement. The proportions of those in the Labour Party, the Co-operative Movement, the ILP and the CPGB are about right, based on the size of these organizations in the interwar years.[4] From a socio-economic point of view, the respondents also represent a fair cross section of the working-class occupations from which labour and socialist organizations drew their support. Their geographical distribution matched the pattern of the movement's regional strength in the interwar period. One group was active in the textile and mining towns of Lancashire and Yorkshire; the second, in the heavily working-class boroughs of north London; the third in the docklands of Liverpool, north-east Kent and Bristol and the rest in railway and industrial towns in the Midlands. Scotland and Wales are a significant omission.

The group does have one clear bias. It consists for the most part of 'lifers'. Nearly all the respondents have dedicated the greater part of their adult lives to the movement and some are still active in their eighties. They are the enthusiasts and the hard workers who have stayed with the movement in spite of disappointments and developments they did not foresee in the twenties and thirties. A high proportion of them held office in their local branches, sections or guilds and served on municipal councils and magistrates' benches. They can therefore be considered representative only of the most active strand of labour men and women, not of those who for a variety of reasons were unable to make such a sustained or intense political commitment. While these cadre activists were numerically few in relation to the total membership of their organizations, there is no question that they wielded disproportionate influence in local labour politics.

FAMILY BACKGROUND

References to the social composition of the Labour Party and the Co-operative Movement in the first two decades of this century suggest that rank and file members came from the 'respectable' section of the working class where male workers were unionized, better-paid and regularly employed. David Howell, for example, found that ILP members before the war were mostly from the skilled working and lower middle classes with a sprinkling of teachers and civil servants. He remarked that 'the Party struck few chords amongst very poor, unskilled, unorganized workers'.[5] Margaret Llewelyn Davies seemed to concur when she described the members of the Women's Co-operative Guild in 1904 as 'almost entirely married women belonging to the artisan class'.[6] These findings make sense because it is hard to imagine that men and women whose lives were a daily stuggle to survive would have had the time or the energy for political activity. It is surprising to discover, therefore, that the information the respondents provided about their fathers' occupations and their own early lives, challenges this interpretation.

Since men are presumed to derive their socio-economic status from their occupations, historians have felt no need to look at parental family background to identify male political activists.[7] In contrast, women have traditionally taken their status from their fathers or husbands. In this study, the questionnaire and interviews given to both sexes placed as much emphasis on the socio-economic circumstances of the respondents' parents as on those of the activists themselves. This focus not only revealed further information about the earlier generation of activists but suggested that interest in labour politics in the first decades of the twentieth century flourished in a wider range of economic and social environments than is implied by the existing profile.

A closer look at Margaret Llewelyn Davies' list of the occupations of Guild women's husbands before the war, shows that she used the word 'artisan' in a very broad sense. She included not only skilled craftsmen but industrial and transport workers, service workers like gardeners, chimney sweeps and van drivers as well as 'unskilled' dock, quarry and agricultural labourers.[8] Twenty years later, the fathers of the men and women in the study had a similarly wide range of occupations. About a third were employed in traditional artisanal crafts like engineering, printing, shoemaking, tailoring, carpentry and upholstering. One-fifth were railwaymen, miners and textile workers, but close to a quarter were manual labourers employed in gas works, the docks, iron foundries, the building trade, agriculture or casually. The rest of the respondents' fathers had lower-middle-class occupations in retail and service industries and a small percentage were middle-class professionals. Even without taking into account seasonal unemployment and the host of other variables that affected working-class living standards, the wage differential between these occupations was wide enough to place some families with the 'better off' and others, particularly those with many children, at or below the poverty line.

The respondents confirmed this conclusion when they talked or wrote about the conditions in which they spent their early lives. Asked to describe their family circumstances as either comfortable (having more than the necessities with perhaps a piano and an annual holiday), adequate for all essential needs, or impoverished, both men and women divided fairly evenly into thirds. Those who described their home lives as comfortable came from families with an average of four children and had fathers who were almost all employed in the better-paid skilled trades or middle-class occupations. In the group whose living standard was 'adequate', less than half of the fathers were in artisanal trades. The majority was made up of railway, dock and foundry workers, miners and low-paid service workers such as postmen and carters. The average family size was larger – six children, with some familes of eleven. The impoverished third had an even higher average family size of seven and problems in addition to low wages which were both the cause and the effect of poverty. A majority of the fathers were manual workers and four of them were habitual drinkers. There was a high incidence of unemployment among them. Two families were fatherless and in three of the largest families of eleven or more, some of the children died in infancy, in one family as many as four.

Although the evidence can hardly be considered conclusive in that it does not allow for life-cycle changes in the standard of living of the activists' families, it seems clear that at least a third of this particular group of labour men and women grew up in homes where supplying the family's essential needs was a daily concern for all its members and where unsettling crises were endemic. Sam Hunter, for example, was the youngest child of a miner-turned-farm labourer in a family of six. Two of his siblings died in infancy. He wrote: 'We lived from hand to mouth, you can say we just barely existed.' Jim Meakin remembered that as a child, he and his friends 'picked coal on the slag heaps of coal mines to keep our own fires burning'. Alice Wood, whose father was a Lancashire miner, said: 'We experienced poverty all our childhood days, no holidays…we visited jumble sales, soup kitchens. Sometimes better-off relatives handed over the clothes they had outgrown.' She recounted one event from her childhood: 'I recall mother having a baby when I was about four years old. Father was ill with pneumonia. I stayed with an aunt at Chorley till after the birth and when she brought me home the house was empty. The rent man had sent the bailiffs and took everything bar one bed so we had to stay at Grandma's and our baby died.'[9]

It is quite possible that respondents from some of the larger families in the 'adequate' group were less aware of impoverishment because of their mothers' household skills. There were seven children in Bill William's family. His father was a shipyard worker who was employed only when ships were in for repairs and if he was 'picked out' to work. Despite this, the family 'never went short of food due to a wonderful mother'. Bas Barker, one of eight children in a mining family made a similar observation: 'Being poor never really seemed to be something we had to be sorry about because we were kept and fed as well as my parents were able to manage.'[10] Edna Hanes remembered that her mother was a 'good manager'. She made all the family clothing, baked their bread and sewed shirts for a local retailer to help support her family. Mrs Ford from Tottenham whose father was a scaffolder subject to frequent periods of unemployment, talked about her mother's strategies to keep the family from resorting to the Board of Guardians. The children were sent to the butcher before school for 'block ornaments', the trimmings from better cuts

of meat, to the soup kitchen and the local church that offered tickets
to be redeemed for a pint of milk.[11]

All the respondents brought up in working-class neighbourhoods
around the turn of the century were aware of poverty either at first
hand or among their neighbours, but women were more inclined
than men to volunteer detailed information about the conditions
they saw around them. Mrs Mitchell from Tottenham said: 'I was a
kid about nine or ten years old and by God did we live in poverty ...
We never ever lived in a house where there was hot water or a toilet
you could call your own.'[12] Marge Tierney recalled that when she
was ten years old, she watched a neighbouring family being evicted,
'thrown out into the street, furniture and clothes taken away, left
only what they wore. It was cold and raining. I went home and
cried.' She remembered seeing children with ragged clothes and no
shoes when she went with her father as he delivered bread in Salford.
Lucy Thirkhill saw similar scenes in Bradford, the children with bare
feet, 'their breeches backsides were torn, their shirts hanging out,
hardly any clothes to their backs.'[13] Hettie Bower spoke of the
children at her school in the East End of London, lining up for meal
tickets and the women who came into her father's corner shop to buy
cheap, stale eggs.

Significantly more women activists than men connected the early
exposure to class-based poverty directly with their decision to get
involved in working-class politics. Describing the slum housing she
had seen in Bradford as a young woman and the children from these
homes whose heads were shaved because of lice, Lucy Thirkhill
explained her reaction: 'I mean, I remember all that you see and ...
something had to be done to get the workers out of conditions like
that, hadn't there? Somebody had to care. That's what influenced
me in politics and the Labour Party, to try and get things to
improve.' Bertha Grieveson recalled seeing 'a woman lying naked on
a mattress, literally starving', and commented, 'I think this was my
turning point.' Amelia Jane Bear confessed that she became
interested in the labour movement 'because of our poor childhood'.
Anna Dagnall explained that she joined the Labour Party after
exposure to 'the rough side of life' and 'the outcasts of the First
World War' while working in her grandmother's cafe near the
Liverpool docks. She wrote: 'Young girl as I was, the impression of
poverty and injustice was pervasive.'[14] Among the men, Fred Price
was one of the few to tell a similar story. In his first job as errand boy

for a pawnbroker, he used to see, 'those dear old people bringing their pathetic little bundles to the pawnbroker on a Monday', which made him think, 'there must be better way or a better system'.

Just as women were more likely than men to single out working-class poverty as their primary motivation for joining the labour movement, they were also more inclined to attribute their strong sense of social justice to a parent or other family member. Twenty-five women cited their fathers as an important influence on their political outlooks, eleven their mothers, two their sisters and eight their husbands. Only four said that they were entirely self-motivated or influenced by friends at work. In contrast, more than half the men claimed to have come to labour politics independently, through their work mates or as an extension of their trade union activities. A minority of nine, cited their fathers as a decisive influence, seven their mothers, three both parents and two their wives.

Respondents' fathers generally had a much higher level of trade union and political activism than the working-class population as a whole. About one-sixth were cadre activists in the same sense as their sons and daughters – that is with a long-term, active commitment to a labour organization. The respondents used words such as 'staunch' 'keen' or 'very active' to describe them. They held office in their union, co-operative society, ILP or in the Labour Party. Some were local labour pioneers. Nina Drongin's father 'built up the trade union movement in the Medway' and Frank Jackson's father started a co-operative society in Walthamstow.[15] In addition to the cadres was a group of fathers, perhaps another sixth, who were socialists but not consistent activists. Some were content just to vote Labour but others participated in socialist culture by sending their children to the Socialist Sunday School, attending the Labour Church or taking a socialist newspaper like the *Daily Herald* or *Reynolds News*. The number of fathers who were labour cadres or supporters was slightly higher for women than men but the difference was too small to explain why so many more women than men cited paternal influence on their political ideas.

The difference might be considered a case of selective memory – individuals choosing memories that illuminated the events and values that subsequently shaped their lives. Certainly selective memory was at work but the variations appear not so much between individuals as between the sexes. When their fathers had been labour activists, sons generally emphasized their contribution to the movement without necessarily citing them as an influence on their own labour careers, but daughters credited them with a direct, personal responsibility for shaping their political views. Olive Davies' father was a dedicated ILP member. She wrote: 'My whole adult life until now has been influenced by his taking me to street corner meetings ... organized by the ILP and on May Day marches in London to hear suffragettes and national leaders speak.' She joined the ILP herself at age sixteen. Anna Dagnell had a similar experience. Her father aroused her interest in socialism when he took her along as a girl of twelve to hear him speak at an ILP open-air meeting on Merseyside. Edith Pennington remembered her father taking her canvassing with him when she was a little girl. He talked to the voters and she marked down 'Yes' or 'No' for Labour. Alice Onions' memory of her father, a bootmaker and a socialist from Wolverhampton, was of him taking her as a child into a local foundry where men and women were working stripped to the waist: 'The women would pick their babies up and suckle them and put them down to play in the corner while they went back to work. They scarcely seemed human to me.' The foundry visit left a deep impression. Alice Onions was later active in the Labour Party like her father, but also became a pioneer in Wolverhampton's birth control movement.[16]

The male respondents with activist fathers present an interesting contrast. Twenty-seven of them said their fathers had been trade unionists or members of a socialist or labour political organization but only nine claimed their fathers as mentors. Frank Jackson's father had been 'a very active member' of the Amalgamated Society of Carpenters and Joiners, the Social Democratic Federation and the co-operative movement. Jackson recalled his father's part in the 'Great March' from Walthamstow to Liverpool Street when workers marched in front of a train to protest an increase in workman's fares on the Great Eastern Railway. He ended the story with the comment: 'That's one of the common incidents in working class history. And they won.'[17] Despite his obvious admiration for his father, Jackson implied that his own political education came from contacts he made through trade union and strike activity in the period from 1910 to 1919 when he worked in various car and airplane factories.

Bas Barker is another example of the tendency for men to cite political influences other than their activist fathers. His father was a miner, a faceworker at the Williamthorpe Colliery near Chesterfield in Derbyshire who became interested in trade unionism as a way to 'break the stranglehold of the company over the whole of the miners' lives'. Barker remembered his father, 'coming out of the pit early every Friday ... to stand in the pit lane ... often getting drowned with the rain, to collect trade union contributions'. Yet Barker attributed his early interest in politics not to his father but to a family friend, Harry Hickens, the general secretary of the Derbyshire Miners' Association. Barker spent his weekends and holidays with the Hickens and 'it was in their house where I met many of the leading figures of the labour and trade union movement ... and became involved in its daily discussions and fortunes, picking up the flavour of political talk and activity at a relatively young age'.[18]

Socialism for most men, including Bas Barker, was primarily about the workplace and organized labour but when women described the socialism they learnt from their fathers, they talked about values relating to the family and the community. The daughters of ILP men in particular emphasized socialism as a life lived according to an ethical code which governed relationships at home, in the community and internationally. In many ways it resembled a religious faith. Mrs Ford described it as such when a friend asked why a nice girl like her was marrying a man who mixed with 'all such [socialist] cac-mac [riff-raff?]'. She answered: 'It's not cac-mac its my religion.' Margaret Mitchell grew up feeling that socialism was her religion because her father, a shoemaker, spoke of it as 'a belief in the natural bounty of God and Nature given to all men to be harvested through their labour'. He urged his children never to waste bread because it represented the hard labour of 'someone of your own class'.[19] Jessie Stephen's father would take in beggars and ask each child to contribute some food from his or her plate to feed the stranger. He then pointed the object lesson: 'You see how many can help one but one can't help many.'[20] Among the men, John Welch said he found inspiration to work for 'a better world, peace and improvements for living', from parents who 'lived their socialism' but neither he nor any other of the men recalled their fathers giving them lessons in socialist morality.

A consistent theme in women's testimony but similarly missing from men's was hatred of war which many said they learnt from their fathers. Alice Onions recounted how her father encouraged her two brothers to become conscientious objectors in the First World War. He helped them to hide out for the four-year duration. Hettie Bower's father was also opposed to the war. He sent his son to Dublin to avoid conscription.   Margaret Mitchell's father, 'ever a pacifist', was unable to prevent her brothers from volunteering but made clear his opinion that the war was being waged for the benefit of international capitalism. She said: 'He hated war; he could see the tragedy of war … that it was a complete negation of all that was good in life.' Nina Drongin wrote that her father came back 'greatly disillusioned by the First World War'; he spoke bitterly about the slaughter of working men. Lily Watson remembered her father teaching her that 'wars were unnecessary' and Nellie Logan her father saying that in the First World War, 'one class (the workers) got the crosses, and the other class got the profits'. Barbara Elliott had a vivid impression of her father's fierce opposition to the armaments industry. He told her that 'we would always have war while people made profit out of the manufacture of arms'. These women respondents and others made a direct connection between their fathers' anti-war sentiments and their own support for disarmament and peace in the interwar period.

Strong paternal influence on close to a half of the women respondents raises the question of fathers' attitudes towards sexual equality. On this issue, women were almost as reticent as men. Only five women and four men said that their fathers supported women's equal rights. Bill Wilson described his father as a feminist and told how he had served 'as part of the bodyguard for one of the Pankhurst family in 1917 when she came to Coventry'. Alice Onions said her father was 'out for votes for women and suffragism'. Marjorie South recalled how her father showed his 'deep belief in the equality of men and women' by accompanying his wife and two other women to the polling station in 1918 where they were the first women to vote in their Birmingham constitutency. These were the exceptions among the majority of respondents who gave negative responses or ignored the question of their fathers' views on women's rights.

Women respondents gave the impression that although their fathers wanted their daughters as well as their sons to become socialists, they did not question traditional gender roles. For the most part neither did the respondents themselves. Only when brothers were given priority of limited resources for education and far more social freedom did some of the women activists complain. Alice Onions mentioned that she and her brother Will were the artists of the family. She won a scholarship to study at Birmingham University but could not go because her father, 'although he was so progressive, didn't think that was quite the thing'. She admitted that she felt, 'very bitter towards him about it for a number of weeks'. Ivy Lovekin whose mother was 'always fighting for women's rights' commented that her father 'did not believe in further education for girls'. One or two women respondents pointed out contradictions between their father's socialism and his private behaviour. Edith Ward's father was a socialist and popular speaker in labour men's clubs but 'he kept my mother very short of money so we often went without'. The message socialist fathers conveyed to their children was that the co-operative commonwealth would end all exploitation, including that of women, but it would not change the traditional division of responsibility between the sexes.

Eighteen of the hundred respondents cited their mothers as a major influence over their political development, eleven women and seven men. In some cases, mothers were active in partnership with their husbands, in others, they were the activists while husbands supported or tolerated their political work. Lucy Thirkhill's mother was the one always out at meetings, not her father: 'He never really took a big active part, not to the extent my mother did.' Ivy Lovekin's father looked after the children while her mother was at 'various meetings.' Mothers generally had a much lower level of trade union and political activism than fathers although it was higher than the average for working-class women.[21] Of the one hundred mothers only six had belonged to a trade union, all of them in the textile industry or sewing trades, and fifteen a working-class political organization. Twelve of the fifteen were members of the Women's Co-operative Guild, a clear indication of how much easier it was for women to get into single-sex than male-dominated labour organizations before 1918. The mothers, like the fathers included a group who were socialists without being activists and they too encouraged their children to attend co-operative classes or Socialist Sunday Schools and taught them social responsibility.

Politically active mothers influenced their children in much the same ways as activist fathers. Once again, daughters were more likely than sons to remember their mothers as role models who involved them in their union or political activities. When Alice Wood started work in the mill at age thirteen, her mother used to take her along to quarterly meetings of the Bolton Weavers and Winders. She soon realized, 'what it was like to fight the employers for every penny we were entitled to'. Marge Evans' mother had been a Labour Party activist before she had a family. While Marge's Irish father urged his children to adopt his hatred for the English, her mother tried to teach them socialist values. Marge Tierney remembered her mother stressing the importance of 'supporting the Labour government and local Labour councillors and [she] bought the *Daily Herald* which I read from being seven years old'. Dorothy Berry's mother was an active member of the Women's Co-operative Guild in Rusholme, Manchester, who introduced her daughter to the movement by sending her to co-operative classes and encouraging her to take part in special events. Dorothy remembered International Day when she rode on a lorry 'dressed as a Belgian and presided over a [mock] meeting wearing the President of Platt Guild's chain of office.'

Male respondents who were socialists, communists or co-operators claimed their mothers as inspiration or teacher more readily than sons who were trade unionists or Labour Party men but they were only seven in number. Peter Buckingham's mother became an enthusiastic co-operator after her marriage. She belonged to the Women's Co-operative Guild and her local co-operative society for about thirty years and held office in both. When Buckingham left school without knowing what he wanted to do, she directed him into the co-operative movement where he could earn a living and take further education courses. He said that it was her 'expression of faith in co-operation as a way of life which influenced me and activated my participation in co-operative bodies'. Stanley Boulton's mother, Emily Allcott Boulton was a keen socialist and he remembered her taking him as a child to meetings in the Margaret Street Socialist Hall in Manchester. He later joined the Young Communist League and went off to fight in the Spanish Civil War. Arthur Sheldon mentioned that his mother was an admirer of Tom Mann who taught him some of Mann's ideas but he attributed his socialism to a work-mate, Jim Davies, whom he met during his apprenticeship as a moulder in a foundry.[22]

Only six respondents, five of them women, said that their mothers had been involved in the suffrage movement. Nellie Logan recalled her mother telling her that as a young woman she 'followed the suffragettes around Manchester'. Anna Dagnell and Mary Towns-end had mothers who worked for women's suffrage through the guild. Edna Hanes never forgot meeting a suffragette who was a good friend of her mother's and eventually became a Labour councillor. Four others described their mothers as 'feminists.'. Peter Bucking-ham wrote about his mother's 'sympathy and support for many feminist aspirations and achievements'. Bill Wilson labelled his mother a 'socialist and a feminist'. Ivy Lovekin's mother 'was always fighting for women's rights' and encouraging them to vote. None of these activists, however, recalled their mothers teaching them feminist ideas or encouraging them to fight for women's social and economic equality. They seemed to think that their mothers' generation had won the struggle for women's rights by gaining the vote and now the fight was for class justice.

Family responsibilities limited the extent to which the majority of respondents' mothers were able to be politically active outside the home. They belonged to the last generation before the widespread use of birth control among the working class and many had large families. When their mothers had more than two or three children, it is not surprising to find respondents speaking of them as too busy with 'domestic duties and family ties' to be active. Gladys Lillywhite's mother was one of many who gave up politics, 'while her children were young'. Marge Tierney's mother 'could not be active. She worked full time and cared for her husband, children and an elderly sick mother.' Alice Wood's mother was a keen socialist but when her miner husband became ill (with black lung disease) she confined her activities to addressing election envelopes at home.

Mothers who were not involved in any area of labour politics could still inspire their children with a desire for social justice. Several men and women said that seeing their mothers overburdened with childbirth and the struggle to maintain a family on low wages, made them question a social system that produced such suffering. Bas Barker believed that his mother's early death at the age of fifty-six was a result of 'the tremendous struggle of trying to keep a family of our size (eight children) on a miner's wage... Like so many other miners' wives, she had born the brunt of the battle throughout those long years of poverty... '[23] Jim Cole said that the sacrifices his mother made 'to bring up her family properly' made him determined to improve conditions for 'any family I might have'. Dorothy Russell helped her mother care for ten other children. She remembered resenting 'the plight of women, just bearing children slavishly to their lords and masters'. With an adult's perspective, she said of her socialist father that he was ' a supporter of women's rights but not his wife's'. Others expressed admiration for their mothers' ability to stretch small wage packets to feed their large families. Gladys Lillywhite thought that she had been influenced by her mother's 'hard work, particularly as a woman and the struggle to bring up a family'. Sarah Seed's mother had one pound a week to feed six children. 'How she did it, week after week, was a mystery to me.'

A group of women respondents said their mothers set them an example of social responsibility by taking care of neighbours and others in need. Edith Pennington described her mother as 'a loving person with feelings for others, always ready to lend a helping hand'. She served on a committee for First World War refugees and took two into her home for three years. Ruby Jobson remembered how her mother made soup for sick neighbours. Hettie Bower's mother gave whatever she could in clothes and food to her poorer neighbours. Marge Tierney commented that her mother was the person to whom neighbours came in times of trouble. Men rarely made observations of this kind. Perhaps the women activists mentioned it because they themselves often served as informal, local 'ombudswomen', helping neighbours solve problems ranging from rubbish collection or holes in the road to paying the rates or trouble with their landlords.[24]

A small core of activists, men and women, came from families in which both parents were active in the labour movement. They had much in common. Labour politics was an inescapable part of their lives from early childhood. Their first sensations may well have been the weight of political pamphlets on their legs as they lay in their prams. If their parents were not out at meetings, they were holding meetings in the living room. Every election day their homes were transformed into committee rooms with a hectic flow of people in and out. As soon as they were old enough, they were sitting at the kitchen table addressing envelopes or out delivering leaflets through every door in the neighbourhood.

Activists with this background were very much aware of having been 'born into Labour politics'. Bill Wilson said as much and John Welch expanded his birthright to include not only the Labour Party but 'the AEU (Amalgated Engineering Union) and the Sons of Temperance'. Lily Watson wrote: 'Having been brought up in a socialist household, I have probably had socialism ground in me and have taken more notice of politics than some young folk do.'[25] Some women felt the need to explain that they had accepted their parents' beliefs because they agreed with them. Lorna Waters put it this way: 'I thought my parents ideals were for me too and I wanted to work for the same [ones].' Lucy Thirkhill made a similar observation. When asked why she thought so many people were not interested in politics, she replied: 'I don't know, maybe they hadn't been brought up amongst it like I had. You see, I wasn't indoctrinated, I mean I believed in it myself.'

One telling statistic from the group of respondents was that sixty-seven per cent of them were first children. It may be that first children are more susceptible to parental influence than their siblings and this study suggests that this is more true of female first children than male. In this period, eldest daughters were expected to take over a mother's role in caring for younger siblings and helping to run the household if she was overburdened, ill or dead. Several women in the study had this parenting role thrust upon them at a very early age. Marge Evans and Elizabeth Wheeler became mothers to their brothers and sisters at age thirteen when their own mothers died. As the eldest of eight, Amelia Jane Bear helped her mother look after her sisters and brothers as well as contributing to the family income by doing housework and washing for other people. One could argue that eldest sons were in a similar position since they were the first to become wage-earners with their fathers, but none of the male respondents seemed aware of this responsibility. The best supporting evidence for the 'eldest child' syndrome is that with the same parental message and example, other children in the respondents' families did not become active members of a labour or socialist organization. Tom Riley was the eldest of fourteen but he was the only activist. He said of his siblings: 'They were all radical but not one of them had any ideas for Labour. None of them belong to a party … I was the real rebel of the whole lot.'[26]

If women were more likely than men to adopt their parents' political beliefs, they were no different from men in their tendency to reject parental religious affiliation. The level of religious practice was much higher among the activists' parents than it was for the respondents themselves. Forty-one of the parents attended a church, chapel or synagogue – more often mothers than fathers. Twenty-two were nonconformists, most of them Methodists or Primitive Methodists, eleven were Church of England, five, Irish Roman Catholic and three, Jewish. Raymond South was one of only three activists who said that they found the inspiration for their socialism in the religious faith they acquired at home. The majority rejected their parents' religious beliefs as antithetical to their developing political ideas. Barbara Elliott made the decision very early. When her father, a Primitive Methodist, sent her to a Methodist Sunday School she found herself unable to accept the teachings there: 'The bible to me was not logical.' Her parents then transferred her to a Socialist Sunday School where she gladly responded to the call to be 'just and loving to all our fellow men and women'. As a young adult, Hilda Nicholas objected to the Baptist Church her parents attended because 'the front pews had cushions for the wealthy'. Hettie Bower rejected her father's orthodox Judaism when she became active in the ILP. Marge Evans responded in the same way to her Irish father's Catholicism and neither Jessie Stephen nor Edna Hanes continued in the Methodism of their parents. Few activists stressed the continuing importance in their later lives of the religious faith with which they grew up.

In the context of the working class as a whole none of the respondents can fairly be described as conformist. They liked to refer to themselves as 'rebels' and the term is apt. From an early age, they developed a passionate desire to fight social injustice wherever they saw it. Alec Lipner said that he was known as 'The Rebel' in his bus garage in Tottenham because: 'I just wouldn't lay down, just wouldn't work under the conditions they wanted me to.'[27] Mrs Mitchell of Tottenham said: 'If I see something going wrong, something that shouldn't be, I revolt against it. I have to do something about it.'[28] The attitudes of their working-class neighbours could re-inforce the rebel self-image. Sections of the working class remained convinced that socialism was a threat to property and savings, monogamous marriage and the family. They treated local socialists with suspicion and open antagonism. As Alice Onions pointed out, 'to be a socialist was to be an absolute outcast'. Women activists were rebels in an additional sense. Merely by appearing on political platforms, they offended popular norms about appropriate behavior for working-class wives. When they spoke in public they invariably had to deal with hecklers who told them to go home and look after their husbands.

Despite the similarities of their socio-economic backgrounds, men and women respondents differed in the way they interpreted their early family experiences and related them to their development as labour activists. In general, women's memories of their families and neighbourhoods were more vivid and detailed than men's and they attached greater significance to this early environment in shaping their political ideas. Male respondents who said they had been concerned about improving working-class living standards in the interwar period, rarely recalled specific or personal examples of poverty; nor did most men make a direct connection between their early experiences in the family, no matter how impoverished, and their decision to join the labour movement. Women were two to three times more likely than male respondents to attribute their labour consciousness to the influence of a family member, usually their fathers. Paternal influence was decisive in their development as activists. Men acknowledged the achievements of activist fathers but often identified men outside the family as their political mentors. The pattern was much the same with activist mothers although as many men as women claimed to have been motivated by maternal suffering and self-sacrifice.

The differences were no doubt the result of a complex mixture of early socialization, individual psychology, the deeply entrenched tradition of separate gender spheres and subsequent gender-specific political concerns. Labour women remembered an ethical, family-based socialism, anti-war messages and the sufferings of women and children because these were the values and issues that were legitimately within their 'sphere' and ones that had most often concerned them during their long years of service in the labour movement. They were more likely to be influenced by family members than men because they had fewer opportunities to find political inspiration outside the home, in the workplace or the trade union. With nothing compelling to displace them, early impressions retained their power over women while men's exposure to class confrontation and labour organization at work may well have diminished the earlier influence of home and family.

THE INFLUENCE OF SCHOOL

The experience of going to school was remarkably similar for both sexes in the group of respondents. With few exceptions, the activists were keen and interested students with a strong desire for education beyond the elementary school. In case after case, family circumstances prevented them achieving this goal. Many of them passed the scholarship examination making them eligible for secondary school but parents who might have scraped together the fees could not afford to maintain their children and forego their wages for another two years. Only twelve of the respondents went on to secondary

schools and five to college or university. The rest left school at
fourteen to go into the workforce. Five of those who grew up in textile
towns became half-timers at the age of eleven or twelve and three
others were taken out of school at thirteen to begin wage-work or care
for their siblings because of the death of a parent.

The sacrifice of education left a sense of loss and frustration that
was still strong years later. Jessie Stephen recalled: 'I was actually in
training as a pupil teacher when the blow fell. It so happened that
that year was a very bad one for all working men and women in
employment and since as I have said before, tailoring was a seasonal
trade, my father suddenly found himself without work. Naturally, I
left school.'[29] Gladys Draper had a similar story. 'I've always
regretted not being able to stay at school till I was sixteen. There was
a scholarship you went in for at eleven and I passed it but they
wanted written permission from the parents that you would stay at
school until you were over sixteen. My father wouldn't have that. He
said he would need any money I could earn when I was fourteen.'[30]
Hilda Nicholas recalled that her mother 'kept me at home on the day
of the exam. She had no hope of paying for the uniform'. Jim Meakin
explained that he left school because: 'there was no opportunity for
advancement; the next stage was grammar school which only the
privileged children were able to go on to'.

A high percentage of respondents tried to compensate for the
disappointment of having to leave school by going to night classes or
teaching themselves through extensive reading. Men were more
likely than women to attend formal classes. Tom Riley recalled: 'I
didn't fall back [after leaving school] I went to night school instead
...' Fred Price, Rees Davies and Arthur Dutton all took Workers'
Education Association (WEA) classes as young men and Davies
became a WEA tutor in later life. Bas Barker joined an adult
education class for miners and he was eventually able to take courses
at Oxford and Nottingham Universities on a Miners' Welfare
scholarship.[31] Edna Hanes took evening classes through the National
Council of Labour Colleges (NCLC) and Peter Buckingham through
the Co-operative Movement. Many more respondents pursued their
education informally by becoming voracious readers. Lucy Thirkhill
was one. She said: 'I read a lot ... I didn't get much schooling ... I'm
more or less self-taught in a lot of things you see.' Norman Green
joined the Left Book Club. He had always been an avid reader and
believed that the LBC 'taught the working class about socialism'. Sid

Osguthorpe was one of a group of young engineers in Sheffield who 'were all good readers and good conversationalists ... Although they were poor, their back bedrooms were filled with books, mostly bought from second-hand shops.'

The common experience of being denied a secondary education fuelled the class and political consciousness of many respondents and created in their minds a link between education and labour politics. They pursued learning not so much to improve their job prospects as to become more effective fighters in the cause of class justice. Bas Barker explained: 'We wanted to get education for our own esteem and knowledge so that we would be more able to argue the cause in support of the working-class movement.'[32] They read books on co-operation and socialism, some even struggling with Marx' *Capital*. Women took advantage of opportunities offered by the Guild and the Labour Party women's sections to study the history of co-operation, the rules of meetings and the structure of local government. At day and weekend schools, they learnt to overcome their fear of public speaking and gained confidence as their knowledge grew. Men and women respondents all placed free education for all to age sixteen high on the list of their social reform priorities in the interwar period.

THE WORKPLACE

Despite limited educational opportunities, the respondents generally had rather better jobs, in terms of wages and status, than their parents. Among the men, there were more teachers and skilled engineers, fewer traditional artisans – shoemakers, for example – and almost no unskilled labourers. Car and aircraft workers increased the numbers in industry and paid political organizers formed a new category. For women too, the generational difference in jobs reflected changes in the structure of the labour market after the First World War. While most of their mothers were domestic servants, textile operatives and hand or machine sewers before marriage, twelve of the respondents were clerical workers, five were shop assistants and one was a teacher. Eleven followed their mothers into woollen or cotton textile mills but only eight were in service as compared to thirteen of the mothers. Four worked in factories and three were dressmakers or milliners. Five did no paid work before marriage but stayed at home to care for their siblings and help to run the household.

While men and women respondents shared aspects of their childhood and school experience, their paths diverged as soon as they entered the labour market. Whether they worked in factories, workshops, offices, shops, schools or other people's homes, gender segregation was the rule. Even when they were in the same profession, trade or industry, men and women almost always worked on different processes, at different skill levels and for different wages. Gender segregation in the labour force combined with male workers' ambivalent attitudes towards women wage-earners produced the most significant differential experience for men and women activists – trade union membership. Forty-two of the fifty male respondents belonged to a trade union during their working lives; they were generally active over many years, held union office and sat on the local trades councils. In contrast, only fourteen of forty-five women who spent time in the labour force belonged to a trade union. Half of them were in textile unions and the rest in the General Workers Union, the National Union of Distributive and Allied Workers (NUDAW), the Garment Workers Union and the Association of Clerical Workers. None of the domestic servants was organized and almost none of the clerical workers, seamstresses and shop assistants.

Male respondents generally commented positively on their trade union experience. William Herbert who worked on the London buses, said: 'I was always interested in the Union, right from when I was at the London General [Bus Company]. I became shop steward there.'[33] Jim Meakin was a shop steward and Branch President of the National Union of Sheetmetal Workers and Coppersmiths. He viewed his period in the union as 'my education in life's problems. I enjoyed trade union responsibility as much as being labour councillor.' Tom Riley was the father of the chapel in the printers' union (NATSOPA) at his firm for twenty-eight years and did a lot of union work. He was tempted to give more of his time to the union than the Labour Party but union work in the printing trade was night work and as he was married he chose the political side. Arthur Dutton discovered while he was in the bricklayers' union that he 'had that natural instinct to be a leader of men' so that 'every job I went on, I was going to be the leading trade unionist'.[34]

Men who had little to say about their early family lives, often had detailed memories of incidents relating to work and trade union activity. Several recalled successful confrontations with managers or employers. Alec Lipner described how he and other militant bus-drivers at Dalston garage in North London gained some control over schedules by sending a message to all the drivers: 'If this schedule's not withdrawn and a new schedule put up to our liking, refer back to the old schedule, work that. Other than that we close the gates.' He commented: 'It took a lot of times before the General [Bus Company] realised that we meant business. We stood outside those gates ... until the General thought, its no good messing about like that, we'll have to get that [changed].'[35] Frank Jackson talked about organizing the shop at Bedford Motors. He said: 'I think I got the sack – in one week I think I got the sack six times – but got re-instated every time! But we organized it, the whole thing, organized it a hundred per cent. It was one of the first closed shops in the motor trade at that time.'[36]

These men straddled the industrial and political sides of the movement with no sense of conflict. Even when they gave more attention to labour politics, most maintained their trade union association throughout their working lives and beyond. A common 'career' pattern for the men began with early trade union membership. As they became more prominent in the union, they formed networks with other trade unionists that extended beyond the factory, workshop or industry into the local labour community. They sat together on the Trades and Labour Councils which were affiliations of local union branches. In the interwar period, the trades councils either merged into Labour's constituency parties or worked closely with them. For trade union cadres, the movement into some form of labour or socialist politics came about as a natural extension of a locality-based trade unionism. The symbiotic relationship between the industrial and political sides of the labour movement shaped men's political consciousness, encouraging them to focus on class conflict, workplace issues and internal power relations as their central political concerns, and organization, agitation and negotiation as strategies.

Women respondents' experience of wage work and trade unions was quite different from the male pattern. Very few found their trade union membership rewarding or a means of entry into local labour politics. One reason for the difference was their relatively short period in the workforce which meant that only six women stayed in a union for more than a few years. Those who were long-term union members had a very similar career path to their male comrades. Four of them achieved elective office. Edna Hanes became secretary of the Leeds branch of NUDAW and was eventually elected to the union's executive committee, the only woman among twelve men. Alice Wood was on the Weavers and Winders committee of the textile union for twenty-five years. Nellie Jackson and Louie Davies served as shop stewards and organizers during their long years of union service in the Bleachers and Dyers and the Garment Workers' Union respectively. Like the men, these women successfully integrated their trade union and political activities.

By contrast, the majority of women activists found little in their trade union experience to encourage either their interest in social reform or their desire to be part of a broad working-class movement. Nellie Whitely's testimony shows some of the frustrations they faced. Nellie joined the union as soon as she entered a Bradford woollen mill as a full-time doffer at the age of thirteen. She found she was the only girl in the winding department who belonged to the union. When the bosses introduced a 'speed up' of the machinery, she was chosen to tell the overlooker that the women workers wanted more money to compensate for the additional work. He refused her request. She explained what happened next: 'They (the bosses) chuntered about a bit and then we decided that we would walk out you see, so we all downed tools.' The next day, all the women returned to work. 'They were frightened of [losing] their jobs, you see.' Nellie was fired for being a 'troublemaker' but subsequently given an opportunity to work in the burling and mending department of the mill. Some time later, 'the unions did take it up' and the women winders were given a small raise.[37]

The incident Nellie described had many of the characteristics of women's trade union experience in the decades before and after the First World War. Women workers were poorly organized and isolated from mainstream union activities. When faced with a shop floor crisis, they produced their own leaders and walked out spontaneously, but usually only for a short time. Their actions then attracted some notice from the union which came in to negotiate a wage increase. Once the incident was over, the union leadership resumed its former neglect. As Nellie put it, 'the unions didn't cause a real stir' among women workers or their employers.

Other respondents commented on some aspects of this pattern. Golda Barr was in the Garment Workers Union 'since the day I started work'. She recalled a workshop in the East End of London where all the men were in the union but none of the women, with the exception of herself. 'When I said to one man why don't you ask us if we are members, he said "well the women don't count very much."[38] Lucy Thirkhill, like Nellie, joined the union under her parents' influence as soon as she began work at Cawthra's mill in Bradford. However, she found that the other girls 'weren't in it.' She stayed in the union but could see little point in attending the male-dominated branch meetings. Alice Wood commented that there were only a small number of women workers from her cotton mill in the union. She found it was very hard to raise the level of organization because they 'had to stay off work for commitments at home' and their attendance was poor. Nellie Logan who was in the cotton weavers' union, tried to organize her fellow women workers when they complained that they could not make enough money due to the poor quality of the yarn which continually broke on the loom. Her efforts proved unsuccessful because the young women's parents were 'afraid of my politics' and warned their daughters to ignore her 'as she would get them into trouble'.

Very few women activists said they either learnt about socialism or met people who influenced their decision to join a labour organization while they were at work. This is understandable for those who worked alone or in very small work groups but it was the same for those in mills and factories. Anna Dagnell spent six years as a piece-worker in a silk-stocking factory in Liverpool before her marriage. There was no union and when the male night workers tried to form one, they suffered 'instant dismissal'. Her workmates chose her to sit on a workers' representation committee but it was under the control of the employers and made only token changes. If she learnt any lesson that influenced her developing socialism, it was that working people were victims of oppression at work as well as in their homes and communities. Only Hilda Nicholas, a tobacco stripper for Wills of Bristol, said she met 'good people' at work who introduced her to labour politics through a Communist Party organization called the Friends of the Soviet Union. For most women in the sample, the workplace was separate from their political activities. The two only came together in a negative sense. Sarah Seed and Nellie Logan, both weavers, were blacklisted by their employers; Sarah for her leadership role in the More Looms strike of 1931, and Nellie because she went to Moscow as a young communist.

The absence of a rewarding trade union affiliation among women respondents widened the gap in experience between them and their male counterparts. By the time men joined a labour or socialist organization, they often had close ties to other male activists in that organization or on the industrial side of the movement. Many had held union office and taken part in bargaining and negotiation within an organized framework. Some had won victories in struggles with employers and realized the power of organized working men to make positive changes in their wages and working conditions. For these men, trade unions were as essential to the fight for the co-operative commonwealth as their political labour organizations.

Women shared few of these experiences or perceptions. They entered labour politics with limited knowledge of formal working-class associations and without much sense of labour power. They had seen poverty and oppression in their neighbourhoods and at work but had rarely been involved in successful, or even unsuccessful, organized struggle against the employing class. Women had no reason to believe from their own experience that trade unions would be effective agents of social or economic change. They were more likely to be fully committed to political action and expect to achieve the co-operative commonwealth through parliamentary social wel-fare legislation. Although they shared with men a determination to end class injustice and improve conditions of life for working people, their vision of how these goals would be achieved and by whom was essentially a different one.

MARRIAGE

Most of the respondents were already active in a labour organization before they were married. Only eight women and two men said they became interested in the labour movement because of their spouses. The more common situation was for labour men and women to meet and marry through their independent political activities in the ILP, the Labour League of Youth, Labour Party or the Co-operative Movement. Twenty-eight women and twenty-one men married fellow labour activists. Three women respondents were divorced and remarried. In each case, apart from any other problems there might have been, their first husbands were not involved in labour politics. The second time they chose men from inside the movement who shared their political interests.

Among the respondents in 'labour marriages', only five said they shared domestic, parenting and political activities equally with their spouses. Elizabeth Wheeler and Golda Barr were proud of their husbands' willingness to take turns with them attending meetings and staying home with their children. Raymond South said he and his wife Marjorie 'were partners in the family as well as in political activity'. The more common pattern was for men to continue their political activities without interruption while women curtailed or deferred their participation to take care of homes and children. Tom Riley noted that before they married, he and his wife were both active Labour Party members. Afterwards, his political work increased until 'nearly every night of the week I was at a political meeting', while she stayed at home with their two sons. Other male respondents rather disingenuously claimed that their wives maintained their political activities without in any way neglecting their families but their descriptions of this balancing act imply that domestic duties came first. Bill Wilson said his wife was active in labour politics with him but 'the part she played was combined with raising our son'. Fred Price's wife 'combined her politics with child-raising'. Jim Cole's wife took part in politics with him, 'where possible'.

Most female respondents seemed to accept the social convention that a woman's first responsibility must be her home and family. When their political careers came into conflict with family needs, they sacrificed politics. Lucy Thirkhill said she curtailed her activities in the party 'quite a lot' when she had children and Mrs Ford put her political work aside when her mother became terminally ill. Several women turned down opportunities to run for local government office. Violet Fletcher explained she did not stand as a candidate for Wolverhampton borough council because she was looking after her sick husband and dressmaking to supplement the family income.[39] Mary Townsend and Nellie Jackson also refused invitations to stand for their local councils because they thought their family obligations came first.

The only women who said they felt some resentment at being forced to make a choice between family and politics were those whose male colleagues 'reminded' them of the conflict. Nina Drongin recalled that when she became pregnant, she resigned the secretaryship of her Labour Party ward. One of the men with whom she had worked closely said to her: 'You'll forget all about socialism now you've started a family.' She said she felt hurt even though she was aware that the common feeling in the party at the time was that 'for a young mother to come to meetings was a shocking thing'. Hilda Nicholas had a similar experience in the Communist Party in Bristol. The District Secretary complained bitterly when she became pregnant with her fourth child, implying that the combination of motherhood and politics was impossible and she was showing disloyalty to the party.

As they tried to balance the competing demands of motherhood and labour politics, women activists from the interwar generation were in a much better position than their mothers. A significant demographic change occurred between the two generations. The average family size among the respondents at all income levels was 2.2 children compared to 5.8 for their parents. Birth control probably made the difference and it meant that women activists could spend less than half the time their mothers did in childraising. With fewer children and better-paid jobs, the respondents generally suffered less from poverty than the prewar generation and presented a more homogeneous socio-economic profile. The majority of women married men who closely resembled the male respondents in their occupations. They were skilled engineers, industrial workers, shop assistants, party and trade union officials and teachers. Very few were unskilled labourers.

Respondents whose marriage partners were not involved in labour politics usually described them as supportive or tolerant of their political activities. Men used phrases such as: 'She supported everything I did'; 'she agreed with me'; 'she encouraged me'; and 'she was able to help and give support and sustain me'. One or two hinted that their political activities caused some domestic tension. Arthur Warren pointed out that his wife 'queried the time I gave to meetings and writing up [the minutes]' and Tom Riley made this ambiguous statement: 'I had no trouble with the family though of course my wife did moan at times.' Women respondents were happy when their husbands tolerated their activities. Amelia Bear said that her husband 'did not in any way stop or deter me from my support for the labour movement', while Mary Townsend's 'did not mind me being active', Ellen Kendall's postman husband was glad she was in the Labour Party 'but I think sometimes resented my social activity in the Guild', Lucy Thirkhill explained that her husband's interest was sport, 'mine was politics which never clashed!'

Labour politics did not necessarily bring spouses together even when both partners were active in the same organization. If they were Labour Party members or co-operators, husbands and wives usually went to separate meetings. Wives attended Guild or section meetings in the afternoons and men, ward, constituency party or co-operative society meetings in the evenings. Separate meetings encouraged distinct agendas and responsibilities so that the area of common ground might be confined to social occasions and special events. When women's activities were interrupted by children, the divergence increased. Women who put their politics on hold, returning in their thirties or later, often had to wait much longer than their husbands to win local elective office. More significantly, the different gender patterns of political activism implied that labour politics was secondary to women's primary roles as wives and mothers while remaining an integral part of men's lives.

POLITICAL IDEAS

In recent interviews, all respondents were asked what they hoped to achieve when they joined labour and socialist organizations in the interwar years. Their answers had a remarkable sameness. Men and women alike expressed themselves in terms of broadly humanitarian ideals with a strong class emphasis. Arthur Warren spoke of 'fire in my belly to work for justice and equity in society'. Nellie Whitely felt strongly that 'working people should be able to have a say in their own destiny'. Tom Riley hoped that 'everybody would have sufficient and we'd become a socialist state'. Jim Cole wanted 'to improve conditions for ordinary people, to achieve a fairer distribution of the nation's resources'. Louie Davies explained that she was 'becoming more and more interested in the rights of the working class'. Edna Mitchell wanted to do 'something useful for the majority of the workers'. Marge Evans felt, 'it was the only way, through political action, to allow social justice'. Ellen Kendall had a 'sense of kinship with working people and a desire to fight for a more just society'.

These comments give some clues to the respondents' general political beliefs. The most common ingredient was an awareness of class-based injustice. The knowledge that working people were 'oppressed' or 'disadvantaged' was at the heart of men's and women's political motivation. They were filled with a determination to fight against oppression in all its manifestations – inequalities in educational opportunities and health care, poor housing, low wages and bad working conditions, the slaughter of working people in war, ill-fed and under-clothed children, mothers dying in childbirth – the dirt, the struggle and the indignities. They were far less interested in identifying or discussing the oppressors. Although one or two referred to 'the ruling class', the 'tories ' and the 'bosses', the majority seemed to want class justice not class war.

Respondents in the interwar period were convinced that working people, once fully organized, would radically change the nature of society. In the foreseeable future, they would replace competitive capitalism with a new system modeled on the co-operative commonwealth and firmly based on the principles of justice, equality, co-operation and international peace. Bill Wilson remembered the younger members in the Coventry Labour Party after the First World War expressing their firm belief that 'the revolution would come and Britain would be socialist'. In the 'new society' every family would have sufficient for its needs and people would live 'with the light of knowledge in their eyes'. With the exception of the communists, they put their faith in the Labour Party as the instrument of peaceful change through the ballot box. Labour as well as communist respondents described themselves as 'revolutionaries' at that time but no-one talked of violent revolution. They appeared to envision some kind of peaceful 'mass action' which would lead to the collapse of the capitalist state and its replacement by a socialist or communist one.

The respondents' socialism – idealistic, humanitarian and ethical – had its roots in the late nineteenth century socialist revival and before that in Robert Owen. It was particularly associated with the ILP and it is worth noting how much more influential the ILP was than its small, regional membership would suggest, particularly among the prewar generation represented by the respondents' parents. ILP socialism was much more accessible to women recruits than the labourism associated with the Labour Party. On the one hand, it promised to end the subjection of women as surely as it would eliminate the exploitation of the wage-worker: 'Under socialism there would be no exploiting class, no tyranny of one sex or race over another.'[40] It was also, like the Co-operative Movement, family-based. ILP socialists argued that equality and social justice could only prevail in the wider society if they were firmly established in its most fundamental social and economic unit.

None of the women activists mentioned such feminist goals as women's legal, economic or social equality when they spoke of their reasons for joining the political labour movement. Even those who went into the Women's Co-operative Guild which devoted more of its agenda to working-class women's interests, expressed their motivation in class, not gender terms. The only clear distinction between women's and men's stated goals was that women more often voiced their interest in the future of working-class children. Ruth Wild, for example, thought that joining the Labour Party was, 'the place to start to try to make things better for my and other folks' children'. Lily Watson wanted working-class children to have 'more chance [than her generation] to discover they have brains and souls and to develop them'. In this respect, these members of the postwar generation of labour women differed from their prewar counterparts in the Guild and the Women's Labour League. Labour women activists like Ada Chew, Selina Cooper, Hannah Mitchell and Annot Robinson who lived through the suffrage struggle were much more outspoken in their demands for attention to women's special needs and equal rights in labour organizations.

Although they avoided the rhetoric of gender equality, many female respondents placed the needs of working-class women and children high on the list of social reforms they advocated and worked for in the twenties and thirties. Twenty-four identifed maternal and child welfare as their major concern and described their attempts to implement reforms in their communities. Violet Fletcher discovered that 'women were very much the underdogs in life' when she moved from a rural area to the Black Country in 1922. Until then, she was unaware that children were still legally the property of their fathers and could be taken from their mothers in the event of a marital separation or divorce. She worked with Mrs Fenn, the Labour Party organizer in the district, 'to secure parliamentary legislation to safeguard a mother's rights in respect of her children'.[41] Nellie Whitely was active in improving the quality of maternity services in Bradford. Marge Evans and her Labour Party women's section persuaded the local council to open two more maternal and child welfare clinics in Bristol. Other activists remembered campaigning for local nursery schools. Hettie Bower worked through the Guild to establish one in her part of North London and Marge Evans did the same in Bristol. About one-fifth of the sample mentioned their support for family allowances. Edna Hanes was proud of the fact that after several years of lobbying she managed to get her union, NUSDAW, to support family allowances at the Labour Party conference.

Sixteen women placed the struggle to get free birth control information for working-class women among their top reform priorities. Mrs Ford remembered Dr Edith Summerskill who later became a Labour MP, coming to talk to their section on the subject and the discussions that followed.[42] Nina Drongin from Chatham and Enid Hyde from Pudsey said that their Guild branch and Labour Party women's section took part in the 'agitation for birth control'. As a mid-wife Nellie Whitely worked to break through the Medical Officer of Health's opposition to birth control in Shipley.[43] Alice Onions helped to set up the first birth control clinic in Wolverhampton in the home of a railway worker who was also a Labour man.

Male respondents contrasted sharply with women in the issues they considered important in the interwar period. They either ignored birth control, family allowances and improved care for mothers and children or placed them at the bottom of their list of reform priorities. At the top they put unemployment and the Means Test. As many as a third of the male respondents had direct or indirect experience of the unemployment crisis in the years following the General Strike of 1926. Bas Barker was an unemployed miner when the strike began and he continued intermittently unemployed for years after the miners' lockout ended. Rees Davies, another miner, was unemployed from 1926 to 1934 except for an eighteen-month period as a checkweighman. Bill Williams, an engineer from the Liverpool area, was out of work from 1928 to 1932, the worst years of the depression. Fred Price's elder brother Tom lost his job because of the strike and his father had to go 'cap in hand' to ask for re-instatement when it was over. Unemployment brought exposure to the harsh conditions of the Means Test. Bill Williams recalled not receiving any unemployment benefit under the Means Test because he lived at home and his father was working.

Even if they were not themselves unemployed in the interwar years, many male activists remembered their efforts to organize or assist the masses who were. As a member of the communist-led National Unemployed Workers' Movement in the thirties, Bas Barker spoke at labour exchanges and organized meetings with trade union and other labour organizations to try to get their support.[44]

Local Labour men who stayed out of the NUWM expressed their sympathy and support for the unemployed by finding food and shelter for the hunger marchèrs who came through their towns. Tom Riley in North Tottenham said: 'We brought them [proper] shoes because some of their shoes were simply no soles at all, just tops.' Frank Jackson found a meeting place for the Tottenham unemployed in the Town Hall. Bill Wilson joined the marchers when they came through Coventry in 1931 and Rees Davies marched with them from Tredegar, South Wales.

Men and women respondents were in broad agreement on the importance of education, housing and a national health scheme. As we saw, many of the activists had been frustrated in their desire for further education beyond the elementary school and this no doubt accounts for their dedication to educational reform. But while the men merely stated their support for a policy of free secondary education to age sixteen, women respondents had often campaigned on educational issues in their home towns. Mrs Ford worked to improve conditions and teaching standards in the Tottenham schools, 'because, after all, you are nowhere without a good education'. Ivy Burston who taught herself tailoring and then went to night school to train as a teacher, campaigned for nursery schools in Birmingham and started classes to educate poor children in co-operative principles. Majorie Evans South, a teacher herself, said that as a member of Windsor Borough Council education committee, she had helped secure 'the best educational facilities for all children, not just the rich', and introduced programmes for children with special needs. Another issue that received about the same level of support from men and women was equal pay. It came in the top four of eight issues for a fifth of men and women. Women who had spent more time in the labour force, tended to rank it high, but so did some dedicated male trade unionists, no doubt because they regarded it as a protection against low-paid women workers undercutting men's wage rates.

More women than men talked or wrote about their passionate support for peace in the interwar period. Nina Drongin could remember feeling a 'revulsion against war ... an instinct against any violence'. She wholeheartedly approved the Guild's pacifism. Mrs Mitchell said: 'We were opposed to war. We knew there was no glory in war, no victors, only victims.' Ruby Jobson, Hettie Birkby, Nelly Logan and Enid Hyde mentioned their dedication to the cause of world peace and participation in No More War marches and demonstrations. Marge Evans said the peace issue was important to her, because she believed that 'I am my brother's keeper' and she wanted a better world for her children. Bill Wilson was one of three men and five women who collected for the Peace Ballot in 1936.

When women evaluated their particular contribution to the political labour movement, the majority emphasized their achievements as social reformers in areas that benefitted working-class women and children. Bertha Grieveson said: 'We were very interested in equal opportunity for men and women and very strong on education and child welfare. We introduced milk in schools and day nurseries for working mothers.' Edna Mitchell believed 'women worked more sincerely than men for issues such as birth control, maternal and child welfare and family allowances'. Mrs Scott spoke of women's influence 'on child welfare, factory and shop conditions, education – making things better for families.'. Ellen Kendall's view was 'by taking part in political activity we could bring pressure to bear on those responsible for dealing with all kinds of social problems, particularly poverty and unemployment'. Amelia Jane Bear thought labour women 'worked hard to get better working conditions and better living for poor people'.

Labour men evaluated their contribution to the movement as politicians as much as social reformers. They emphasized what they had done to help the party hold its own in election campaigns and how they worked as labour councillors to provide the best possible municipal services. Sid Osguthorpe from Sheffield was proud of canvassing for Labour candidates in *twenty* general elections starting with the Coupon Election of 1918. Arthur Warren, a borough councillor in Dartford, Kent, described his contribution as making sure 'the money raised by rate was spent on services for all and not at the whim and cry of those able to pay their own way'. As a member of Manchester City Council, Jim Cole had 'improved housing standards and welfare services'. He said he 'always provided an ear for constituents with complaints'. Ray South worked for 'the highest possible standards in civic amenities, housing and parks' in Windsor and Fred Price from Merseyside had managed to push through the Council, plans for 'that magnificent building known as the [Ellesmere Port] Central Library'.

Men and women with a background in the ILP or the Communist Party were more likely than Labour respondents to identify the same achievements. Both sexes worked in the NUWM; both were active in the successful struggle against fascism in the thirties and both highlighted any contribution they had made to the republican cause in the Spanish Civil War. For these respondents and many others, the conflict in Spain was the most memorable event of the interwar years. It embodied their ideals of international working-class solidarity, anti-fascism and socialist humanitarianism and showed them in stark contrast to the appeasement policies of western capitalist governments. Labour men and women remembered raising money, urging the Labour Party to take a firmer stand on the need for allied intervention, marching, demonstrating and holding meetings on street corners and in labour halls. Arthur Dutton probably spoke for many socialist men when he said: 'I should have gone across, I should have gone across to Spain ... I didn't do enough.'[45]

It is clear that the respondents had broadly similar political goals and aspirations centred on improving the condition of their class and transforming capitalist society into the co-operative commonwealth. They differed along both gender and ideological lines on issues and strategies. Labour women put their emphasis on social welfare reform in the interests of working-class women and children as the best way to improve living standards for working-class families and communities. They looked to the state to pass the necessary legislation once Labour came to power but showed little interest in the mechanics of political power. Labour men stressed issues that had to do with the workplace and municipal amenities but they recognized the need to devote time and energy to winning political power. They gave more attention than women to political in-fighting and electoral battles. Communists of both sexes focused on class struggle, not social reform. They remembered the days of the United Front and the popular communist-led movements against unemployment and fascism.

THE GENDER ISSUE

Interviews and answers to the questionnaire also provided information on attitudes towards women and gender relations among rank and file labour activists. Respondents answered questions about the gender division of responsibility in their local Labour party, ILP or Communist Party branch, whether men or women were dominant, and how far their organization encouraged equal opportunity for women to hold office and stand as candidates for local and national government. Well over half the men were of the opinion that the sexes were equal partners in every aspect of local party business even when they noted that as a general rule men sat on committees, made speeches and ran as candidates, while women canvassed, raised funds and ran social events. One of the men who argued for equal partnership pointed out that women were actively encouraged as 'a basic tenet' of co-oporative policy; another that women were legally eligible to sit on all committees (whether they actually did so or not); and still another that the Labour Party ' always tried to be fair'. Bill Wilson commented that as far as he could remember, 'the issue of equal opportunity never arose' implying that it was never in dispute.

The minority of male respondents who thought men were dominant in their organizations agreed with Jim Cole, an electric welder from Merseyside, that 'basically the women ran the social side leaving the politics to the men'. The reasons they gave for this division of responsibility were connected with women's primary commitment to their families. Cole pointed out that 'it was not so easy for women to get away for conferences' and Rees Davies, a miner, explained that although miners' wives 'supported their men in all their political activities, large families restricted women's full activities'. Davies went further when he suggested that 'women did not consider it [labour politics] a part of their lives'. The other argument the minority gave for male dominance was that women attended their own sections and the men only consulted them on party business when they were considering joint activities.

Women's answers to the questions on gender were the mirror images of men's. Over half the women said that men had been dominant in their organizations in the interwar period. Annie Cain remembered that it was 'mostly the men who held office'; Nellie Jackson that 'women had very little say in policy forming in that period'. Marge Evans thought labour women had learnt only 'recently' to refuse the 'menial or unattractive jobs' in the local party. None of the women condemned the party or their male colleagues for encouraging the imbalance of power. Instead they suggested that separate sections had solved the problem. Ellen Kendall explained it this way: 'Women needed separate organization in order to ensure that their views were made known.' Amelia Bear admitted, 'men did tend to dominate the meetings. Women organized separately became more effective.' One or two women blamed their own sex for male domination, arguing that women did not attend meetings regularly and were timid in challenging male authority. Edna Hanes, the only woman on the NUDAW executive, observed that she had found 'male colleagues often encouraged women' who showed consistent interest in the union.

The minority of women who claimed gender equality in their organizations tended to be from 'mixed' organizations, the ILP or the Communist Party, or women who had successfully penetrated the male office-holding hierarchy at the national level of the Labour Party. Hettie Bower, Nina Drongin and Nellie Logan all commented that men and women shared the political work in their Communist Party branches on a completely equitable basis. Nellie said: 'We were all in it together, no time to think what sex you were.' Barbara Elliott, a full-time paid organizer in the Labour Party emphatically denied any 'bias against women' in the party. In her opinion, if women were unequal it was because they shut themselves off from the mainstream movement in women's sections. 'I never encouraged women's organizations.'

The testimony about gender relations revealed a difference of perception between the majority of men and women about the meaning of sexual equality in the context of local labour politics. Most men took 'equality' to mean a relationship based upon a clear gender division of responsibility and power such as often existed in working-class marriages. They reserved their highest praise for wives or other women activists who gave their first attention to home and family and fit their politics around this primary obligation. They were satisfied that their organizations supported women's equal rights and put no constitutional barriers in the way of women's access to office-holding power. A minority of women agreed with this definition. Most women, however, defined equality in light of their own experience. They remembered men doing most of the talking and decision-making in the constituency parties and leaving them to make the tea and organize the Christmas party. Because they did not feel like equals in this situation, they chose to meet in separate sections where they could express their points of view and make their own decisions. They seemed to find this arrangement met their expectations of equality and fulfilled the Labour Party's claim to stand for women's equal rights.

CONCLUSIONS

According to the testimony of this particular group of a hundred interwar labour activists, the new women members who came into the movement after 1918 had a great deal in common with their male comrades and significant differences. The common denominators were their working-class backgrounds, an ethical socialism and long-established conventions of gender difference. While class interest and socialist ideology united men and women in the movement, the shared conventions about gender roles tended to drive them apart. Women's experience at home, in the workplace, and in trade unions diverged from men's in ways that encouraged a division of political interests along gender lines and raised barriers to their full and equal participation in the movement.

Not surprisingly, the most powerful interest that bound these labour men and women together was their class. Although they came from families with a wider range of occupations and incomes than other studies have implied, they shared a working-class identity. Whether their fathers were skilled engineers or dock labourers, they experienced economic insecurity due to unemployment, large families or the illness of the breadwinner. Even respondents from better-off families remembered the struggle to make ends meet, shopping for food bargains, wearing hand-me-down clothes, 'scrimping and saving'. Almost without exception they had grown up in urban working-class neighbourhoods, physically separated from the middle class. Despite the differences between mining, textile, railway and dockland towns, the working-class neighbourhoods they described had a lot in common, with their streets of rowhouses, corner shops, nonconformist chapels and Victorian schools with small railed-off concrete playgrounds. Just over a third had a background in non-conformist religion, mostly Methodist or Primitive Methodist and about the same number had a shared socialist culture that included Socialist Sunday Schools, the Labour Church, the *Daily Herald* or *Reynolds News*. The respondents assumed the existence of a common working-class culture and their testimony supports this assumption.

Within this common culture, the respondents in the study shared certain characteristics as labour activists, regardless of their gender. With few exceptions, they had become aware of social injustice at an early age. As they were growing up, they reached the conclusion that their families, neighbours, and by extension all working people, were unfairly deprived of basic needs and opportunities. At least a third owed this consciousness to labour or socialist parents; others learnt the lesson from experience and observation. Perhaps they were particularly receptive to parental influence and prone to develop a precocious sense of responsibility because so many were eldest children. Another common formative experience was the frustration they felt at having to leave school at fourteen because their parents could not afford to send them to secondary school. In many cases, they used the disappointment as a spur to self-education and labour politics. Most characteristic of all, women as well as men were self-described rebels who refused to accept things as they were and set out to build a better world.

The evidence is strong that men and women drew their inspiration from the same political ideology. It would be unfair to judge the complexity of their ideas on the basis of the brief descriptions that they gave, but some general conclusions emerge. Their's was a visionary socialism which owed more to Robert Owen, Christian Socialism and the Independent Labour Party than Karl Marx. Its goal was the co-operative commonwealth, the antithesis of competitive capitalism, in which everyone would co-operate in the production and distribution of goods and services for the benefit of all. The co-operative commonwealth would end all exploitation and inequality, economic, social or sexual, and bring peace based on international working-class solidarity. This essentially teleological ideology explains the respondents use of idealistic terms to describe their aspirations as socialists in the interwar period. They wanted 'a better world', social justice for their class and equal opportunities for their children. They were much more confident of achieving the co-operative commonwealth in the interwar years than they are today. Labour men and women expected a Labour majority in Parliament to achieve their goal; socialists and communists thought more in terms of a workers' uprising.

A key tenet of the respondents' socialism was the equality of the sexes but it was usually an unexpressed assumption. Only a few women cadres mentioned it as a reason for joining the Labour Party and their male comrades seemed puzzled that women's equal rights in the movement should be an issue for discussion. But the socialist ideal of sexual equality was a poor fit with long-established conventions of gender difference. The majority of men and women activists accepted a gender division of social and political responsi-

bility which at its simplest assigned all things domestic and maternal
to women and all things public, industrial, commercial and financial
to men. Merely by going into politics, the women in the study pushed
out the boundaries of their sphere but they continued to justify their
activities as legitimate extensions of their domestic or maternal
authority. Though a majority remembered male domination at
'mixed' meetings and chose to meet in their own sections or guild
branches, few were conscious of having been victims of gender
inequality. Men and women alike assumed that separate and
different was still equal.

Gender differentiation began in the activists' homes. Almost as
many men as women had parents who were either in the labour
movement or were sympathic to socialism. But women were twice as
likely as men to attribute their political ideas to their parents, usually
their fathers. They remembered their fathers teaching them socialist
values through stories and moral lessons and taking them to meetings
and rallies. In fewer cases, mothers performed a similar function,
motivating their daughters by setting an example of political activism
and social responsibility. To a much greater extent than men, women
had detailed memories of the poverty in their homes and streets,
children without shoes, destitute women and evicted families. Men
certainly had similar experiences but women identified them as the
main reason for their years of dedication to the labour cause.

While women derived most of their political inspiration from their
families and neighbourhoods, men's contacts and experiences in the
workplace and trade union either reinforced or displaced family
influence. Men's route to the Labour Party, the ILP or the CPGB
often lay through their trade union where they learnt the lessons of
organization, class confrontation and negotiation. They acquired a
distinct set of political goals and strategies in an environment where
industrial and political activities were closely integrated. In contrast,
most of the women in the sample, had only a short-lived and often
disappointing experience with trade union membership. They found
that most of their fellow workers were not in the union, and that the
male leadership took little interest in them. The union therefore
offered women none of the companionship and office-holding
experience that it gave men nor did it impress them as an effective
means for creating social change.

This was a significant divergence. Women activists thought of
themselves as social reformers, working to improve the conditions

that they experienced in their homes and communities. They did not use feminist rhetoric but they made domestic and female-centred concerns their main political focus. Their agendas included birth control, family allowances, equal pay, more and better education and peace. The men who served their political apprenticeship in a mostly male trade union, on the other hand, were inclined to see their politics in more organizational and confrontational terms and to focus their reformism on work-related issues and power politics.

According to the women studied here, gender roles affected other aspects of the experience of labour activism. The demands of home and family changed the pattern and the intensity of women's participation. No matter how ingenious they were in finding ways to balance family and political responsibilities, the former had a way of asserting their primacy. A majority found that they had to put politics aside while their children were small or when family crises occurred. Only one or two indicated that they were conscious of this difference as a source of inequality with male comrades. They were more aware of the social conventions that frowned on women taking part in public life. As a result, they tended to exaggerate the extent to which labour organizations supported the equality of the sexes and were grateful to husbands and male colleagues for allowing them to pursue their political interests.

Historians who have assumed that the new women activists of the twenties and thirties were of no historical interest because they were indistinguishable from their male counterparts, clearly failed to take into account the impact of ideas about appropriate gender roles and behaviour on working-class labour activists. Beneath the rhetoric of equality that all interwar labour and socialist organizations used, lurked the reality of gender difference quietly insisting that politics for women was a thing apart while it was a man's entire existence. With the same backgrounds and ideology, a majority of the labour men and women in the study were concerned with different policy issues and had different overall strategies. In the Labour Party, they often met separately and assumed different political responsibilities. The result was nearly always unequal power in men's favour. Without some understanding of this pattern of class resemblance and gender difference among male and female activists, it is impossible to evaluate the significance and the outcome of the gender conflicts that occurred in the Labour Party in the twenties over birth control, family allowances and women's autonomy.

CHAPTER 3

' ... *But the seats are reserved for men' the gender struggles of the twenties*

The decade from 1922 to 1932 was a generally disappointing and difficult period for labour men and women after the heightened expectations of the postwar years. The reappearance of mass unemployment in late 1920 marked the end of the postwar boom and heralded an economic recession that lasted, with short periods of recovery and deep depression, into the early thirties. This economic downturn was accompanied by an overall political swing to the right. With the exception of two short-lived minority Labour governments in 1924 and 1929–31, the period was one of almost uninterrupted Conservative rule. Strike defeats and declining membership weakened the trade unions while the political labour movement grappled with the problems posed by the formation of the British Communist Party in 1920. Organized women had to fight for their social welfare programme in an environment of government cutbacks and attacks on married women workers.[1]

These hostile conditions provoked very different responses from the men and women in the labour movement. On the male side, the Trade Union Congress (TUC) moved towards defensive strategies following the defeat of the General Strike in 1926, while the Labour Party strove to differentiate itself from the Communists, by sticking closely to the straight and narrow path of parliamentary politics.[2] Organized women, on the other hand, still growing in numbers and with all the vigour and enthusiasm of the newly converted, were in no mood for retrenchment.[3] They were determined to help working-class women survive the return of the prewar pattern of unemployment and family poverty. Ignoring government cutbacks and the anti-feminist backlash, they embarked on an ambitious and controversial programme of social welfare reforms which included state-supported birth control, family allowances and extended care programmes for mothers and young children.

The pursuit of such divergent policies inevitably led to gender conflict in the Labour Party. At almost every annual party conference from 1923 to 1930, the male majority voted down or refused to discuss reforms that the women had overwhelmingly endorsed at their own national conference a few weeks before. The women argued that birth control and family allowances were class concerns because they would raise the living standards of working-class families, while the men labelled them 'special interest' issues that threatened party unity. Labour women leaders with a foot in both camps gave timid and belated support to the rank-and-file or sided with the mainstream opposition. After repeated efforts to reverse the negative decisions, Labour Party women turned to the source of their weakness and tried once more to change the party constitution.

The gender struggles of the twenties were not merely policy disagreements but a continuation of earlier attempts to define women's place in the party. When organized women asked their own leaders and the mainstream party to support reforms that were of special concern to their sex, they were trying to establish the principle of equality of gender interests in labour politics. Those who refused to give that support claimed that they were acting to prevent the party splitting along gender lines into distinct and antagonistic groups. The two points of view clashed in the struggles over birth control, family allowances and the party constitution.

THE BIRTH CONTROL CONFLICT

The birth control campaign should be viewed as just one part of a broad social welfare policy which Labour, Guild and ILP women pursued with remarkable consistency throughout the twenties and into the early thirties. Their overall goal was to remove working-class mothers and their children from the cycle of poverty associated with the capitalist wage and employment structure. They insisted that the state provide workers' families with a standard of health and well-being comparable to that enjoyed by the wealthier classes. Access to free birth control, family allowances, nursery schools and the proper care of maternity were all intended to accomplish this end. Of all these reforms, birth control generated the greatest fervour and unanimity among organized women and the most determined resistance from the male majority.[4]

Birth control became the pivotal political issue for Labour and Co-operative women only after the war. Before 1914, the few League and Guild women who mentioned the subject at all, expressed varying degrees of ignorance, confusion and moral outrage about its use. The subject was first raised publicly in letters written to *Labour Woman* in the autumn of 1913. Four authors, sounding distinctly middle class, made the case for and against 'family limitation'. Those opposing argued that birth control was a moral evil to which the working class in its greater purity had not fallen prey or that socialism, not birth control, was the answer to family poverty. Those in favour pointed out that working women did not go on having children out of moral superiority. The truth was they wanted to limit their families but did not know how. As A. Caroline Sewell put it: 'I find that the honest, simple poor want to know how "rich ladies manage" as they consider it hard on them to be kept in the dark.'⁵

In a remarkable collection of letters written in 1914, Guild women confirmed Sewell's perception that many working-class mothers were indeed desperate to limit the size of their families. The Guild's central committee had asked local branch members to answer questions about the size, age and condition of their families as part of the 'fact-finding ' to promote a national scheme for maternity care. The response was overwhelming. In addition to the questionnaires, three hundred and eighty-six Guild women sent personal and often harrowing accounts of their experiences of pregnancy, childbirth and marriage. A hundred and sixty of their letters were published in 1915 under the title of *Maternit:y Letters from Working Women*.⁶

The letters were a moving plea for relief from the burdens of repeated child-bearing. At a time when convention spoke of motherhood as 'that sacred calling', the majority of correspondents dreaded the prospect of another child. As one explained: 'All the beautiful in motherhood is very nice if one has plenty to bring up a family on, but what real mother is going to bring a life into the world to be pushed into the drudgery of the world at the earliest possible moment because of the strain on the family exchequer?'⁷ Many of the Guild women who wrote letters had suffered miscarriages, their babies had died in infancy or been 'sickly,' 'delicate' and 'hard to raise'. Some described going without food during pregnancy as the only way to save money for their confinement; others wrote about the lasting physical problems they endured as a result of difficult deliveries and insufficient rest. They used phrases such as 'I am a ruined woman'; 'I dragged about in misery'; 'I am nearly used up.'

Although the letters give the strong impression of an almost universal demand for some means to control family size, very few writers mentioned birth control. They wanted the state to take responsibility for healthy motherhood and enact the Guild's National Care of Maternity programme. Capitalizing on the growing political concern about what could be referred to in the relative innocence of the post-Darwin, pre-Nazi years as the 'health and vigour of the race', they demanded state doctors and mid-wives, maternity hospitals and financial aid. As one said: 'Our children are a valuable asset to the nation and the health of the woman who is doing her duty in rearing the future race should have a claim upon the national purse.'[8]

The six Guild women who mentioned 'preventives' were apologetic and defensive. One explained that although she could be accused of 'commiting race suicide' she felt the decision justified by the misery and suffering of repeated pregnancies. Another confessed that she had 'disgusted' some of her fellow Guild members by 'advocating restrictions'. A third explained: 'I had a fight with my conscience before using preventives.' The other three implied that they themselves did not use birth control but could understand the state of mind and body that might lead women to such a course. One said: 'When we know what the working women have to go through you need not wonder at them trying to curtail the family.'[9] The infrequency with which the subject was mentioned and the shame-faced reluctance of its advocates suggests that before the First World War, artificial birth control was still a socially taboo subject among the respectable working class. Despite their deeply felt need to control their fertility, the majority of Guild women seemed to look upon birth control as an offence against nature, associated with immorality and the upper classes.

The First World War broke down the taboo and some of the misconceptions about birth control among the working-class. Increased mobility, higher wages and more independence among young women workers, disruption of working class family life and the frightening decline in life-expectancy for soldiers at the front, all contributed to a change in sexual mores. Wartime publicity about unmarried mothers, sexual promiscuity and veneral disease made these once unmentionable topics part of working-class discourse. More soldiers and civilians began to use condoms in response to public warnings about the spread of veneral disease.[10]

In some working-class families, war conditions affected the gender distribution of power and responsibility. With the men away, married women became heads of households and for many this was a liberating experience, increasing their self-confidence and encouraging them to expect more from life than endless pregnancies. Robert Roberts remembered local soldiers' wives in Salford who experienced the war as a ' great release' from the heavy hand of male authority.[11] In an interview, Mrs. Ford of Tottenham expressed a similar view. She said: 'Its only since the first world war and since women began to take an interest in politics that the women have been people. They were always the ones that stopped at home and put up with everything. After the war, after the women had worked in factories and been on the buses, they began to show that they were just as equal as men are. That's what first started all this.'[12] Certainly, the postwar generation of labour women discussed birth control without any of the inhibitions and defensiveness found in the *Maternity Letters*.

The influence of Marie Stopes and the middle-class birth control movement is harder to assess. It is doubtful whether many married working-class women would have read her best-selling books on the subject, *Married Love* and *Wise Parenthood* although some labour women activists may have done so. The Guild Central Committee purchased these books for their office in 1923 and advised the branches to do the same.[13] Jill Liddington mentions that Selina Cooper owned a collection of pamphlets and books on human sexuality and birth control which may have included them. Even if they did not read Miss Stopes' writings, they would have known who she was. So much publicity was given to the opening of Stopes' first birth control clinic and her unsuccessful lawsuit against the Catholic doctor, Halliday Sutherland, that her name became a household word. Working-class women were among the thousands who wrote asking her for advice. Their calls for help, like the *Maternity Letters*, testify to the intensity of working-class women's need and desire for family limitation.[14]

By the time mass unemployment was once more straining the health and ingenuity of working-class mothers, labour women were beginning to identify birth control as a vital aspect of their social welfare policy. In this environment, it needed only a small spark to light the fire of their enthusiasm for a campaign to make birth control available to those who were so sorely in need. That spark was the case of Nurse E. S. Daniels, a health visitor employed by the Edmonton

Public Health department in north-east London. Nurse Daniels was dismissed in December 1922 for 'insubordination and refusal to comply with the instructions issued to her in relation to maternity and child welfare.' She had in fact been telling women attending the Maternity and Child Welfare Clinic where they could get contraceptive advice. Following the publicity given to the case in *The Times*, the Minister of Health, Sir Alfred Mond, issued a ruling that maternity centres were not to give birth control information but should refer women with medical problems relating to child birth to a private doctor or hospital.[15]

Labour women rushed to Nurse Daniels' defence. They sent appeals to the Edmonton council and the Minister of Health to reconsider their decisions and in this way launched their birth control campaign. At their Annual Congress in May 1923, Guild women passed a resolution urging the ministry and the local health authorities to allow all maternity and child welfare centres to offer birth control information to married women who requested it.[16] A month later, at their national women's conference, several Labour Party women's sections submitted a similar resolution. After a short discussion, the matter was referred to the SJC, Labour women's advisory committee, to report on before the next conference.[17]

Once the rank-and-file had taken the initiative, a new cadre of young socialist feminists most of them outside the Labour Party power structure, came forward to organize and direct their efforts. They included middle-class women, Dora Russell, Rose Witcop and Frieda Laski and working-class activists, Alice Hicks and Jennie Baker. The ILPers, Dorothy Jewson MP and George Lansbury's daughter, Dorothy Thurtle, also gave their support. In May 1924, these women organized a deputation to John Wheatley, the Minister of Health in the first Labour government, asking him to lift the ban that made it illegal for local health authorities to dispense birth control information. John Wheatley was a Roman Catholic, keenly aware of the strong opposition that the Marie Stopes' case had aroused among his fellow Catholics in the Labour Party. He denied the deputation's request saying that in any case an administrative order would not be enough to reverse the Mond decision. Such a change would require parliamentary approval. Although the meeting failed in its object, it did help to identify an appropriate strategy. Labour women would have to win their party's overwhelming support in order to get a birth control measure passed in the House.[18]

From the beginning of the birth control campaign, Labour Party women leaders, notably Marion Phillips, the Chief Woman Officer and the party-controlled SJC, opposed their rank-and-file. In March 1924, Dora Russell and the other birth control advocates, impatient with the lack of response from the SJC to the 1923 conference resolutions, protested in a letter to *Labour Woman* that the committee had failed to carry out the instructions of the delegates. Marion Phillips responded angrily in a lengthy statement printed in *Labour Woman* in which she listed the reasons why the sections should not try to make birth control a party political issue.

Marion Phillips' arguments represented the official Labour Party position on birth control which remained unchanged throughout the entire debate. Members of the National Executive Committee appeared convinced from the outset that the mere mention of birth control on its agenda would split the party and damage its electoral prospects. Marion Phillips therefore began her statement with an appeal for party unity. Referring to the Irish Catholic minority among the working class, she said that since the party contained 'people of different religious and moral views', Labour women were, 'bound in our loyalty to the common cause of labour not to force them to separate themselves from us on an issue that is not a political one but is in a very special sense a matter of private conviction'. Secondly, she argued that if women put all their efforts into the primary struggle for socialism, they would find that with the achievement of a socialist society, there would be no economic need to limit family size. She ended by pleading with Labour women not to make the 'intimate relations of husband and wife' a political issue at all but to confine themselves to calling for a full expert investigation of the medical side of the question.[19]

The arguments were forceful and coming from the most powerful Labour woman propagandist ought to have had considerable impact. Yet, they seem to have had no affect at all on rank-and-file determination to get Labour to support working-class women's right to free birth control information. The number of local sections sending resolutions calling for such a measure to the 1924 women's conference, tripled. Instead of accepting the clearly stated wishes of the membership, however, Marion Phillips assumed the role of policing agent for the male party leaders and tried to weaken and contain the struggle. According to Dora Russell, just before the conference opened, Marion Phillips confronted her and demanded that she withdraw her birth control resolution. When Mrs Russell said that she could not ignore the instructions of her section, Miss Phillips replied: 'Sex should not be dragged into politics – you will split the Party from top to bottom.'[20]

This remark reveals the deep gulf of misunderstanding that divided the mainstream party, including the women leaders, from the rank-and-file women on this issue. Labour women conference delegates did not refer to birth control as a private, sexual matter. They talked of it in terms of maternal health, child care and the responsibility of the state to the citizen, thus identifying it with other social welfare measures to which the Labour Party was already committed. In their enthusiasm, they were inclined to place it in an even broader political context. For example, in her speech at the 1924 Labour Women's Conference, Mrs Palmer of Southampton declared, amid conference applause, that birth control was an essential factor in the abolition of poverty, 'the civilized substitute for war, for famine, for pestilence, for disease.'[21]

Labour women's birth control campaign drew its fervour and unity from a deep well of resentment at the sufferings of excessive child-bearing and the frustration of efforts to give working-class children a 'fair chance in life'. When Dora Russell listened to delegates at the 1924 Labour Women's Conference, she was shocked by the vehemence with which the women spoke out against child-bearing, repudiating 'what had been preached at us as the noblest fulfillment of our womanhood'.[22] Mrs Lane from Houghton-le-Spring was one of them. She saw in women's demand for birth control evidence of their emancipation. This generation was prepared to 'rise up to fight against the things that oppress us'. The old fatalism about the sufferings of child-birth, 'enduring patiently that which they believed could not be altered,' was gone and women wanted to avoid subjecting children to the pain and suffering of a world of deprivation.[23] The only answer that the NEC offered, indirectly, to these concerns was that socialism, when it came, would provide all the answers. Most labour women rejected this solution. As one delegate put it, 'while they had the disease among them, they must take the only medicine they had'.[24]

While Marion Phillips and the NEC rejected the birth control measure for its potentially negative effect on national electoral politics, Labour women demanded it in the name of class justice. Mrs Jones of Greenwich was one of several delegates at the 1924 women's conference who wanted working women to have the same right to control their fertility that middle-class women enjoyed: 'We feel as working women, the working woman should have the right to say how many children they are able to have ... The wealthy woman says how many children she can have because she can afford to pay for the knowledge and we say that the working mother should be able to get the knowledge although she has no money.'[25] Others pointed out that working-class children from large families began their lives with such grave disadvantages in health, social training and education, that they were rarely able to escape from the confines of poverty. From this point of view, as Mrs Lane explained, those who were agitating for birth control were clearly those who had the 'social welfare of the community at heart'.[26]

The party's argument that any birth control measure would alienate Catholic party members and voters carried less weight with Labour women because they knew that many Catholic women were on their side. At the women's 1925 conference, Miss Quinn, an Irish Roman Catholic and member of the Tailors and Garment Workers' Union was among only six delegates out of just over a thousand who voted against the resolutions on birth control. She referred to birth control as 'an impure and unchaste matter ... a device against God and humanity'. These statements produced such an outraged response from the other delegates that the conference was disorderly for several minutes. A fellow Catholic, Mrs Simpson, was incensed that Miss Quinn, a single woman, should presume to lay down rules of conduct for working-class mothers. She herself had given birth to thirteen children and wished that she had had 'more knowledge'. While there were undoubtedly many Catholic working-class women who regarded any birth control measure as against the teachings of the Church, Labour women Catholics, with the exception of Miss Quinn, did not publicly raise their voices against the lifting of the local government ban.[27]

While there was clearly no meeting of the minds between Labour women and the mainstream movement over the birth control issue itself, a more profound disagreement lay at the heart of the dispute. The two sides held widely divergent views about the place and function of women in the party and the meaning of the party's commitment to sexual equality. For Marion Phillips and the NEC, equality meant that women would have the same opportunity as men to hold office and be elected as delegates to the annual party conferences where policy decisions were made. Even though this constitutional equality was unlikely ever to become a reality because of women's virtual exclusion from the large industrial trade unions, any special concessions made to women as a group would be 'privilege' not equality. Labour women, on the other hand, interpreted equality to mean that women's political concerns would receive equal weight with men's in policy-making. They pointed to the women's conferences and women's guaranteed representation on the NEC as evidence that the constitution laid the foundations for women's separate but equal power.

This difference in perspective fuelled the birth control debate. The NEC argued that the women in the party were acting as a separate, special interest group trying to impose their minority opinion on the majority who represented the interests of the working class as a whole. Labour women denied this charge, insisting that their proposal to provide working-class women with access to free birth control information was a social welfare reform entirely compatible with the broader goals of the class party. As far as they were concerned birth control was as valid a way of raising working-class living standards as any industrial reform. It seemed to them to be just the kind of issue that the constitution intended as women's contribution to party policy. Furthermore, they were convinced that the party had an obligation to support their majority conference decisions. In 1924, Mrs Palmer made the confident assertion that the party had 'a responsibility to take the lead in pushing for this important reform whether it was a popular position or not'. She wanted the party 'to be the leader of women's thought in this country'. She added with some belligerence that 'if Labour refused to give that word of hope and of life to working-class women which they are waiting to receive ... then someone else will'.[28] In this spirit, Labour women began their fight to lift the birth control ban on local clinics and at the same time win the right to make policy on issues of concern to working-class women.

Immediately after the 1924 women's conference which had passed the birth control resolution almost unanimously, Dora Russell, Frieda Laski, Dorothy Jewson and two hundred other delegates from the sections whose names we do not know, formed the Workers' Birth Control Group (WBCG). Their purpose was to identify themselves as Labour birth controllers, quite distinct from the Malthusians and the eugenicists who had long been regarded as enemies of the working-class because they advocated family limitation only among the 'inferior' classes. Labour women did not want to be associated with the middle-class birth control societies like the New Generation League and Marie Stopes' Society for Constructive Birth Control in which similar eugenic ideas survived.[29] The WBCG had a single goal – to make it possible for working-class women to get birth control information and treatment, safely and without charge through the local state-supported maternity clinics. For six years from 1924 to 1930, the group kept in close touch with the women's sections around the country, encouraging them to set up local birth control groups. They sent out speakers, distributed letters and pamphlets, organized public meetings and lobbied Labour members of Parliament.

The WBCG was an outstanding example of an effective single issue lobbying organization. The minutes of local sections show how it rallied Labour women's support. In York, for example, on 17 June 1924, only days after its formation the WBCG sent a circular stating its position and goals, asking women from the section to join and enclosing a list of speakers. On 1 July the minutes refer to an enquiry about the WBCG from a Mrs Green, who was probably the section's representative on the local party executive committee. The section instructed the secretary to write to Mrs Green about bringing the birth control issue before the mostly male committee 'as we feel they ought to take an interest in this subject'. On 15 July 1924, the WBCG sent a circular informing the section of a new edition of Nurse Margaret Sanger's pamphlet on birth control. The section decided to order a dozen copies. On 16 September, the WBCG sent a letter requesting 'we try to arrange meetings for some of their speakers in our area and suggesting we get a number of sections to join in as this saves expense'.[30] Other section minutes show the same intense level of communication in the years 1924–7. During those years, many women's sections including York, Gorton, Stockport, Tottenham and Willesden reported the formation of WBCG branches.

The women's campaign did not fail for lack of good organization, intelligent strategy or tenacity. Over the next four years (1924–27) Labour women passed almost unanimous birth control resolutions at each women's conference, persuaded local constituency parties to submit birth control resolutions to national party conferences, met with local trades councils and labour federations to try to gain union support and lobbied local Labour councillors and members of Parliament. They pushed the SJC to give a full report of the progress of the campaign to the NEC and urge its members to support the birth control resolutions.[31]

Year after year, the NEC thwarted women's efforts by preventing the subject of birth control ever coming up for general discussion at the annual party conferences. In 1924, the conference ended abruptly because of the crisis over the Campbell case that forced the first Labour government out of power.[32] The birth control resolutions were among those that were never brought to the floor. In 1925, the NEC issued a statement declaring that birth control was not a party political matter and therefore had no place on the conference agenda. The statement which became the party's final word on the issue, read: 'That the subject of birth control is in its nature not one which should be made a political Party issue, but should remain a matter upon which members of the Party should be free to hold and promote their individual convictions.'[33] In 1926, because resolutions continued to appear, the NEC banned the subject under the 'three year rule' which forbade discussion of any resolution which had already appeared at three successive conferences and on which a ruling had been made.[34]

Why did the NEC repeatedly find ways to keep the birth control issue off the conference agenda? The opposition of the Roman Catholic minority was certainly one reason. John Wheatley was an influential member of the party leadership and Catholics were heavily represented in the large industrial trade unions, especially transport, textiles and mining. The Manchester and Salford Catholic Association was one of several regional organizations putting pressure on the NEC to oppose the birth control measure. Just as important, however, was the NEC's preoccupation in the years from 1924 to 1927 with its own political priorities. While Labour women were absorbed in the birth control campaign, the NEC and the male side of the labour movement were struggling with internal policy issues that they saw as critical to the survival of the party and the industrial labour movement.

At the top of the list was the threat from the Communist Party of Great Britain (CPGB) which absorbed more of the male leadership's attention in these years than any other single issue. Every year from 1921, the CPGB requested affiliation to the Labour Party and every year the party turned it down after long, often acrimonious debates. Labour leaders feared that the Communists would steal their members, split the party, cause dissension in the unions and undermine social democratic representation in Parliament. Their fears were partially confirmed in 1924 when the taint of association with Communism caused the party to fall from power after less than nine months and to lose the next election. The following year, the party finally banned Communists from its ranks but the NEC remained preoccupied with the enemy to the left.

Labour women took no part in the debates over the Communist Party. The handful who attended annual party conferences only contributed to discussion on women-related topics. Male delegates considered anything to do with internal party organization completely outside women's legitimate sphere. For this reason, Labour women had no direct involvement in the men's other major concern during these years, the events surrounding the General Strike. Locally, women raised money for miners' families, took miners' children into their homes and served on local strike action committees, but the men in the movement assumed responsibility for finding appropriate political strategies to deal with the crisis. When the defeated miners went back to work, the government pressed home its victory by passing the Trade Disputes and Trade Unions Act, a vindictive piece of legislation limiting the right to strike, denying civil service unions affiliation to the Labour Party and trade unionists' automatic party membership. As a direct result of the act, the party lost well over a million affiliated union members which crippled its finances. The NEC and the unions were grappling with these problems just when Labour women were pressing their birth control resolution.

The NEC's efforts to keep the subject of birth control from surfacing at party conferences make sense in the context of men's preoccupation with what they regarded as the critical issues facing the movement. With the party under pressure from the left and the right, Labour leaders found the question of whether women should be able to get birth control advice at their local clinics at best irrelevant, at worst, subversive. After the 1924 election defeat, the NEC consistently directed the party towards one over-riding objective, regaining parliamentary power. Victory at the polls would reaffirm Labour's place in mainstream democratic politics and allow the repeal of the Trade Disputes Act. Committee members argued that including birth control in its platform, would antagonize the sizeable minority of Roman Catholics in the party, alienate working-class Catholic voters and probably a host of other potential supporters.[35] It made no sense to them to weaken Labour's election prospects at a time when the whole labour movement was desperately in need of political power.

From Labour men's perspective, women were showing 'separatist tendencies' when they persisted in demanding that the party adopt their specialized agenda and change the constitution to increase their autonomy. The NEC was especially sensitive to 'separatism' in the mid-twenties, in part because of the long struggle over Communist members and in part because they feared the negative impact of party disunity on the voters. Labour leaders were determined to prevent the party splitting into warring interest groups. On a least two occasions, they reminded women that the party would not tolerate 'separatism'. For example, when Labour women formally applied for the 1926 Labour Women's Conference to be held in Huddersfield, Ramsey MacDonald proposed a motion: 'That future Reports show more clearly that the Conference is held under *the auspices of the Labour Party and not of the women's sections.*' [my italics]. On another occason, NEC members reminded Labour women that: 'if they (the NEC) advised the Party to take a stand on birth control then they would run the risk of allowing the Party to be used for *all sorts of specialist, non-party purposes*, with the consequent risk of offending good Labour Party members and supporters' and thus playing into the hands of their political enemies.[36]

Nothing demonstrates more clearly than the birth control struggle, the extent of gender segregation in the national Labour Party of the nineteen-twenties. With men and women pursuing their own policies and strategies, neither could well understand the other's point of view. Labour women seemed remarkably unaware of the political pressures behind the NEC's consistent opposition to their birth control resolution. Because of limited opportunities to participate in the debates over party policy and organization, they were slow to develop a sense of their responsibility for maintaining unity or making the compromises necessary to win national elections. On its part, the NEC never fully explained the political imperatives influencing its decision to reject the women's birth control proposal. The committee merely repeated its original statement that birth control was a private not a political matter, that it would upset religious minorities within the party and create disunity. Even in their own meetings, male committee members deliberately shunned discussion of the resolution. The NEC minutes for the years from

1924 to 1927 show that whenever Dr Adamson or Susan Lawrence raised the subject, it was invariably dismissed with motions for 'next business' or 'no action be taken' or 'further consideration of the subject be deferred'.[37]

National Executive Committee members' reluctance to discuss birth control as they would any other political issue hints at the possibility that their opposition went beyond purely political concerns to traditional working-class attitudes towards sex and gender roles.   Biographers and social historians of this period, including Richard Hoggart and Robert Roberts recalling their own working-class communities, have noted male public reticence on sex-related subjects.[38] This aspect of working-class culture was certainly represented in the Labour Party. Women in the sections and local parties often complained of difficulty in getting the men to discuss a birth control resolution.[39] Birth control may have threatened Labour men's domestic and sexual authority. Although Labour women never discussed types of birth control, they always implied that it should be the wife's responsibility, a means for her to gain control over her fertility.[40] Just as Labour men fought hard to prevent women exercising independent power within the party, they may have decided that they also had to fight against any erosion of their traditional control in marital relations and the family.

Despite their male comrades' discomfort and their party's repeated rejections, Labour women went on with the campaign, convinced that their cause was just. With the support of some of the constituency parties, they formally protested the NEC rulings and increased their efforts to reach local trade union members and Labour councillors. In February 1926, the WBCG tested the parliamentary waters. Two of their keenest supporters, Ernest Thurtle and Lord Buckmaster, both Labour members of Parliament introduced bills in both houses based on Labour women's birth control resolution. Neither bill had the backing of any political party; they were private members' bills on which members of Parliament could vote according to conscience. Such bills rarely become law but they are a useful barometer of parliamentary opinion on any issue. The Commons defeated the bill but the Lords passed it – and Labour women felt encouraged by the result. They had succeeded in getting members of Parliament to take their resolution seriously and a respectable number had given their support. In April, they had another boost. The ILP passed their birth control resolution at its annual conference.[41] Lastly, in spite of the party's ban, several constituency parties sent in birth control resolutions to the Labour Party's upcoming conference.

With some optimism, therefore, the leaders of the WBCG, Dora Russell and Dorothy Jewson moved a resolution at the 1926 Annual Labour Party Conference that the NEC reconsider the three-year ban and give delegates the opportunity to discuss the birth control resolution. Dora Russell set out to persuade the male trade union delegates that birth control was a matter of women's occupational safety. She asked them to imagine how they would feel if, as engineers or miners, they brought a proposal to the conference that they thought was vital to their lives, health and well-being, only to be told that the NEC refused discussion on the matter. 'Would it not make them wild? Well the women were wild.' Appealing to the miners with their powerful block vote, she compared the demand for birth control with their demand for a seven-hour day. 'She wanted them to realize that to the women it was as important as the seven-hour day was to the miners and their opinion ought to have the same weight as the Miners' Federation had in their matters.' She ended with a plea for equality in gender interests. 'If they wanted the women to march shoulder to shoulder with them, they must pay as much heed to a resolution they put forward as they would to that of any of the trade unions or affiliated organizations.' When the vote was taken, the women had won the right to further discussion of their resolution by a narrow margin of 1,656,000 for and 1,620,000 against.[42]

It appeared that Labour women had found a way to win the support of the only group that could help them, the industrial trade unionists. In this case, it was undoubtedly the miners, with the largest number of conference votes, who tipped the scale in their favour. The miners were not known for supporting feminist issues. They had been the last big trade union to back women's suffrage. What brought about their change of heart? Although Dora Russell's comparison of the dangers of child-bearing to those of coal mining may have moved them, they probably acted more out of a sense of reciprocity than conviction. Earlier in the same conference, the miners' delegates had lavished praise on Labour women for the support they gave the miners throughout the General Strike and in the early weeks of the lock-out. Mr Horner of the Miners' Federation had gone so far as to say that 'the women had saved the British Labour movement from disgrace. Had it not been for what the women had done, except for one or two unions, nothing would have been done.'[43] It would have been inconsistent with such sentiments to turn the women down flat. After all, they might have argued, they were not endorsing birth control, merely allowing conference discussion of the party's ban.

Buoyed with hope, Labour women prepared to push their birth control resolution one step further at the 1927 Annual Party Conference. This time a successful vote would send the resolution back to the NEC with a strong message to reconsider its 1925 decision that the subject of birth control was a private, not a political issue. Once again Labour women directed their message to the miners. Mrs Lawther from the Blaydon District Labour Party reminded them of their special obligation: 'Surely you will not turn the women down on this question because it was the women who stood four square with you in your dispute. It is four times as dangerous for a woman to bear a child as it is for you to go down a mine. You are seeking legislation to make your occupation safe, will you still go on allowing your wives to suffer under this ban?'[44] The same appeal produced a very different result. The resolution to refer back the Party's 1925 ruling on birth control was soundly rejected with only 275,000 in favour and 2,885,000 against.

The explanation for the defeat is not hard to find. The miners had just returned to work, defeated, after the gruelling seven months lock-out and the government had passed the Trade Disputes and Trade Unions Act. Together with the rest of the trade union movement, the miners looked to the party to reverse this disastrous piece of legislation. They could not afford to flout the NEC's rulings or do anything that might jeopardize the party's electoral success. They may also have been influenced by the energetic Catholic lobbying of the trade union block vote during the year.[45] The birth control resolution fell victim to political circumstances but in a broader sense, gender segregation caused the defeat. Segregated in the labour market as well as in labour politics, women had neither industrial nor political leverage. Under certain conditions, women's interests might appear to complement men's but when there was a crisis in the male sphere, women's concerns became secondary. If the women had succeeded in sending back their resolution to the NEC in 1927, only the wildest optimist could believe that they would have cleared the next two hurdles, persuading the NEC to withdraw its objections and getting a majority of trade union delegates to accept women's right to birth control.

From this time on, the cause was lost. In 1928, Arthur Henderson attended the Labour Women's Conference to 'promote better feeling' by explaining why the party had overruled their almost unanimous demand for the birth control measure four years in a row. His intent was no doubt to get this emotive subject off the agenda of future party conferences. He reasserted the party's unwillingness to 'legislate in advance of public opinion... on this question which touches the deep religious convictions of large numbers of people'. Surprisingly, he received the public backing of Ellen Wilkinson, the only Labour woman MP at the time and always a strong supporter of the rights of wage-earning women. Perhaps out of concern for her Catholic constituents, she argued that the measure had a better chance of passing if it was not made a plank in the party programme but was left to the pressure of women of all parties.[46] Another woman trade unionist, Mrs Bamber of the National Union of Distributive and Allied Workers, urged the delegates to accept the NEC ruling and concentrate their attention on vital issues such as housing and unemployment 'on which progress must be made before we could hope to secure the limitation of families'.[47] The birth controllers wearily repeated their arguments for this 'fundamental need' but when the vote was taken, the women delegates accepted the party line by a narrow margin of three votes with many abstaining. Either their party loyalty proved stronger than their commitment to birth control or they recognized that they lacked the power to succeed.

What were the results of this lengthy and seemingly futile campaign? Despite its failure within the Labour Party, the birth control campaign did produce some positive results. Labour women's efforts to convert local authorities to their point of view helped to change national policy. In 1930, the Labour Minister of Health sent all local health authorities a discreet memorandum (153/MCW) informing them that maternal and child welfare clinics were allowed to give birth control information to women 'in cases of medical necessity'.[48] British historian, Linda Ward argues that this minimal concession was an unintentional result of the Local Government Act of 1929. This act replaced the percentage grant system to local authorities with a block grant, making it difficult for the minister to use the sanction of withdrawal of government funding to prevent local councils from sponsoring any particular programme.[49]

However, there is evidence that the Minister was also responding to pressure from some local authorities who wanted to distribute birth control information. Guild and Labour women could take a major share of the credit for this pressure. In Edmonton, for example, where Nurse Daniels' dismissal had ignited the campaign, the women's section persuaded the Urban District Council to ask the Minister of Health to lift the ban, and when that was refused to continue to demand a change in the existing prohibition.[50] In some boroughs, like Shoreditch in London, where Labour women birth controllers were especially active, borough councils defied the ban and went ahead with a birth control programme forcing the minister to bring the law into line with the reality.[51] Rank-and-file activists vigorously lobbied their local health authorities for similar programmes all through the early thirties.[52]

These limited, local successes, however, could not hide the fact that at the national level, the birth control campaign had failed in its bid for Labour Party support. Labour women had put gender politics to the test and lost. They had proved to have less power and influence within the party than Roman Catholics. The party had rejected their idea of sexual equality as parity of women's concerns with men's in policy-making. It was clear that 'women's interests' existed in the Labour Party only as a verbal concession to gender difference not as a distinct area of authority. Labour women learnt the hard lesson that under the existing constitution, no matter how strongly they united on any particular issue, the men would always be able to overrule them.

The birth control campaign, therefore, forced Labour Party women to recognize that the only possible solution to their problem was to try once more to change the party constitution. Unless they could get some of their resolutions placed directly on the national agenda, make the women on the NEC directly responsible to the sections and increase their representation at party conferences, they would remain powerless. In 1929, the NEC pushed the lesson home when its members rejected another of Labour women's policies, one which they had also struggled for years to achieve – family allowances.

THE CAMPAIGN FOR FAMILY ALLOWANCES

At the same time as they were struggling to get party support for their birth control measure, Labour, ILP and Co-operative women were trying to secure some form of state endowment for working-class mothers and their children. The 'family allowance' campaign, however, did not generate the same level of enthusiasm or unanimity among local activists nor such dramatic clashes with the mainstream party. This was largely because it required Labour women to reconcile a number of conflicting interests. They had to weigh the value of state money payments to working-class mothers against the possible negative effects on the family wage and the cost to a Labour government. What makes the campaign of special interest is that it shows organized men and women debating the merits of competing claims, but while Labour women moved steadily towards a more radical and women-oriented formula for family allowances, the TUC and the Labour Party leadership marched just as surely in the opposite direction.

Labour women's interest in some form of state endowment for women and children pre-dated the war. In 1913, *Labour Woman* published a debate among members of the League's London branches entitled, 'How shall Women Live?' The participants considered three possible ways to ensure married women's economic survival: childhood pensions; special provisions for married women in the work force including equal pay, training programmes and day nurseries; and payment of the wife out of the husband's earnings. The least controversial at the time, was childhood pensions in the form of a weekly state payment to all mothers for every dependent child. Those who supported it argued that it would enable mothers to stay at home with their young children if they so wished; it would give working-class mothers a measure of financial independence and was the best hope for getting equal pay.[53]

Marion Phillips who was taking part in the debate, opposed the scheme. In her opinion, money paid to the mother would 'increase the irresponsibility of fatherhood'. She suggested that an extension of social services in the form of the provision of free milk and bread, baby clinics and schooling would still enable mothers to stay at home with their children while not depriving fathers of their incentive to work. Her proposal of services in kind rather than direct cash payments was a preview of how the battle lines would be drawn up in the campaign for family allowances after the war.

As in the case of birth control, the war encouraged Labour women to develop a policy of family endowment. Most importantly, the war offered the opportunity to see a model programme in action. Separation allowances were cash payments to the wives or mothers of servicemen, paid every week through their local post offices.

Although Labour women complained of the inadequacy of the allowances, they recognized the significance of the government's acceptance of financial responsibility for women and children who were unable to support themselves. They reasoned that what could be done in wartime when the nation's resources were being diverted to munitions, could be accomplished with less financial strain in peacetime. The war also increased the need and therefore the demand for such a scheme. The number of widows with dependent children and young mothers with husbands who were mentally or physically too disabled to work, grew by the tens of thousands. All the political parties accepted some responsibility for these domestic war casualties but Guild and Labour women adopted their cause as their own. They believed that the contribution of these women to the war was no less than that of the men in the armed forces. They argued: 'The mothers deserve a pension for services if soldiers and sailors do.'[54]

As an immediate answer to this war-related problem, Labour women in 1919 urged the party to adopt a scheme for mothers' pensions. They wanted all mothers with dependent children who were without male breadwinners to receive financial support from the state. This would include not only widows but women with husbands who were incapacitated or those who had been deserted 'through no fault of their own'. The Labour Party introduced a bill along these lines into Parliament in 1920 making it clear that the pensions were to be given on a non-contributory basis. The bill was defeated but the Labour Party continued to pass resolutions calling for mother's pensions until 1925 when a Conservative government passed a contributory Widows' Pensions bill. The only year when the party conference did not pass the resolution was in 1923, when, in anticipation of a Labour government, the delegates decided that the cost of the programme would be too high.[55]

Mothers' pensions had some relationship to the child allowances discussed before the war. They were to be neither connected to the Poor Law nor contributory in nature, but direct money grants by the state to the mother in accordance with the number of her children. However, they were much more limited in application than the earlier proposal implied, since they were to be given only to mothers who were 'husbandless'. From the Labour Party's point of view, they were justified not only on social welfare grounds but because they would help to keep married women out of the labour force and would not affect the wage structure.[56] Labour and Co-operative women, however, regarded them as only a partial solution to a much larger problem of deprivation among working-class women and children which was growing worse with the spread of unemployment. From 1920, they were at work on a comprehensive scheme that would ensure an adequate standard of life and health for all mothers with young children, whether they had husbands or not.

In developing their ideas for such a scheme, Labour and Guild women were influenced by proposals made during the Maternity Convention held in Washington D. C. in 1919 as part of the International Congress of Working Women. The rules laid down at this convention for the protection of mothers and infants included full maintenance payments and free medical care for six weeks before and after the birth of a child. Labour women wanted to extend these provisions to cover the entire period of a child's dependency. At the Labour Women's Conference in 1921, the delegates passed a resolution calling upon the Labour Party to undertake an inquiry into 'schemes of motherhood or child endowment and their relation to ... the general life of the community'. Mrs Hood of the Guild who proposed the resolution thought that any scheme worthy of Labour Party support should give pensions 'as a right, without inquisitorial questions'.[57]

The Labour Party duly appointed a special committee of the Joint Research Department of the TUC and the Labour Party which produced its report on Motherhood and Endowment in 1922. According to Marion Phillips who was on the committee, three considerations guided the members. The first was that state endowment of the family would have far-reaching economic and political consequences. It 'would greatly influence the whole system of wage organization and negotiations and also greatly influence votes at all elections'. Secondly, committee members wanted to limit their proposals to what they thought a Labour government could carry out and lastly, in accordance with this principle of political feasability, their recommendations were to be a first step and not 'the millennium at once'.[58] As might have been expected under these conditions, the report failed to break new ground. It merely adopted Marion Phillips' prewar proposal in calling for an extension of the existing social services – free school meals and milk, school medical inspection and treatment – to include the provision of free school clothing and boots for all children. Thus, even in the early twenties, the Labour Party was clearly unwilling to interfere with the traditional gender division of responsibility in the working-class family by considering cash payments paid by the state direct to mothers with wage-earning husbands.

In the women's conference debates and the written responses from local sections, the weight of opinion generally opposed the idea of payments in kind proposed in the report. Among the leaders, only Marion Phillips and Mrs Harrison Bell spoke in its favour because of their views on the effect of money payments on the working-class father's sense of responsibility. Ellen Wilkinson, Mrs Hood, Dorothy Jewson, Margaret Bondfield and later Jennie Lee, opposed it, arguing that mothers ought to have direct control over a money payment instead of communal handouts. Mrs Stocks, a middle-class feminist and friend of Eleanor Rathbone who had pioneered the idea of family endowment just after the First World War, agreed with the opponents that the only satisfactory form would be a state maintenance fund for all mothers and children which would prevent them being used as pawns in the struggle between capital and labour.[59]

Among the working-class delegates who gave their opinions of the report, most disliked the idea of free boots and clothing because it smacked of charity and the Poor Law – 'pauper relief'. They also resented the implication that working-class women were incapable of managing a money allowance. The comments of Mrs Bradbury, a delegate from Chipping Norton, were typical of several:

Her father was an agricultural labourer and had only earned a few shillings a week. But, thank God, he was a socialist and this meant they had no charities ... It is an insult to the mothers of the country to think that we are not capable of managing our own affairs.[60]

A number of local activists argued for money payments from a more positive, feminist point of view, very similar to that of middle-class advocates of family allowances. Mrs Clayton of Bradford, for example, wanted endowment of mothers 'whether they had husbands or not'. Jessie Stephen wanted them to serve as wages for women 'the same as the men so that they could spend the money as they best thought fit'. Mrs Johnson of the ILP urged cash payments direct to mothers as 'the first step towards the full emancipation of women'.[61] According to Marion Phillips, the local sections who were most critical of the joint TUC/Labour Party report, argued for endowment in the form of money instead of, or in addition to, services

and commodities, out of 'a desire to secure the economic independence of women as a first object'.[62] The same argument
appeared in Guild resolutions.[63]

In spite of this strong body of opinion against 'handouts' and in
support of cash payments to all mothers, a majority of the women
delegates to the conferences in 1922 and 1923, endorsed the
TUC/Labour Party report. While it is possible that the majority
really did favour allowances in goods and services but chose not to
express that viewpoint, it is as likely that there were other reasons for
their apparently contradictory action. Mrs Hood's comments in 1922
suggest one reason. She said that, 'she sympathized with those who
did not like things being doled out to them but Mr Emil Davies who
was on the committee had pointed out that it was impossible at the
present time to pay an endowment in money'.[64] Working-class
women were used to 'cutting their coat according to their cloth' and
while they had no hesitation in demanding a fair share of Tory
budgets, they were more reluctant to overburden a Labour government. Mrs Hopper, the delegate who presented the report to the
Labour Party conference in 1923, suggested another reason for
accepting payments in kind. She argued that 'money allowances
would be rendered insufficient by the rise in prices which follows any
rise in wages or allowances' and referred to the experience of
housewives during the war.[65]

The decision to compromise on the question of the form of the
endowment in 1923, however, appears to have been primarily a
response to the worsening economic conditions for working-class
mothers and children in the period 1920–3. Mrs Hooper told the
conference delegates that in the two years since she had first become
convinced of the need for family endowment, 'the suffering among
women and children in her town had increased to such an extent that
they could not afford to wait'.[66] She mentioned women with young
children in an agricultural district of the Isle of Wight who had had
no new underclothing since marriage. Jessie Stephen who voted for
the report even though she much preferred cash payments, also
referred to the 'very low' economic position of women in 1923. 'It
was said that the hand that rocks the cradle ruled the world, and yet
the ordinary comforts of life were denied to these rulers of the
world.'[67] In view of the urgency of the economic situation, organized
women calculated that they would be more effective if they endorsed
improvements in social services which the Labour Party was prepared

to support with legislation, than if they refused this in favour of apparently unattainable money grants.

Although there was no overt gender conflict over the issue of family endowment in the early years of Labour women's campaign, it was already clear that organized women wanted a more radical measure than the mainstream party would support. In the euphoria following the 1923 general election that brought Labour to power for the first time, Labour women anticipated the passing of a Mothers' Pension bill which would include some of the social welfare provisions of the 1922 report. Phillip Snowden, Labour's Chancellor of the Exchequer assured them that the legislation was planned but asked them to be patient while he worked out the details of his first budget. In March 1924, *Labour Woman* announced 'Mothers' Pensions Are on the Way!' but within a matter of months the party was out of power without having introduced the promised bill.

Labour women did not falter in the face of this disappointment. They continued to press the party to extend its mothers' pensions scheme. In 1925, Dorothy Evans asked that pensions be given to women whose husbands were not just incapacitated but unable to provide adequate support for any reason. Using a very popular argument of the time, she said that women were anxious to see 'some form of remuneration for mothers for the state service of rearing children'.[68] Mrs Rosalind Moore of West Willesden asked the Labour Party conference to appoint a committee to re-examine the whole question of women's pensions and formulate a definite and comprehensive scheme as part of the party's programme. She argued that pensions were needed not just for widows and married mothers but for all homemakers. Arthur Henderson complained that Mrs Moore's suggestion was too vague and the party did not respond to either request.[69]

Just when it seemed as if the campaign might repeat that of birth control, with the women asking for a radical reform and the men rejecting their proposal, the ILP produced the first coherent socialist family allowance policy and thus broadened the debate. In its 1926 policy statement *Socialism for Today*, the ILP outlined the steps to be taken to secure a 'living wage' for all workers. Family allowances were integral to this policy. The ILP proposed a statutory minimum living wage for all workers to be supplemented by children's allowances of five shillings for each child to be paid out of direct taxation which would fall most heavily on the wealthy. The justification for the policy was that it would not only give the workers' children the chance of a better life, but would increase the purchasing power of the working-class family, help to redistribute the nation's wealth and undermine the economic basis for paying women less than men.[70]

The ILP policy statement gave the subject of family allowances much greater prominence in the labour movement than Labour women's resolutions and speeches had achieved. As soon as the reform had ceased to be a 'women's issue' and had become a question involving socialist principles and union wage bargaining, it was immediately placed at the top of the party's agenda. Although the 1926 party conference rejected the ILP's resolution calling upon them to adopt the scheme at once, the delegates agreed to set up a national joint committee of the TUC and the Labour Party to prepare a recommendation on family allowances and the Living Wage policy.

Because of its relative simplicity and specificity, the ILP's family allowance proposal both clarified and polarized opinions in the labour movement. By 1927, Labour women had adopted a position very close to that of the ILP. They had abandoned allowances in kind in favour of cash payments by the state to the mother for each dependent child, the cost to be met out of direct taxation and 'not by any contributory system of insurance'. Mary Agnes Adamson the member of the SJC who proposed the resolution reminded the delegates that this scheme had existed during the war and 'during that period children had been better fed, clothed, etc.; there had been deterioration ever since'.[71] The resolution left open how much the allowance should be and precisely who would get it. The following year, however, the SJC was obliged to pay more attention to these details, because it was asked to present its views before the Labour Party's national joint committee. Eleven of the members of the SJC supported the ILP's proposal to give five shillings to every mother for each child but twelve were opposed. The majority were reluctant to commit the Labour Party to too large a financial outlay, preferring a smaller sum for each child. The least popular proposal made by Marion Phillips was for an extension of the maternity benefit to cover the first two years of the infant's life combined with free nursery schools.[72]

While Labour women moved closer to the ILP position on family allowances, first the TUC and then the Labour Party backed away.

The national joint committee which was mandated to decide on the policy was unable to reach agreement because although the Labour Party members eventually accepted the ILP proposal for a monetary endowment, the trade unionists were convinced that state-paid cash allowances would have a negative effect on wages and future wage negotiations. As one committee member put it: 'Trade unionism finds that wherever there are emoluments, wherever there are special social services, they are acting detrimentally not only to our getting better conditions for our people, but even to our trade union organization itself.'[73]

In 1929, after three years of fruitless debate and under pressure from the NEC, the committee published a majority and a minority report. The majority recommended the party endorse the ILP family allowance policy while the minority, led by the General Council of the TUC refused to accept any form of financial grant to mothers for their children. Faced with a split between the political and industrial sides of the movement, Arthur Henderson decided, as he did in the case of birth control, that party unity could not be sacrificed for the sake of any one social reform measure. 'We have enough to do to improve social services in areas agreed upon so we should leave the question of family allowances which appears to divide the labour movement into industrial and political sides.'[74] Family allowances disappeared from the party's agenda until the end of the Second World War.

It is reasonable to ask at this point that if the male-dominated Labour Party abandoned the ILP's family allowance policy in 1930 because male trade unionists refused their support, what role, if any, had women played in the campaign? Even as their own views became clearer and firmer, they had not been successful in pushing the party conference at any stage to accept a cash endowment to married women with wage-earning husbands. They had not even been responsible for formulating the scheme to which the party gave serious consideration. Their only contribution was to have initiated and sustained the party's commitment to the lesser measure of mothers' pensions just after the war, a measure that the party overlooked during its short periods in office.

Ignoring for a moment their constitutional weakness, were there any other reasons for this singular lack of effectiveness? One that deserves consideration is that the family allowance campaign produced considerable gender tension in the Labour Party. There were men who deeply resented cash allowances paid to wives whose husbands were earning wages because it threatened the traditional division of responsibility in the working-class household. Rhys Davies, a trade union delegate to the Labour Party's 1930 conference, complained that family allowances would mean that, 'instead of the working man getting his wages at the factory pay office or colliery pay office, his wife would draw his wages for him at the Post Office'. As far as he was concerned, the idea of family allowances was an insult to the working man and to the trade union movement since it was 'based on the false assumption that the average working-class father was devoid of feelings of responsibility for his wife and children and a confession that the married man could not, either by personal qualities or by trade union organization, secure an adequate income to maintain himself and his family'.[75]

One Labour man who opposed family allowances chose to hit back by criticizing women's capabilities as household managers. In May 1930, Mr Somerville Hastings, Labour MP for Reading wrote a letter to *Labour Woman* rejecting state money payments to the wives of working men on the grounds that 'working-class women don't have the requisite knowledge to spend an allowance in the right way. They would spend the money in private enterprise shops with adulterated food'.[76] Labour women could be as sensitive to attacks on their traditional gender responsibilities as the men in the party. Somerville Hastings' views brought a number of angry letters from *Labour Woman* readers. They pointed out to the new member for Reading that of course working-class mothers knew what food was good for their children, the problem was they could not afford to buy it! They argued that thousands of mothers went without food themselves in order to feed their children as best they could. Only a cash allowance would relieve the anxieties of the struggle to make ends meet and ensure that workers' children were properly fed. Mrs Frances Edwards made the point in her letter that the family budget was a woman's concern and one that few men could understand: 'Children's allowances are the woman's opportunity and she must fight if necessary in opposition to the men who are seldom the Chancellor of the Exchequer in their homes and so do not understand.'[77]

Disagreement between Labour men and women over how family allowances would affect the wage structure, exacerbated gender tension. The majority of Labour women reached the conclusion by 1927 that state money payments to mothers for their children would not adversely affect men's wages but would even improve their competitive market position. Mrs Read from the Orpington women's section explained how this would work. She wrote to *Labour Woman*: 'Men are supposed to be paid higher wages because they have families. The extra amount might just as well be paid straight to the mother leaving the men a little nearer to an equal footing in the scramble for a job.'[78] In addition, many argued, because family allowances offered the best hope for achieving equal pay, they would prevent men's rates from being dragged down by women's cheaper labour. Once working-class women and children were removed from the wage-bargaining table, the 'rate for the job' would prevail.[79]

Male trade unionists, on the other hand, found this argument unconvincing. They shared the view of Ernest Bevin that 'family allowances would interfere with the delicate mechanism of the wage structure'.[80] In future wage bargaining, employers would be certain to argue that since workers with families were receiving state money payments, then wages could be reduced without causing hardship to women and children. Men's wages would come down to the level of women's and no one would benefit.

By supporting family allowances with increasing determination, Labour women were not merely placing themselves in opposition to the broader national goals of the trade unions and the Labour Party but challenging ideas about gender roles that were deeply embedded in working-class culture. Taken in conjunction with trade union caution after the General Strike and the Labour Party's limited power during its short periods as a minority government – the last during the global economic crisis – success in achieving this particular reform was highly unlikely.

In 1929, labour women were facing their party's rejection of two reforms, birth control and family allowances, that they had come to see as vital to any long-term improvement in the lives of working-class mothers and their children. Their response was to try once again, as they had in 1921–2 to change the 1918 constitution to give the housewife's point of view as much weight in Labour's policy decisions as that of the miner or the railwayman.

CHANGING THE 1918 LABOUR PARTY CONSTITUTION

The failure of their campaigns for birth control and family allowances reminded labour women of the anomalies in their position under the 1918 constitution. As a result of unresolved differences between the Women's Labour League and the Labour Party over women's place in the party, the constitution relegated women members to a literal no-man's land. Treated as a distinct group for some purposes but as equal to male members for others, they had no access to power in either capacity. By 1929, the majority of Labour women were eager to extend those provisions in the constitution that allowed for the existence of a distinct women's organization to give them power comparable to that of male trade unionists, to contribute to party policy on women's issues. A minority, including the women leaders, accepted the dominant male view that if any changes were made, they should be in the direction of eliminating gender distinction altogether. The struggle between the two points of view – separate but equal or fully integrated, took place in 1929 and 1930 while the Labour Party was in power and was to be the last attempt until the seventies to give women a distinct voice in the political labour movement.

The most glaring constitutional weakness the birth control and family allowance campaigns revealed, was the extent to which Labour women leaders were cut off from their rank-and-file. The 1918 constitution had deliberately made no provision for women members to have leaders who were directly responsible to them. The Chief Woman Officer, Marion Phillips, was on the party payroll and was accountable to the party agent and the NEC, not to the women in the sections. Of the eight members on the Standing Joint Committee, only four were chosen by the sections, the others were party appointees. The four women on the NEC owed their election to the big trade unions who controlled the annual conferences and therefore did not regard themselves as the representatives of women members only. This last situation had proved especially damaging in the birth control campaign when one of the women most frequently on the NEC, Mrs Harrison Bell, ignoring the wishes of the majority of women in her party, strongly opposed the campaign and publicly denounced Labour women birth controllers as tools of the Communist Party.[81]

The separation of the leaders from the rank-and-file accounts for their often divergent attitudes. The women who achieved some prominence in the party could not afford to be identified solely with women's issues. They had to compete for office with their male colleagues and therefore had to put the party's interests, as defined by men, before those of the women members – 'the whole before the part' as Marion Phillips was fond of saying. The women rank-and-file who thought of themselves as having a distinct place in the party, found that they had no one in the party's power structure with any responsibility to support them or to represent their viewpoint. Those Labour women who had perceived this weakness when the constitution was first outlined were joined at the end of the twenties by others who had learnt the lesson at first hand from the birth control fight. Dora Russell led the demand to have the women on the NEC chosen and elected by Labour women at their annual conference, but she was undoubtedly expressing a view that was shared by many local activists.[82]

The other area of controversy at the centre of the debate in 1929 was the Labour Women's Conference. When the NEC agreed in 1918 to the League's request for a separate women's conference, they seem to have envisioned it as a practice arena for the women who were new to politics. Anxious to avoid 'separatism', the members of the NEC carefully ensured that the women's conference had no means of making independent political decisions. Resolutions passed there were reported to the NEC but could not be placed on the annual conference agendas. As we have seen, this barrier became a major source of frustration among Labour women activists in the twenties. In 1928, Dorothy Jewson proposed that the party allow just three resolutions a year to go forward from the women's conference to the national party conference. Her resolution was passed at the women's conference by a two-thirds majority; the minority argued the case for giving up separate women's conferences altogether.[83]

In 1929, as the NEC prepared to streamline the constitution at the start of the Labour Party's second period in office, it had before it women's proposals for the direct election of the women members on the NEC and for changing the status of the women's conference. The NEC discussed the first proposal and decided not to change the method of electing the women to their committee but offered as a concession to increase their number from four to five.[84] The other proposal was ignored. It was irrelevant to the main purpose behind the revision of the constitution which was to increase the party's unity and efficiency. In order to make the annual party conference a more manageable size, the NEC proposed a proportional reduction in the number of delegates from the trade unions and constituency parties. As part of this plan, the 1918 provision allowing a constituency with 500 or more women members to send a second delegate to the conference, a woman if they chose, would be changed. Under the new ruling, no second delegate could be sent unless the local party had 2,500 women members.

This proposal sent shock waves through the local women's sections and constituency parties, bringing to the surface all the frustration of the growing numbers of individual party members, men and women, with trade union domination. In the debate at the 1929 conference, the delegates from the local parties made strong appeals for the party to reject the proposal. They argued that since so few of the local parties had 2,500 women members, it meant the virtual elimination of the second delegate and therefore of women members from the party conference. The trade unions, almost without exception, sent male delegates, so that once the local party's delegation was reduced to one, women would lose their only opportunity. As Mrs Thomson, the delegate from Coventry pointed out, 'one does not need any spectacles or any super intelligence to know that when only one delegate has to be chosen, it is the man who is sent by the Constituency Party'.[85]

The debate over the constitutional changes, shows that men in the local constituency parties took a very different view of women's conference representation from the NEC. They wanted to raise it, partly out of a desire to increase the power of local parties at the expense of the trade unions but also in recognition of the important contribution women made to the survival and running of the local parties. Mr Broad from the Edmonton CLP, for example, reported that 'nine-tenths of my canvassing is done by women ... and the bulk of the money is raised by women'.[86] Councillor Alex Griffin of the Edge Hill District Labour Party (DLP) said that in his opinion, it was 'the women of Liverpool who have broken down Tory rule in Liverpool once and for ever'.[87] Mr Setchell from Bermondsey expressed his disgust at the party's hypocritical attitude towards its women members. It eulogized them for their hard work and support and then turned round and denied them any participation in the running of the party.[88] Mr G. T. Garratt, from the Cambridgeshire DLP, pointed out the difficulties local parties would have in attracting women members if the proposed change in the constitution was enacted. He asked the conference how he, or any other party member could say to local women '"Come and join the Labour Party; if you do you will have a voice in running the Labour Party"' when he knew, 'that in practice their votes are entirely ineffective'.[89]

No doubt, Labour women valued this evidence of appreciation and comradeship in their hour of need. Unfortunately, it did not amount to an endorsement of their demands for a distinct women's voice. None of the male delegates appeared to support any separation of the sexes. Mr Garrett referred to the women's conference as an example of an 'old-fashioned' idea of sexual division. It was the one woman delegate who spoke in the debate, Mrs Thomson of Coventry DLP, who urged the importance of women being able to put their special concerns before the whole party in conference. She said: 'We have heard speeches on Maternal Mortality, Birth Control, Family Allowances, and so on, put before this Conference by men. Well, one appreciates their championship of the cause, but it does seem to me we could put our own point of view better.' She went on to address the question of the 'unfortunate dividing of the sexes'. She looked forward to the day when men and women would be organized together in the party as equals but insisted that that would only happen if provision was made in the constitution for the women's point of view to be fairly represented.[90]

These arguments failed. The proposed change to the constitution which would reduce women's already very small conference representation to almost none, was carried. Susan Lawrence, the most powerful woman in the Labour Party at the time, justified the decision for the NEC. She argued that it would be resorting to privilege to double the representation from constituency parties while halving that of the trade unions and privilege to grant any special concessions for women to attend the conference. She said that there was no rule to prevent all the delegates from the local parties or all the members of the NEC from being women. She advised the women of the party to get rid of their existing privileges, represented by their guaranteed seats on the NEC and their separate conference, and work to get to the party conference by 'fighting and scrapping with [their] male comrades on terms of perfect equality'.[91] Such a view was alien to most Labour women who thought the Labour Party stood for co-operation and much preferred the idea of co-operating than competing with their male colleagues. It seemed unjust to be accused of seeking privilege, a powerfully pejorative word in the labour movement in 1929, when all they wanted was the removal of the existing constitutional impediments to gender equality.

The struggle was almost over. The following year, the women's conference debated its own future. Mrs Johnson of Norwich moved and Mrs Cusden of Reading seconded the following resolution: 'That this conference urges that the Labour Women's Conference should be an official gathering and official recognition should be given to their resolutions.' Mrs Johnson assured the delegates that 'she was not a Feminist – she was a Socialist' but she wanted a women's conference that could send resolutions straight to the party conference and then to members of Parliament. In what was the catch phrase for the 'equality of gender interests' group, she wanted the party to give its attention to 'the housewives' point of view'.[92] The counter-argument echoed the views of Susan Lawrence. Mrs Duncan Harris from Croyden urged Labour women to get out of the nursery represented by the separate women's conference and stand upon their own feet and help to shape policy at the national conference. Otherwise, they would end up with a 'women's Labour Party and a men's Labour Party'.[93] Marion Phillips assured the delegates that the women's conference was an influential body which 'materially affected the actions of the NEC'. She pointed out that the committee could not afford to ignore the 'opinion of a gathering of women who did work for the Party'.[94] The delegates, with the party's response to their demand for birth control and family allowance reforms still fresh in their minds, remained unconvinced. Once again, they endorsed separate but equal power for labour women. Mrs Johnson's resolution calling for a constitutional change to give teeth to the Women's Conference decisions by allowing them to be discussed by the whole party in conference passed by 542 votes to 165. Predictably, the NEC took no action to implement the majority decision of its women members.

There was a postscript to this constitutional defeat. In 1932, Marion Phillips' death prompted the National Agent to review the position of women in the party. The report criticized Labour women's independent activities under Marion Phillips' leadership, attributing it to the influence of the suffrage generation who transferred their 'sex consciousness' to the labour movement. However, according to the report's author, this stage of the women's movement was over.

The new generation of Labour women, lacking the suffrage experience, 'is not swayed to anything like the same extent by sex
antagonisms or merely sex interests'. Among this generation, there
was a growing disposition to abandon separate sex activities in favour
of 'joining together in all phases of common Party work', a
development encouraged by the increasing numbers of young wage-
earning women in the party who attended evening meetings.
According to the report, the women's sections had become a section
of a section of the party since they catered only to married women
with family responsibilities. The National Agent asked the NEC to
consider whether or not the time was ripe to strip away all the
institutions that catered specifically to women so that women's
activities could be 'dovetailed into ... general Party activities'.[95]

Oddly, the NEC did not take advantage of this opportunity to
eliminate the separatist gender interests that it had complained about
for so many years. It left intact the structure of women's sections,
separate women's conferences and guaranteed representation on the
NEC. The committee was content with maintaining the isolation of
this structure from policy-making power and tightening its control
over the new Chief Woman Officer, Miss Mary Sutherland. Whether
or not the thirties generation of Labour women was a different breed
from its predecessors with no interest in specifically women's concerns
remains to be discussed in another chapter but there were no further
attempts in the interwar period to change the constitution to give
women the power to represent those concerns or incorporate them
into party policy.

CONCLUSIONS

In the twenties, a majority of Labour women tried to get the Labour
Party to accept what may be called a women's interpretation of their
place in the party. They expected to represent the special concerns of
working-class women and their children and to have those concerns
carry equal weight with male interests when policy decisions were
made. When they tried to explain their idea of women's place in the
party, they liked the analogy to a large trade union. Labour women
wanted a position similar to that of the railwaymen or the miners who
used the party platform to support their special industrial and
political interests without being accused of separatism. In Labour
women's minds, such an arrangement was quite in keeping with the
broader political interests of the working class.

Neither the Labour women leaders nor the mainstream party accepted this interpretation. It offended the women leaders because they believed that unless women competed on equal terms with men without any special concessions, they would never achieve true equality or integration. It worried the male-dominated mainstream party by raising the spectre of gender antagonism which would destroy party unity and undermine its electoral strength. However, because no one denied the existence of gender differences, the special provisions made for women in 1918 were allowed to remain as long as they had no connection to power.

Both interpretations of gender equality would have been hard to implement. Labour women would certainly have been in a stronger position to get women's issues onto the party agendas if they had been organized as a trade union with their conference representation based on total numbers.[96] But, in spite of the concerns they shared, particularly if they were married with children, working-class women were not an occupational group. They had no organized power base and were connected directly or through marriage with a range of different occupations. More significantly, it was inconceivable that the male party would have been prepared to accept a women's 'trade union'. As the birth control and family allowance campaigns showed so clearly, sometimes volatile emotional responses characterized gender relations in the Labour Party due in large part to the underlying conflict between traditional working-class patriarchal values and the socialist ideal of sexual equality. The men who objected to working-class wives receiving 'wages' in the form of family allowances from the government would have been even more unhappy with unionized wives bringing their 'labour disputes' into the party and the home.

The weakness of the arguments of women leaders and the Labour Party was that they were either unjustifiably optimistic or they constituted a deliberate attempt to maintain male domination under the guise of constitutional equality. The provisions in the 1918 and 1929 constitutions which supposedly offered equal terms to men and women for election to policy-making bodies, were in reality heavily weighted against women. It was not only a question of having to overcome the prejudice among local Labour men against sending women delegates to party conferences. In individual cases, that was always a possibility. Far more difficult to change was the control that large industrial trade unions exercised over conference decisions. The chances of women being able to penetrate these unions in large numbers in the interwar years were remote. Consequently, a fair conference representation based on their numerical strength was out of the question for women members. By obliging them to compete with men with one hand tied behind them, the framers of the constitution assured male-dominance and forced women into a supporting role. Party officials insisted that it was all in the interests of unity but the truth was it involved a considerable loss of enthusiasm and energy especially at the constituency level. After 1929, the great period of growth in women's membership was over. The sections which had willingly accepted the major responsibility for fundraising, canvassing and social events, remained static or declined.

Because the outcome of the struggle between these two points of view was never very much in doubt, it is easy to underestimate women's achievement. Few political campaigns connected with the Labour Party have produced either the unanimity or the enthusiasm that the birth control issue generated among Labour women and a small minority of Labour men. Scarcely a decade after it had been a taboo subject, women's sections all over the country were involved in open discussion of birth control between themselves and with male Labour councillors and members of Parliament. Despite their failure to gain the support of the party, the campaign stimulated the female membership and led to the conversion of a number of local councils. Less tangibly, it spread the message of the benefits of birth control to unknown numbers of working-class women.

The argument can be made that the women's reform programme was politically inappropriate to the times and that it demonstrated a lack of understanding of the nature of power politics. Because they were largely excluded from the Party's power structure, it would be understandable if Labour women did not share the same concern for electoral strategy and internal unity as the men. Labour women still wanted to act on the ideals for which in their mind, the party stood. While Labour's male leaders abandoned the postwar goals of gender equality, social justice and the living wage in the harsher economic and political climate of the twenties, these were still the primary concerns for the majority of Labour women.

Oddly, Labour women showed no bitterness towards the party after their defeat on the one issue that they cared so much about. Women did not leave the Party in droves or refuse their valuable support services during strikes or elections. Stella Browne commented after the defeat of the birth control struggle that 'had there been a systematic and resolute feminine refusal to pay a penny's subscription after Blackpool, the result would have been very different'.[97] Perhaps she was right but Labour women never even hinted at the possibility of such action. The loss of vitality and membership in the women's sections in the thirties was primarily because more women after 1930 chose to join the constituency parties with the men.[98] Because they believed in the party as the best hope for improving the conditions of life of the working class and saw themselves as deeply involved in that struggle, the majority of committed activists stayed with the party and concentrated their reform efforts at the local level.

CHAPTER 4

'A sex question or a class question?' – Labour women and feminism in the twenties

As labour women struggled in the nineteen-twenties to define their place in working-class politics, they began to reassess their relationship with the middle-class women's movement. Before the First World War and right up until the suffrage grant, the relationship had generally been one of co-operation and mutual support. The suffrage struggle was only one of several campaigns in which women reformers worked together across class lines.[1] Once the vote was won, however, organized women faced a choice between their class and gender loyalties. They could either join the national political party most closely identified with their class interest or continue as a women's lobby outside the party-political structure. Nearly all the working-class activists and a handful from the middle-class chose the Labour Party while the majority of middle-class reformers formed 'non-party' organizations pursuing a variety of feminist causes.

Despite their division along class and political lines, organized women debated many of the same questions and drew up very similar agendas in the post-suffrage years. While Labour Party women discussed women's 'equality' versus their 'special needs' within the party, the middle-class movement divided on the same issue in relation to national goals. 'New feminists', as they called themselves, differed from the liberal egalitarians in believing that discriminatory social welfare legislation, not just legal parity with men, was necessary to achieve true equality for women. After 1925, the 'new feminist' agenda was almost indistinguishable from that of labour women. It included family allowances, birth control, nursery schools and the prevention of maternal mortality. At the same time, labour women and the new feminists joined equal rights feminists in supporting married women's right to work and equal pay.

In view of these common agendas and labour women's difficulties in persuading the Labour Party to accept their reform programme, it would seem that there was every reason for organized women of both classes to resume their prewar pattern of co-operation. Instead, tension mounted between them. Middle-class 'non-party' feminists became highly sceptical of the sincerity of the Labour Party's claim to support sexual equality, while labour women came to associate feminism with 'leisured' women who had no understanding of the problems of the poor and no sympathy with the labour movement. This mutual distrust culminated in a particularly bitter, public fight over protective laws for women workers.

The deterioration in relations between labour women and middle-class feminists in the twenties was directly linked to women's entry into the class-based political structure. Before 1918, women reformers of both classes had recognized the value of working together to achieve the legal rights and social welfare reforms a male-controlled political system denied them. The intransigence of the national parties, particularly on the suffrage question, reinforced the need for co-operation. Their joint campaigns, however, obscured significant differences in long-term goals. Despite their considerable diversity, most middle-class activists were working towards some form of gender equality while most working-class activists wanted the betterment of their class. Once women had the vote, they acknowledged the class difference in their choice of organization and found the need for co-operation far less compelling.

LABOUR WOMEN AND MIDDLE-CLASS FEMINISTS

When the Labour Party became the mass party of the working class after the First World War, it adopted a new policy towards the middle-class women's movement. Before the war, Labour had been the only party to give official support to the suffrage campaign through its 1913 alliance with the National Union of Women's Suffrage Societies (NUWSS). After 1918, the party withdrew from the feminist alliance and began a sustained campaign to drive a wedge between its women members and the 'non-party' feminist groups that replaced suffrage organizations. In the eyes of party leaders, these groups were serious competitors for working-class women's votes and Labour women's loyalty.

The historian, Harold Smith, has suggested that because of its hostile attitude, the Labour Party was largely responsible for the breach between organized labour women and middle-class feminists in the twenties.[2] A case can certainly be made for his viewpoint. At every annual conference from 1919 to 1925, the party warned its women members to resist the call of the feminist sirens. Conference reports referred to the 'specious attempts to appeal to them by so-called non-political but Anti-Labour women's organizations'.[3] In 1921, the National Executive Committee denied conference representation to the National Union of Societies for Equal Citizenship (NUSEC), the successor to the NUWSS.[4] In 1925, a resolution that would have *forbidden* Labour Party women to be members of the NUSEC's Women's Citizens' Associations was only narrowly defeated.[5]

Guild and Labour women leaders quickly fell into line with the party's stand and spread the word to the rank-and-file. Margaret Llewelyn Davies and Marion Phillips repeatedly urged their members not to divert their time and energy to groups that were not only politically ineffective but also unsympathetic to the working class. The Standing Joint Committee of Industrial Women's Organizations (SJC) actively discouraged joint lobbying or demonstrations with middle-class feminist groups even for causes that both classes of organized women supported.[6] Before conceding Harold Smith's argument, however, it is relevant to know if there were any other reasons for the deterioration of relations between labour women and middle-class feminists and whether or not labour women actually took any notice of their party's strictures.

In the post-suffrage years, organized middle-class feminists began to express misgivings about a Labour alliance. They were especially uneasy about the change in the status of the Labour Party. Before the war, middle-class feminists like Mrs Fawcett and Ray Strachey tended to see Labour as the socially responsible wing of the Liberal Party. Its anti-authoritarianism and commitment to social welfare seemed compatible with their own reformist views. Labour was far less acceptable to them after the war when it became a mass working-class party with collectivist aims. Eleanor Rathbone, the guiding spirit of the NUSEC in the twenties, was representative of a broad strain of middle-class feminist opinion in her mistrust of the working class as an uneducated and irrational political force. She preferred what she described as the 'impartiality' of the educated middle-class voter.[7] Her view prevailed in the NUSEC because many of the prewar socialist and radical feminists abandoned the women's movement after the war. With the passage of the suffrage grant, these activists either gave their first attention to the Labour Party, went into the international peace movement or retired from political life.[8]

Labour Party policies and actions in the postwar years fuelled organized feminists' growing disillusionment. Labour's insistence on the Restoration of Pre-war Practices Act in 1918, for example, appeared as a serious betrayal of the feminist cause. The act allowed all returning servicemen who had belonged to trade unions to claim their prewar jobs and rates of pay, thus sweeping away most of the wartime economic gains made by women industrial and clerical workers. While labour women, by and large, accepted this as a matter of fairness, middle-class feminists blamed the Labour Party for allowing wage-earning women to be sacrificed indiscriminately to the wholesale claims of organized male workers.[9]

Middle-class feminists were further dissatisfied when the first Labour government in 1924 failed to carry out its pledges to extend the franchise to women on the same terms as men and pass bills for mothers' pensions and equal guardianship rights. They resented the disparity between words and deeds in the party's treatment of women's concerns. With little sympathy for the difficulties of a minority government, they characterized the party's record as deliberately anti-feminist. In 1925, the Six Point Group, formed in 1920 by Lady Rhonda with a programme of egalitarian reforms, commented that the members of the Labour government, 'not only failed to do anything whatsoever to forward it [feminism] when it was in their power to do so easily but have actually gone out of their way to obstruct it'.[10]

Labour women, too, disappointed their middle-class sisters even before protective legislation brought the two groups into open conflict. The *Women's Leader* published a report of the 1925 Labour Women's Conference which criticized the delegates for their inconsistency on feminist issues. It referred to the juxtaposition of two contradictory resolutions. The first called on the Labour Party to 'deal stringently with any representative of the Party who does not support sex equality, economically, educationally and politically', while the second opposed married women's right to work when men and single women were unemployed. The *Leader* report failed to mention that labour women delegates passed the first resolution unanimously but rejected the second after Jessie Stephen denounced it as reactionary. Clearly, middle-class feminists were more than ready to doubt labour women's commitment to the woman's cause.[11]

Since organized feminists were almost as suspicious of the motives and actions of the Labour Party as the party was of theirs, they must share some responsibility for undermining the alliance. The determinedly 'non-party' stance of most of the postwar feminist groups, the Women's Citizens' Associations, Six Point Group, the Open Door Council, the National Council of Women and the Women's Local Government Society, often seemed to be in effect an anti-Labour position. All the feminist organizations maintained much closer personal and political ties with Liberal women than they did with either Guild or Labour women.[12] The Women's Liberal Association joined the NUSEC and the Open Door Council in their campaigns for gender equality in women's pay, franchise, moral standard, and guardianship rights. Edith Picton Turberville, who ran as Labour candidate for Stroud found that while she had the help of the NUSEC organizer, the local societies shunned her 'in the fear that public opinion would label the NUSEC as being Labour in sympathy'. There were no reports of such fears being expressed in relation to Liberal or even Conservative candidates.[13]

The Labour Party's concern that feminists would invade their electoral territory and carry off their women members appears to have had little foundation. Although the patriotic Women's League of Empire reported having 40,000 working-class members, there is no evidence that any of the other middle-class groups actively courted a mass working-class membership. The NUSEC addressed its propaganda to an educated middle-class constituency and made few attempts to recruit working-class women to its local Women's Citizens' Association branches. The Open Door Council, an off-shoot of the NUSEC, established in 1926 to fight for equal economic opportunity, sought the endorsement of prominent labour women in its campaign against sex-based protective legislation. It approached Selina Cooper, for example, and she spoke on the council's behalf.[14] However, its purpose was not to lure working women away from the Labour party, but to show that there were some among them who opposed sex-based protective legislation.

This brings us to the question of labour women's response to the party's attempts to prevent them joining any of the middle-class feminist organizations. In March 1925, the NUSEC journal, the *Women's Leader*, reported that many Labour Party, ILP and Guild women were ignoring the party's injunction and continuing to play an active role in the organization. According to the article, labour women were serving on the executive committee in defiance of their leaders' 1919 ruling. This was true to the extent that the names of several well-known labour women appeared in the NUSEC committee minutes up to 1927. At one time or another in the first half of the decade, Barbara Ayrton-Gould, Madeleine Symons, Edith Picton Turberville, Dorothy Jewson and Monica Whately all served on the committee.[15]

The errant women were all educated, middle-class socialists who had been active in the prewar women's movement and held prominent positions in labour politics. Their participation in the NUSEC can be explained in a number of ways. They may still have had strong personal ties to their former sisters in the suffrage fight with whom they also shared a commitment to such feminist reforms as equal pay and married women's right to work. Since the Labour Party officially supported many of these same reforms, they probably did not see their membership in NUSEC as a conflict of interest. Another compelling reason for their continued association with middle-class feminists was for the help that the 'non-party' groups gave them in their parliamentary election campaigns. Labour women rarely had access to trade union funds for their campaigns and were often saddled with very 'unsafe' seats. The NUSEC and the Local Government Society offered financial and organizing assistance to all women candidates. The three most powerful Labour Party women of the twenties, Susan Lawrence, Margaret Bondfield and Ellen Wilkinson, who were almost certainly out of sympathy with non-party feminist groups, all wrote to the NUSEC in 1924 to acknowledge the value of its electoral support.[16]

Rank-and-file labour women seem to have had far less involvement with the non-party, middle-class feminist organizations than their leaders. A few familiar names appear in the NUSEC records. Selina Cooper was active until 1922 and Jennie Baker, the birth controller, until the early thirties. Again, both were veterans of the prewar suffrage fight. Emily Hoeter of the Ashford-under-Lyne and District Power Loom Weavers mentioned at the Labour Party conference in 1925 that she had been a member of the Women's Citizens' Association 'for a long time' and had received its support when she ran for the town council in Stalybridge.[17] There is nothing to indicate her class background or that of other women whose names appear in the NUSEC minutes but the weight of the available evidence suggests that only a tiny minority of postwar Labour or Guild women joined the WCAs.

If working-class women had been flooding into the WCAs in the post-suffrage years, one would have expected the number of local associations in working-class areas to grow. But, in 1920, the *Women's Leader* referred to the closing of many of their associations in northern industrial towns. Selina Cooper's branch was one of them. Labour women in Nelson apparently did not support this feminist organization and it closed after only a few months.[18] The Bolton Women Citizens Association continued into the thirties but an observer for Mass Observation reported that the women who attended the meetings appeared well dressed and middle class.[19] Among the activists who were interviewed or filled out a questionnaire for this study, the vast majority said they had never heard of either the NUSEC or the WCAs. Ellen Jane Kendall who joined the Labour Party in 1922 wrote: 'We had little knowledge and no contact with such organizations. We would have thought that they were not sufficiently aware of the problems of working women.'[20]

Ellen Kendall's comment may be the key to what kept labour women away from middle-class feminist groups. There is no reason to assume that it was merely a case of going along with the party's wishes. Their struggles with the party over the birth control issue and their repeated demands for more policy-making power belie an attitude of slavish obedience to the party line. A more likely explanation is that they believed with Ellen that middle-class feminists had little understanding of their problems as working-class women. The majority of the postwar generation of labour women had taken no part in the suffrage struggle and had never worked closely with middle-class women reformers. Rather than seeing them as sisters in a common struggle, they tended to characterize them as 'rich, but idle, ladies'.[21] The Labour Party certainly encouraged this point of view, but the evidence is strong that working-class women who joined the party after the war were already class-conscious and suspected the motives of those who claimed to be speaking on their behalf without personal experience of the hardships of working-class life.

A series of letters that appeared in *Labour Woman* in the spring of 1916 suggests that war conditions heightened class consciousness among politically aware working-class women. The letter writers were incensed about a government proposal to set up war-savings committees to instruct working-class housewives in economical housekeeping and persuade them to invest their savings in war bonds. They wanted to know how the middle-class women who were likely to sit on such committees could presume to instruct working women in the skills of economic housekeeping that they had been forced to practise all their lives. One woman wrote recommending that League women refuse to sit on the war-savings committees. The letter stated: 'It is no good at all for one or two Labour women to be on committees wholly composed of the well-to-do class who have not the slightest sympathy with those who have to struggle on all the time.' Another echoed the sentiment although she advised labour women to sit on the committees if they had the opportunity. 'As working women, we feel that we cannot economise any more than at present, as we were brought up with it from the cradle but we think that if members of the League got on these committees they might be able to teach those who have never known what want is, the horrors of poverty such as some women endure.'[22]

It is no easy matter to recapture the nature and depth of class resentment from a distance of time and experience. Public records and journals rarely offer insight into class attitudes. The 'thrift' letters are exceptional. In speaking or writing about their lives, rank-and-file women activists from the interwar years referred directly and indirectly to the wide gulf in income, education and experience separating them from middle-class women, including some of their own party leaders. Equally clearly, they expressed a strong sense of identification with their own class. As we saw in an earlier chapter, when asked their reasons for joining the Labour Party or the Co-operative Movement, all the women respondents for this study, like their male counterparts, emphasized their desire to improve conditions of life for working people. It is not surprising that the first enthusiastic generation of citizen members of the Labour Party viewed middle-class women's organizations with lack of interest or suspicion and did not rush to join them.

The increase of class tension among women reformers after the war, did not immediately induce either side to abandon their common roots in the late nineteenth century women's movement. Throughout the twenties, labour women continued to demand reforms specifically for the women of their class. They used language resonant of the women's movement which they inherited from their prewar socialist feminist leaders and the suffrage struggle. Similarly, the NUSEC, the largest of the non-party feminist organizations, drew upon the same feminist tradition when it took up the cause of improving working-class women's domestic and maternal conditions. Both groups called for birth control, family allowances, maternity care and nursery schools. The overlap did not stop there. Labour women and officially the Labour Party itself, were committed to the same legal reforms as liberal egalitarian feminists – equal pay, equal guardianship rights for mothers and married women's right to work.

In the aftermath of women's suffrage, leading activists from the suffrage generation, middle and working class, expected organized women to overcome their political differences and transform their common agendas into a united drive for women-centred reforms. It soon became clear, however, that the common agendas masked divergent aims. In the new political situation, organized women put class loyalty before their shared interests as women. Even feminists who preferred to remain outside the class-based political parties revealed class and political preferences in their stated goals, language and strategies. The class difference can be seen by a closer look at the arguments labour women and middle-class feminists used in calling for their common programmes.

MARRIED WOMEN'S RIGHT TO WORK

With the onset of a recession in 1920, the social and economic climate for women worsened. In 1922 wage-earning women were still being forced out of their jobs to make way for ex-servicemen and their unemployment rates were rising faster than those for men. In March, the London County Council (LCC) fired Dr Miall Smith, a Medical Officer of Health in the borough of St Pancras, as well as a number of school cleaners, charwomen and ambulance attendents because they were married. The Labour Party and the Women's Co-operative Guild joined with the NUSEC in protesting this attempt to make married women workers the scapegoats of the unemployment problem. Susan Lawrence, a prominent Labour member of the LCC, managed to save the school cleaners by showing that those who were married were not in fact being supported by their husbands, but this did not prevent local councils across the country from instituting a marriage bar which mainly affected school teachers and municipal employees.[23] In the period from 1921 to 1933, government agencies, employers and the press attacked married women's right to engage in paid work each time the economy slumped and unemployment rose. With the same regularity, the subject appeared on the agendas of both labour and middle-class women's organizations. The debates offer an opportunity to analyse the range of different perspectives among and between labour women and middle-class feminists.

The Open Door Council (ODC) represented the middle-class liberal feminist position on the issue. The council declared that any restriction on married women's right to work was 'tyrannical, anti-social and uneconomic.' Its members used the classic liberal argument that such an impediment was, 'an impertinent and unjustifiable interference with the private rights of another'. They dismissed the view that married women must stay at home to fulfill the responsibilities of marriage with the argument that domestic responsibilities belonged equally to husband and wife. They emphasized that the denial of married women's right to work would perpetuate the low status and low pay of all women wage-earners since employers would be unwilling to train women for jobs that they would leave on marriage.[24]

Under Eleanor Rathbone's leadership, the NUSEC took a rather different position. While defending married women's right to wage-work on the grounds of individual rights, Miss Rathbone made it clear that she did not consider work outside the home ideal for married women with children. Since the jobs that most married working-class women did were low paid, low status and often physically demanding, she felt that they would be better off at home especially if they had young children. She wanted to improve the conditions of life and the status of women as wives and mothers so that they would have at home 'an environment as suitable for them as is the outside industrial world for the father and breadwinner'.[25] State-paid family allowances would relieve married women of the financial necessity to seek wage-work and, most important from the NUSEC point of view, give them a degree of economic independence from their husbands.

Officially, the Labour Party's position on married women's right to work was very similar to that of the middle-class feminists. In 1923, the party produced a statement drawn up by the Standing Joint Committee of Industrial Women's Organizations (SJC), condemning the practice of firing married women and declaring that 'in principle', it was 'against any discrimination against workers on the grounds of sex or marriage'. The arguments that the SJC made in support of this stance, however, were quite different from those put forward by either the egalitarian or the new feminists. The report emphasized that the question of married women's right to work was, 'not so much a sex, as an unemployment question'. Married women were being forced into the labour market by widespread unemployment and the failure of the government to protect them from its consequences. The solution lay in state provision of work or maintenance for the unemployed and mothers' pensions which would enable married women with children to stay at home. Unlike family allowances, these pensions were to be paid only in the absence of a male breadwinner and were not intended to give married women with working husbands an independent source of income.[26]

The Labour Party's position on married women's right to work had much more in common with the prevailing attitudes among male trade unionists than with any feminist point of view. With some exceptions, trade unionists had a clearly stated preference for 'keeping their wives at home', where they could 'look after their domestic duties'.[27] However, they feared that any attempt by the state to determine married women's right to work on the basis of family need would bring men's wage packets under scrutiny and could reduce all employment to the level of relief work. If the state were to decide what constituted an adequate family income, there would be no need for collective bargaining and trade unions would lose their power.[28] These fears, rather than a commitment to the right of married women to equality of economic opportunity, dictated the Labour Party policy of support for married women's right to work.

The majority of Labour and Guild women seemed to agree with the party's official policy. They soundly defeated every conference resolution opposing married women's right to work. In 1925, for example, when the Association of Women Clerks and Secretaries called for a ban on the employment of married women with other means of support in times of economic depression, Jessie Stephen labelled it 'the most reactionary [resolution] they had had put before the conference up to the present time' and the union withdrew it.[29] The Crewe women's section proposed a similar resolution in 1932, the worst year of the Depression, but the delegates defeated it by 237 votes to 177.[30] Delegates also refused to support another resolution at the same conference which would have excluded married women from paid work on the party staff. The Chairman commented: 'It is fatally easy to make a case against the married woman in these times of great unemployment, but if intelligent, organized women once let the principle go of having a woman's work judged on its merits, apart from the personal circumstances, as a man's is judged, then good-bye to any real equality.'[31]

Labour women activists who supported married women's right to work, however, used arguments that were much closer to the middle-class feminist position than to that of their own party. Some argued on the basis of the right of the individual, regardless of gender or marital status, to self-development and economic independence. Dorothy Elliott, a prominent member of the National Union of General and Municipal Workers (NUGMW), said that 'women whether married or single had the right to develop their capacities and put their creative powers into that work which they could best perform'.[32] Mrs Palmer of Southampton expressed her belief that as a matter of social justice 'women had a right to be economically free'.[33] A conference resolution from Manchester described the LCC's proposed firing of married women teachers in 1922 as an 'unjustified interference with the freedom of employees who should be judged not by their private circumstances but by the value of their work as teachers'.[34]

Others saw the prohibition of married women's wage work as an example of unfair discrimination against women. Annot Robinson, for example, pointed out the injustice of singling out married women to sacrifice their jobs when 'there were scores of young unmarried women and hundreds of men occupying posts and taking incomes although they had otherwise sufficient to maintain themselves.'[35] Emma Sproson from Wolverhampton, refuted the assumption that just because a woman's husband was working she was being supported by him. 'She knew perfectly well that men did not give wives their money. There were very few men who did give their wives everything.'[36] Monica Whately placed the responsibility for discrimination against married women workers firmly at the door of the industrial labour movement. She said that trade unions were quick to defend any member who was unjustly treated by an employer, but she did not know of a 'single union having called a strike because a woman had been dismissed from her job because she was married'.[37]

The majority of those who expressed their support for married women's right to work in liberal feminist terms, had been active in the prewar suffrage movement. Dorothy Elliott, Selina Cooper, Annot

Robinson, Jessie Stephen, Monica Whately and Emma Sproson all belonged to that pioneering generation of feminists. Selina Cooper and Monica Whately, both socialists, were also active members of the Open Door Council. Although their opinion prevailed at the women's conferences, it is hard to judge from the evidence whether the delegates were responding to the feminists' arguments or to those of the women leaders who were emphasizing the class aspect of the issue. Certainly, there is something in the tone of the feminist speeches that suggests a rather defensive posture. Dorothy Elliott appealed to the conference 'not to be led away by the fact that there was so much unemployment among single women or by the talk of a dual income in some households'. She urged the delegates to 'stand firmly upon the principle' of economic equality.[38] Annot Robinson 'regretted the importance attached to two incomes going into one home'.[39] Jessie Stephen felt the need to remind the delegates to be 'logical' and 'perfectly honest' in their thinking on the subject.[40]

Their remarks were directed at the significant minority of rank-and-file labour women who opposed the liberal point of view and argued against married women's right to work unless they had no other means of support. The main proponents of this perspective were the white collar unions – the Post Office Workers, the Women Clerks and Secretaries and the Civil Servants Clerical Association. On three separate occasions, the delegates from these unions introduced resolutions at labour women's conferences arguing that 'in times of excessive depression' preference for employment should be given to women, married or single, whose earnings were their sole source of income. Working under a marriage bar themselves, the clerical workers argued that when there was a scarcity of jobs, married women who went on working even though they had husbands to support them were depriving single women of work and condemning young school leavers to 'the terrible curse of aimless idleness'.[41]

Some local section delegates backed the clerical trade unions on the issue of married women's right to work. Mrs Ward, from the Crewe Central women's section, for example, explained why she and her fellow members thought that 'in these days of changing conditions where so many people were without the means of livelihood, it was very strange to allow married women to have paid jobs when their husbands also had good jobs'. She reminded the delegates that 'in the Labour movement the policy had always been, "one man one job."' – a slogan that she interpreted to mean one household, one income. In support of Mrs Ward's resolution, Mrs Lee of York dismissed the argument that married women's knowledge and experience were needed for administrative posts. That might have been true 'in the old days' when people were badly educated. Nowadays young people were being educated to fill such jobs but when they left school, they found 'married women occupying all the available positions'.[42]

A number of Labour women guardians and councillors publicly disagreed with the official party ruling on this issue. Responding to a Liberal woman councillor arguing for married women's right to work, Mrs Ball, a Labour member on the Manchester Board of Guardians, refuted her suggestion that when married women worked, they provided work for other women as housekeepers. Working mothers could rarely afford housekeepers, she said. They either did both jobs themselves at the cost of their health and the comfort of the home or they used the unpaid labour of their eldest daughters whose market value was less. She described 'these little mothers' as 'undeveloped, wan and fragile ... the arduous work they have to do at home blights their whole future'.[43]

It appears that there were three different points of view among labour women on the issue of married women's right to work. However, in effect there were only two. The small group with connections to the prewar suffrage movement were the only ones to argue for it in feminist terms. Labour women leaders and probably a majority of members supported the principle on class, not feminist, grounds. As they saw it, any attempt by the state to determine married women's right to work on the basis of family need would threaten male trade unionists' control over wage bargaining. The third group, although it opposed married women's right to work, also wanted to protect the working-class family wage but in this case by giving priority in the labour market to the male breadwinner. The prevailing attitude on this issue among labour women was more a class than a liberal feminist perspective. The apparent agreement between middle-class feminists and labour women on the question of married women's right to work concealed a fundamental difference in motivation and purpose. Was the same true of another shared agenda item, that of equal pay?

EQUAL PAY FOR EQUAL WORK

The significant break down of sex segregation in the labour force during the First World War gave an enormous boost to the demand for equal pay. Large numbers of women in industry and commerce who had proved their capacity in jobs normally done by men, came to believe that there was no good reason why they should be paid any less. At the same time, the trade unions, fearful of the effects of dilution on skilled wage rates, insisted on the 'rate for the job' for women substitutes. Although the ruling proved hard to enforce, reformers like Beatrice Webb were convinced that it was the solution to the whole problem of equal pay for male and female workers.[44] Most encouraging of all, when women were more evenly spread through the workforce, the demand for their labour in traditional women's occupations increased and forced up the rates of pay until a statutory minimum of one pound a week could be established.

The optimism generated by the war soon evaporated in its aftermath. A Committee on Women in Industry set up by the War Cabinet in 1918 to investigate and report on equal pay decided in a Majority Report that the only basis for paying the same wage to men and women was equality of output.[45] This meant that where women were doing the same jobs as men, they would receive the same piece rates, but not necessarily the same time rates. Equal pay on these terms, however, implied a sexually integrated job market. For women wage-earners to benefit from this proposal, they would have had to stay on in their wartime jobs or the peacetime equivalents. Unfortunately, as soon as the war was over a two-pronged attack by government and organized labour forced wage-earning women back into the traditional female sector of domestic service and unskilled, low paid and segregated manufacturing processes. In this environment, equal pay for equal output was irrelevant. Apart from cotton textiles, where men and women weavers continued to get the same piece rates, women remained in sufficient numbers doing similar work to men only in teaching and the civil service. Consequently, the battle for equal pay made the greatest progress on the professional front.

While all middle-class feminist groups supported equal pay for equal work, they differed in where they placed their emphasis. The Six Point Group and the Open Door Council generally adopted the arguments presented by Beatrice Webb in her Minority Report to the

Committee on Women in Industry. She argued that 'for the production of commodities and services, women no more constitute a class than do persons of a particular creed or race'. She advocated opening all occupations to any individual who was qualified for the work irrespective of sex, race or creed. The same qualifications, conditions of work and rates of pay would apply to all persons in any particular job. They would be determined through collective bargaining within the framework of a national minimum in regards to 'rest-time, education, sanitation and subsistence' prescribed by law and applicable to all workers.[46] Her proposal met the requirements of the liberal feminist position in that it opened all jobs for free competition and tied the wage to the job and not to the sex of the worker.

Eleanor Rathbone, president of the NUSEC and a 'new feminist' found this argument weak on at least two points. She felt that it did not satisfactorily address the prevailing convention that men must have higher wages because of their family responsibilities. Her answer was family allowances which, by withdrawing dependents from wage bargaining, would undermine the theoretical basis for unequal rates of pay. Her second concern was that in a situation of free competition between men and women, employers would continue to choose male rather than female workers, leaving large numbers of working women to face unemployment. Her solution here was to raise the status and the financial security of women's work as housewives and mothers as an alternative to labour market competition.

The industrial labour movement endorsed equal pay for equal work as early as 1882 and the Labour Party reiterated the commitment in its 1918 policy statement *Labour and the New Social Order*.[47] The parliamentary party put its words into action when it supported the equal pay claims of teachers and civil servants just after the war. However, as in the case of married women's right to work, Labour's stance was dictated primarily by a concern for the interests of male industrial workers who, under existing conditions, were responsible for maintaining working-class living standards. As a reserve army of cheap labour, women wage earners were a permanent threat to male wage rates. If they were going to compete with men for the same jobs, which the labour movement hoped they would not, then they must demand the male rate so as not to throw men out of work or force down wage levels.

Labour women leaders followed the party's lead and made a conscious effort to stress the class rather than the gender aspects of equal pay. Ellen Wilkinson, for example, in a phrase that was becoming standard in dealing with feminist issues, declared that equal pay, 'was not a sex question but emphatically it was a class question. It was a question of where women workers should say that they wanted the rate for the job and would not be used to undercut the men.'[48] The SJC in its *Report on Equal Pay for Equal Work* also made a point of reminding wage-earning women that equal pay must be achieved by 'levelling up' their wage rates to those of male workers and not dragging down the men's rate. It recommended trade union organization as the surest way for women wage-earners to secure this goal whether they worked on the same jobs as men or in sex-segregated processes. For those women in the poorest paid and sweated sector of the labour market, the trade boards which established a legal minimum, still offered the best hope of raising wage levels.[49]

Limited evidence indicates that rank-and-file Labour Party women endorsed these essentially class-oriented arguments. The York women's section, for example, passed a resolution stating, 'that the delegates to the conference support the equal pay for women and men for equal work done or else if cheaper rates of wages be given the employer would always whenever possible take women and the men would remain unemployed'.[50] This was in March 1930, at the peak of the depression and shows the same concern for the male breadwinners that we found among local activists who thought it wrong for married women with other means of support to work outside the home. This is the only specific reference to equal pay in the available minutes although local Labour women regularly passed resolutions condemning employers' attacks on the wages of miners, builders, farm workers and other manual workers. It may be that as most of the section members were married and non-wage-earning, their first concern was for the preservation of male rates of pay and they accepted equal pay as a means to this end. However, it should also be noted that in a conference decision, the delegates by a large majority endorsed family allowances as a way of securing equal pay – a much more feminist position but still one that, they argued, would not involve a threat to male wage rates.

As was the case with married women's right to work, a group of mostly older, prewar suffragists argued for equal pay in very similar terms to those of liberal feminists. Dorothy Elliott, asked Labour women to recognize the difficulties of proving that women were doing the same jobs as men. In her view, it was time to get rid of all sex distinctions in the labour market and to insist on payment for the job. Ellen Wilkinson argued that if women refused to undercut male workers, employers would treat them like 'human beings', instead of as a 'special class of workers'.[51] Not surprisingly, women from the cotton textile towns in Lancashire, the only industry where women workers received equal pay for equal work, also argued in favour of the 'rate for the job'. However, these labour women did not regard equal pay either in purely feminist terms or as an end in itself It was still a means of protecting male wage rates and improving the conditions of life for the working class as a whole. As Dorothy Elliott put it, 'They must get beyond the idea of the man and woman worker and get down to the worker producing wealth for the employer.'[52]

Labour women were not as deeply divided over the issue of equal pay as they were over married women's right to work but they were just as distant from the middle-class feminist position. Even the minority of prewar suffragists who argued for equal pay in similar terms to the egalitarian feminists, still placed women's economic equality in the broader context of working-class progress. From the majority viewpoint, wage-earning women would be the secondary beneficiaries of equal pay; wage-earning men and their families would be the first.

SOCIAL WELFARE LEGISLATION

After 1919, labour women and the middle-class 'new feminists' in the NUSEC shared a policy of supporting discriminatory social welfare legislation directed particularly at working-class married women. In the twenties, both groups of organized women ran campaigns for birth control, family allowances and maternal and child welfare. In many ways these issues offered the best chance for cross-class co-operation because they could be viewed as an extension of the prewar joint campaigns for divorce law reform, maternity benefit and maternity and child welfare clinics. However, in the twenties the reform campaigns ran along parallel lines without the joint deputations, lobbying or mass meetings that had characterized the prewar period. What brought about the change?

Eleanor Rathbone, whose point of view dominated the NUSEC in the decade 1920–9, owed her brand of welfare feminism to the nineteenth-century nonconformist reforming tradition to which Margaret Llewelyn Davies, Enid Stacy, Katherine Glasier, Esther Roper and Eva Gore Booth also belonged. It was a strongly humanitarian and philanthropic tradition with its focus on working-class women and children as the most vulnerable sector of society. Like these reformers, Eleanor Rathbone wanted to reconcile women's distinctive social role as wives and mothers with the feminist ideal of equality of opportunity. She shared their perception that this could only be done by securing legislative protection for women to make their vital contribution to society under the best possible conditions. Only when this was achieved, would women be able to 'attain the same freedom of self-development and self-determination which men enjoy'.[53]

Labour Party leaders' views on social reform legislation in the twenties were poles apart from those of the NUSEC. As we saw in the debates over birth control and family allowances, they measured all reforms on the yardstick of the electoral needs of a mass party. But how far did rank-and-file Labour and Guild women share the NUSEC perspective? Labour women certainly had a similarly humanitarian, even altruistic approach to politics which encouraged the common interest in welfare reform. Organized women from both classes expressed strong support for social justice and help for disadvantaged working-class women and children. Both labour women and the NUSEC members believed in ameliorating working-class women's existing social and industrial conditions rather than waiting for either socialism or equal rights legislation to take care of the problems. This approach differentiated them from the 'liberal' feminists who were prepared to sacrifice women's immediate needs as workers and mothers to the long term goal of equal opportunity. Neither labour women nor the NUSEC had any difficulty in reconciling special legislative protection for women with a firm belief in their equality with men. If the NUSEC view was that 'family allowances and birth control were not a side-show, an excrescence on feminism, but part of its very core', labour women would have agreed while substituting the word 'socialism' for 'feminism'.[54]

The substitution, however, is an indication of a fundamental divergence between labour women and the NUSEC in their approach to social welfare legislation. For Eleanor Rathbone and the NUSEC, the purpose of such reforms as birth control and family allowances was to eliminate the barriers to gender equality that had their origin in the unequal distribution of power in the working-class family. For the majority of labour women, the reforms were ultimately a means of eliminating the barriers to social equality represented by the impoverishment of the working-class family. The difference is clear in the case of family allowances. Eleanor Rathbone advocated state-paid allowances as a way of achieving equal pay, as a means of raising the status of motherhood, and giving wives some measure of economic independence from their husbands. The majority of labour women wanted the allowances to relieve the anxiety of working-class mothers trying to make both ends meet, to enable them to feed and clothe their children and eat properly themselves.

Another very important difference in the attitudes of the two classes of women reformers also derived from their class perspectives. Eleanor Rathbone and the NUSEC advocated social welfare reform to benefit working-class women out of a middle-class sense of social responsibility. Labour women urged the same reforms for their own class and on the basis of their own class experience. In the case of birth control, for example, Eleanor Rathbone's support for working women's access to birth control information was influenced to no small degree by the old malthusian fear of over-breeding among those least fitted to become parents.[55] Labour women's passionate and sustained support for this cause drew on their personal experience of 'terrible housing conditions, the lack of means to support and educate a big family, the weary life of such a mother, the tragedy of the birth of the unwanted baby ... '[56] They thought it only just that in a situation involving the health and well-being of mothers and their children, working-class women should have the same options as the middle-class women who could afford to pay for birth control information.

Clearly, the common agendas of middle-class feminists and labour women in the 1920s concealed a wide divergence in perceptions and ultimate goals that would have made cross-class participation difficult to achieve. Even though the ideological division between egalitarian and social-welfare feminists overlapped class and political divisions, the overlap was never numerically large enough or sufficiently influential to counteract the strong sense of class loyalty among the postwar generation of labour women activists and middle-class feminists' growing sense of disillusionment with the Labour

Party. The prewar suffragists who supported feminist and socialist measures into the twenties – Selina Cooper is probably the best example – were a diminishing minority.

The Labour Party's support for equal rights legislation after the war was in almost every case motivated by the need to protect organized male workers. Social welfare measures which would benefit working women had always to be measured on the yardstick of party unity. Labour women leaders with a place in the party's power structure, made a conscious effort to put women's issues in a class context and to relate them to the broad policy goals of the male-dominated party. Rank-and-file labour women accepted the priority of class loyalty but argued for women's issues in terms that were neither those of the party nor of middle-class feminists.

While middle-class feminism, especially the liberal variety tended to be logically consistent and theoretical with clearly defined goals, labour women's support for women's issues, seems to have been much more pragmatic in that it was a response to existing circumstance and firmly based in working-class women's experience. Among its most consistent themes was a popular idea of 'fairness' as a measurement of women's rights both in relation to the men of their class and party and to middle-class women. It was also characterized by a desire to protect women who were poor and often without the means to help themselves against the rich and strong. Most labour women advocates of women's special needs did not share the middle-class view that all women had a common oppression that crossed class barriers. On the contrary they expressed the opinion that since middle-class women already enjoyed all the material goods, well-being and opportunity they needed, they could have no under-standing of the problems of poor women. The class focus of the postwar generation of labour women was the main reason for their lack of interest in a working relationship with middle-class feminist organizations.

PROTECTIVE OR RESTRICTIVE LEGISLATION?

The class tensions and ideological differences between labour women and middle-class feminists developed into open conflict over the question of support for sex-based protective legislation. The precipitating events were the attempts of both Labour and Conservative governments to introduce a new factory act – Labour in 1924 and the

Tories in 1926. Although neither act was passed, the prospect of a legislative change in the conditions of women's industrial employ-ment was enough to bring the debate between the two classes of organized women out of the realm of the abstract and unattainable and onto the battleground of political reality. Liberal egalitarian feminists were eager to sieze the opportunity of a new factory act to establish the principle that industrial regulation should be based on the nature of the job, not the sex of the worker. Labour women, on the other hand, were anxious to give additional protection to a female labour force made more vulnerable by the economic recession.

Just as British feminists and labour women prepared to do battle over sex-based protective legislation, feminists across the Atlantic were engaged in a similar struggle over the same issue. In the American case, the focal point was the Equal Rights Amendment to the Constitution proposed by Alice Paul and the National Woman's Party. Paul came to oppose all sex-based protective legislation because of the difficulty of reconciling it with equal economic rights. The voluntarist feminist groups associated with working women, Florence Kelley's National Consumers' League and the Women's Trade Union League, however, refused to abandon the fruits of their long struggle to relieve wage-earning women of the worst excesses of capitalist exploitation. Like British labour women, they questioned the value of exchanging concrete gains in terms of hours and working conditions for an abstract right to equality.[57]

In analysing how and why the confrontation over protective legislation proved to be the decisive break between labour and feminism in Britain, it is useful to look at the way the same conflict developed under the different political and economic conditions that prevailed in the United States. The key questions are these: Did the economic recession in Britain strengthen Labour's case for sex-based protective legislation in a way that did not happen in the United States? Did it make any difference to the dispute or its outcome that the supporters of special protection for women workers in Britain spoke as members of a mass working-class political party while their American counterparts did not? Were working-class women activists more involved in the conflict in Britain than in America where it was largely confined to middle-class women reformers?

The struggle over protective legislation in Britain was organized women's response to the declining economic power of female wage-workers in the recession conditions of the twenties. During the

postwar boom, 1918 to 1920, labour women's leaders seemed ready
to modify their traditional support for special industrial protection
for women. The wartime experience, when thousands of women
worked successfully in trades previously considered unhealthy and
unsafe, encouraged the Standing Joint Committee of Industrial
Women's Organizations (SJC) to call in 1918 for a revision of prewar
restrictions on women wage-workers. The following year, the
committee endorsed Beatrice Webb's *Minority Report on Women in
Industry* which included a recommendation that there be no more
'special provisions differentiating men from women' in any future
factory act.[58] In their turn, a majority of middle-class feminists in the
NUSEC supported the maternity provisions of the 1919 International Labour Organization's Washington Convention which
demanded six weeks paid leave for working mothers before and after
the birth of a child.[59] In the favourable economic climate of the
reconstruction years, the gap between labour women and organized
feminists on the issue of sex-based protective legislation seemed to be
closing.

As economic conditions for women wage-earners grew worse after
1920, however, the gap widened once more, driving the two classes of
organized women into more extreme positions. In the years 1920–4,
women's trade union membership declined by one third. According
to Sheila Lewenhak, this decline encouraged a host of other ills.[60]
Employers took advantage of women workers' lack of organization to
drop their basic wage rates to the lowest level set by the trade boards
which established minimums in the poorest sector of women's
employment. After 1921, even this minimum standard was
threatened when the government responded to employers' complaints by cutting back on the number of new trade boards. Hours
regulations, relaxed during the war, continued to be widely ignored.
A sixty-hour week was common and in some factories, women were
working a two shift system that meant either leaving home at four or
five in the morning or returning after ten at night.[61] At the same time,
women workers were facing unemployment and underemployment
on a proportionate scale to men but with minimal trade union or
insurance support. The government's answer was to push them into
that catch-all uninsured occupation – domestic service. Finally in the
harsher economic climate, married women workers were the subject
of repeated attacks and suffered discrimination in the allocation of
unemployment insurance benefits.[62]

Labour women leaders had two solutions to the crisis. The first was an intensive campaign to encourage women's trade union membership. The evidence was compelling that the one-fifth of women workers still unionized had been the only ones able to resist the downward pressure on their wage levels and working conditions. The other was to call for further protective legislation. Unorganized wage-earning women were probably no more subject to economic exploitation than unskilled and unorganized male workers, but since their wage rates were generally lower, they had less far to go to reach and fall below subsistence level. In addition, their vulnerability was considered a threat not only to themselves but to their children, born and unborn. For labour women leaders, state protection seemed to offer the only practical way of halting women's decline into a permanent underclass of wage workers. In 1923, the SJC outlined provisions for a new factory act which set a maximum forty-eight-hour week for women and young persons, no more than nine in a day and no more than four and a half without a break. It called for the abolition of the two-shift system and reiterated the ban on night work and on work in dangerous and unhealthy trades. These provisions were incorporated into the party's 1924 Act.[63]

British middle-class feminists diagnosed the economic problems of wage-earning women very differently. In their view, the evil of women's low wages would only be cured through free and open competition between and among the sexes for all jobs. Protective legislation applied only to female workers was in effect restrictive legislation since it prevented women from exercising their right to compete on equal terms in the labour market. To treat women workers as different from men, classing them with children, was a denial of the basic adult right to pursue one's self interest which for women workers as for men lay in maximizing their earnings. From this perspective, the Labour Party's Factory Act with its special provisions for women workers was likely to confirm their low status as well as giving legal justification for the differential wage structure. When the act was introduced into Parliament, NUSEC leaders immediately wrote letters of protest to members of Parliament and the press against legislation which 'imposes restrictions with regard to the sex of the worker'.[64]

Although women wage-earners in the United States suffered under the same constraints of low wages, a sex-segregated labour market and declining trade union organization as their British counterparts, the United States did not undergo a comparable economic crisis until right at the end of the twenties. Unemployment rates did not reach abnormal levels nor did unorganized women workers experience to the same degree, a deterioration in their wages and working conditions. These conditions, together with hostility and discrimination directed at the married woman worker, came later in the thirties. While British women's employment was still expanding into new and unregulated areas of manufacture, particularly in the electrical and consumer goods industries, for American wage-earning women in the twenties, the general trend was a movement out of manufacturing and into clerical jobs.[65]

The protective legislation debate in each country showed the influence of the different economic conditions. British labour women's arguments in favour of the expansion of sex-based protective legislation gained credibility from evidence of the vulnerability of women wage-earners in periods of recession. Aware of the dire economic problems that working women were experiencing, labour women united with male trade unionists and the parliamentary Labour party in support of further industrial protection. Some of the staunchest egalitarian feminists in the Labour Party, Ellen Wilkinson and Dorothy Elliott had to admit that 'whatever may be the ultimate ideal of sex equality in industry, the time is not yet ripe for the removing of any legislation which protects women workers'.[66]

In contrast, Florence Kelley and the leaders of the American Women's Trade Union League were attempting to make the same case in a time of overall economic growth and defend a body of legislation which applied to a decreasing percentage of industrial women workers. Economic conditions had far less relevance to the debate in the United States than in England. The political and legal constraints imposed by the constitution shaped the issue there. The historian Vivien Hart, points out that to secure any kind of industrial protection for wage-earning women under the constitution, feminist reformers had to argue that women workers were unable by their very nature to protect themselves. This distinction was the only legally acceptable justification for federal intervention in their right to freedom of contract.[67] It implied a permanent female helplessness unrelated to specific economic circumstances. American feminists therefore had to align themselves with one of two inflexible positions. They could either support the equal rights amendment that would allow no special legal provisions for wage-earning women at all or stay with protective legislation on grounds which established women permanently as a special and weaker class of worker.

Neither labour women nor middle-class feminists in Britain were forced into such a rigid stance. Because they argued for further protection for women workers in response to specific economic circumstances, labour women not only left the door open to a change in policy once those circumstances improved, but they were also able to defy the apparent logic of such a policy by continuing to call for equal pay. They had the luxury of ambiguity. They could say, with Mrs Wignall, a cotton operative from Preston, that they believed in the equality of men and women while also believing that working women needed special protective laws.[68] However, the greater flexibility in Britain meant that there were splinter groups of organized women on both sides of the dispute who adopted divergent positions. After 1927, the NUSEC, for example, changed its outright opposition to any form of sex-based protective legislation to a conditional support which allowed it to consider the views of the workers affected and whether or not the legislation would benefit the community. This change caused a defection of the egalitarian feminist members to the Open Door Council.[69] A minority of labour women, including Selina Cooper and a very vocal Mrs White from the Radlett women's section opposed any restrictions on women's economic freedom.[70] Dora Russell wanted protective legislation applied to workers of both sexes except in the case of maternity provisions.[71] ILP women, led by Dorothy Jewson, wanted to keep the existing sex-specific protective laws but to base all future legislation on the nature of the work, not the sex of the worker. The American context did not allow for this range of opinion.[72]

At first sight, the fact that the supporters of sex-based protective legislation in Britain belonged to a mass working-class party appears to have had very little influence over the terms of the debate or the development of the conflict. The arguments of the two sides in Britain and in America were so similar as to be almost interchangeable. The British Open Door Council and the American National Woman's Party both presented the liberal egalitarian case that it was essential to free women wage-earners from anachronistic laws that confined them to a separate and unequal status in the labour market. Both groups seemed less interested in the complexities of labour issues than in securing recognition of the principle of economic equality. The Open Door Council may have held a more radically *laissez-faire*

liberal position than the National Woman's Party. It published a
report expressing the view that the Mines Act of 1842 preventing
women being employed underground in coal mines was an in-
fringement of their rights.[73] It lobbied against the maternity clauses
of the Washington Convention which it described as 'a serious attack
on the personal freedom of a woman as an individual and on her
rights as an earner' and argued that maternity should be treated like
any other illness that might temporarily incapacitate a male
worker.[74] It called the designation of work as unsuitable for women
because it involved heavy weights or dangerous chemicals, a policy of
'doctrinaire sentimentality based on a false ideal of gentility'.[75] The
National Woman's Party preferred to talk in terms of 'industrial
equality', a 'fair field and no favor' and 'human legislation' but
these ideas had the same implications as those the Open Door
Council expressed more openly.[76]

The defenders of sex-based protective legislation in both countries
also used similar arguments. The main point the defenders made was
that women wage-earners could not be treated in the same way as
male workers because they were not the same. They were mostly
young, only worked until marriage and worked for the most part in
segregated, unorganized trades. They were not as physically strong
as men, had domestic responsibilities not shared by male workers and
were potential or actual mothers. They argued that these differences
would not simply disappear if protective laws were revoked and free
and equal competition introduced. Instead of creating economic
equality, the change would leave wage-earning women with no
defence against exploitation by employers. Even if some women
workers, the women in the printing trade, for example, might benefit
from the removal of night work restrictions, hundreds of other
women in unskilled trades would find themselves obliged to work at
night to the detriment of their health and family life.[77]

American and British supporters of sex-based protective legislation
were at pains to stress that these laws had a proven history of success
in increasing the employment of women, raising their status and
spreading the benefits of industrial protection to male workers. They
both argued that in opposing protective laws, liberal feminists were
risking the loss of these benefits and a return to *laissez-faire*
capitalism.[78] Pauline Newman, the American WTUL leader, for
example, bitterly recalled that before any legal limit to working
hours, women had been '"free" and "equal" to work long hours for

1 Marion Phillips in her 'Lady Member's Uniform', 1929. (Photograph by courtesy of the National Museum of Labour History)

2   Margaret Bondfield. (Photograph by courtesy of the National Museum of Labour History)

3 'Labour believes in International Friendliness' Faversham Constituency Labour Party, 1925. (Photograph by courtesy of the National Museum of Labour History)

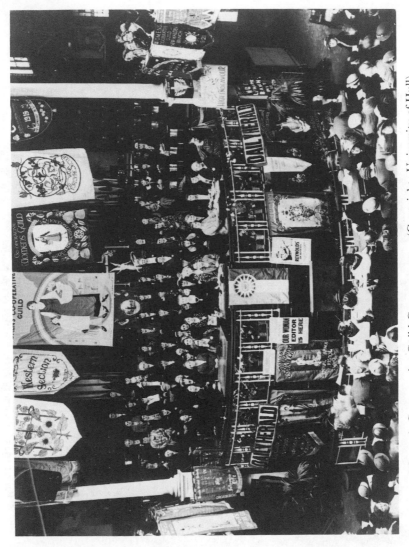

4 Women's Co-operative Guild Congress, 1925. (Copyright: University of Hull)

5(a) 'Separation of the Sexes': Annual Labour Party Conference, Leicester, 1932

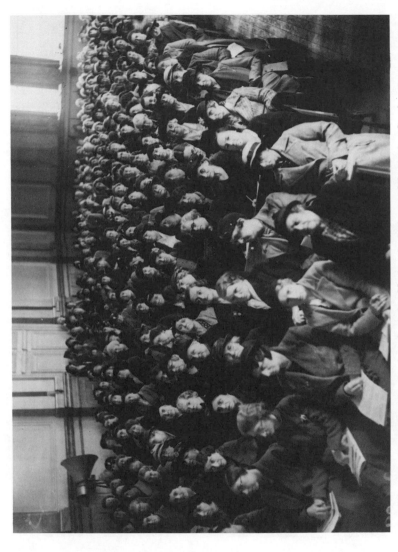

5(b) 'Separation of the Sexes': National Labour Women's Conference, Leamington, 1936. (Photograph by courtesy of the National Museum of Labour History)

6   Dorothy Jewson. (Photograph by courtesy of the National Museum of Labour History)

7　Ellen Wilkinson, 1945. (Copyright: The Labour Party)

8 'With Babies and with Banners'. A Labour Women's March through Faversham in support of extending the vote to women on the same terms as men, 13 June 1925. (Photograph by courtesy of the National Museum of Labour History)

9   Mary Sutherland – Labour's Chief Woman Officer. (Copyright: The Labour
Party)

starvation wages, or free to leave the job and starve!'[79] In a similar tone, Marion Phillips asked her opponents rhetorically, 'Would they prefer that the employer maintain his right to sweat his workers in the name of equality?' She explained that while the 'ultra-feminists' saw any protective legislation as a restriction on the rights of employers and workers to pursue their own self-interest, 'we, on the contrary, see in such legislation a growing code of humane and decent conditions for the worker adapted to age, sex and average strength'.[80]

Women in both the Labour Party and the American Women's Trade Union League who had had industrial and trade union experience were particularly incensed that middle-class women with no experience of wage work except perhaps in the professions, were presuming to judge what was in the best interests of women shop floor workers. An American WTUL officer Elisabeth Christman, a former glovemaker, wanted to 'put some of the "equal righters" in a boiler factory or to work at a conveyor belt in a highly speeded up mass production industry'.[81] In similar vein, Mary Bell Richards of the National Union of Boot and Shoe Operatives in Britain, doubted that middle-class feminists had any idea 'what it was like to sit continuously for five hours with your eyes glued to the needle of a power machine'. She was appalled that reformers would suggest any change likely to worsen conditions rather than improve them. In her view, it was time that women 'demanded something for themselves'.[82]

Labour women leaders, not the Labour Party, set the terms of the protective legislation debate in Britain. They also conducted the pamphlet war and the public confrontations with the Open Door Council without the active support of the party which limited its role to giving approval to any official publications. After the defeat of the party's 1924 Factory Act and the introduction of the Tory bill in 1926, Ellen Wilkinson introduced a private member's factory bill incorporating the protective measures that labour women wanted.[83] The women on the SJC wrote the party's official rebuttal to the liberal feminist attack in the form of a pamphlet entitled, 'Protective Legislation and the Woman Worker'. Marion Phillips put the case for sex-based protection in a BBC radio broadcast debate with Elizabeth Abbott of the Open Door Council in February 1929 just as she had replied to the letters written by the Council to *The Times* earlier in the year.[84] When the Council took the fight to the international arena in an effort to convert the Women's Advisory

Committee of the League of Nations, the Women's Committee of the
Labour and Socialist International and the International Labour
Organization to its point of view, Labour women leaders used their
representation on these committees to rally labour interests against
the council.[85]

Because of the Labour Party's lack of involvement in the protective
legislation fight, it is easy to assume that the conflicts over sex-based
protective legislation in Britain and the United States were almost
identical versions of a struggle between mostly middle-class proponents of the two points of view. This assumption seems to be borne
out by the fact that the issue did not generate a very strong response
among working-class women activists or wage-earners in either
country. Judging from the local women's section minutes, the subject
of protective legislation was of little interest to rank-and-file Labour
Party women members, perhaps because most were married and
outside the labour market. Those who spoke on the issue at the
National Labour Women's Conferences were for the most part
officials in the trade union movement whose work brought them into
close contact with the problems of women wage-earners.[86]

Yet the comparison with the United States does reveal a significant
difference of emphasis in the British case. The fight over protective
legislation in America was essentially a struggle between middle-class
feminists with divergent views about the nature of women and their
social and economic roles. The National Woman's Party leaders
viewed women workers, not as a distinct group, but as autonomous
individuals capable of complete social and economic equality with
men once all legal barriers fell. In their view, women's biological and
physiological differences were personal characteristics irrelevant to
their public functions. Florence Kelley and the National Consumers'
League, on the other hand believed that these differences could not
be ignored since they defined and limited women's economic and
social roles. As such, they ought to form the basis for any policy
decisions relating to women. Thus, gender provided the framework
for the debate in the US. The class issue that clearly underlay the
dispute, although of vital concern to Florence Kelley, was secondary
since none of the organizations involved claimed to represent an
exclusive class interest.

In Britain, however, the protective legislation fight was as much
about politics and class as about gender. From the moment when the
NUSEC opposed the Labour Party's 1924 Factory Act, Labour

women leaders saw themselves engaged in a political struggle with middle-class 'non-party' feminists over the right to decide an appropriate industrial policy for wage-earning women. They based their claim to make the decision on class interest. As representatives of organized women workers and as members of the working-class party they felt they were empowered to interpret wage-earning women's needs and wishes. 'Non-industrial' middle-class 'armchair philosophers' with few working women supporters could make no such claim.[87] Middle-class feminists, for their part, challenged labour women's right to force 'restrictive' legislation on women wage-earners. They were convinced that the male-dominated party dictated the policy in the interests of working-class men who wanted to limit women's opportunity to compete with them in the labour market. The ideological differences became divergent class identifications rather than differing views about the social significance of gender.

In contrast to this aggressive class confrontation conducted as part of an on-going political debate, the American dispute had all the appearance of a family row. Despite their ideological differences, Florence Kelley and Alice Paul were both active in the broad context of the American women's movement. Their relationship with the national political parties and the trade unions is unclear but seems to have consisted of personal contacts with prominent men from all parts of the power structure who were sympathetic to their cause. Neither leader emphasized a party political affiliation. Rather, as women reformers, they expected to serve the interests of their different women constituents in a gender context by using, not joining, the male political establishment. When it became clear that they were deeply divided on the subject of sex-based protective legislation, both leaders moved towards the conflict with considerable reluctance and dismay. When it finally came, the fight was personal, bitter and largely confined to the family of middle-class women's organizations.

In Britain, the debate was suffused with the rhetoric of class antagonism. Labour women leaders encouraged women members to see protective legislation as something that benefited working-class women but that middle-class feminists did not want them to have. In an article in *Labour Woman* entitled, 'Pet Bogey of Extreme Feminism', for example, the author reminded her readers that organized women textile workers outnumbered men in their industry, received equal pay and still enthusiastically supported more factory legislation. She asked: 'Why should they be treated as if their opinions were dictated to them by men and not worthy of consideration? What right have non-industrial middle-class women who are not representing them to throw their wishes to the winds'?[88] In another article, 'Equality, Real and Pretended', the author accused middle-class feminists of putting the interests of the employing class before those of the workers. She wrote: 'Industrial women do not accept these efforts of non-industrial women in the National Congress of Women who pretend to assist them while in reality, though perhaps unknowingly, assisting the employers in their fight against new factory legislation.'[89] On another occasion, Marion Phillips raised doubts about the sincerity of the Open Door Council's professed concern for all workers' hours by asking: 'Why did the women who were so keen that women's hours should not be restricted if men's were not, do nothing to prevent the miners' working day being extended?'[90]

Although the evidence is scanty, the comments of the handful of local labour women who spoke at conferences suggest that they accepted the class view of the protective legislation debate. At the 1930 conference, Mrs Corner, a Fabian, commented that: 'The women in industry must decide for themselves what they wanted. They did not want the people who were not in industry deciding what industrial women should have.'[91] Mrs Wignall, the cotton operative from Preston, put it this way: 'She wanted women to stick to their protective legislation and get into trade unions. They had fought for protection for years and years and were not going to give it up for a wild feminist principle.'[92] For the first time in Labour records we find a member apologising for her middle-class origins. Monica Whately wanted the conference delegates to accept that her opposition to sex-based protective legislation was based on her socialism not her class: 'She knew that when she said that protective legislation was opposed to socialist principles, that some people would speak of it as being, the "middle-class view". It was not her fault that she happened to be born in the middle-class.'[93] Her protest implied that most labour women saw the dispute over special industrial legislation for women in class, rather than gender terms.

The difference of emphasis showed in the outcome of the struggles in the United States and Britain. In America, the quarrel had its biggest impact on feminist organization and gender ideology. It split the feminist movement into two broad irreconcilable camps and forfeited the support of labour and labour-minded feminists for an equal rights amendment. According to Nancy Cott, it left behind a memory of 'warring outlooks among women', and confusion resulting from the unresolved question of the nature of women. Were they the same as men or different and how should this influence future social policy? Faith in simple all-embracing formulas for achieving gender equality was gone to be replaced by a realization of the complexity of the problem of integrating women into a world run according to male norms.[94]

In Britain, the equally bitter struggle left a political division between feminism and socialism, middle- and working-class women's reform movements. The protective legislation fight gave credibility to the view that feminism was a middle-class point of view which was hostile to the interests of the working class. After 1930, the Labour Party abandoned its earlier commitment to the equality of the sexes in its rhetoric, publications and policies. The subject of gender disappeared from public discourse in social democratic politics. The word 'feminism' was rarely heard and if mentioned was usually accompanied by a disclaimer to indicate that the speaker or writer had something different in mind from the feminism associated with middle-class women.[95] The number of party pamphlets directed specifically at the women in the movement decreased significantly from a high point in the immediate post-suffrage years. While this rejection of feminism owed something to a widely expressed feeling among the general public that women had 'come too far, too fast' it was justified for the party by the mistrust of middle-class feminists generated by the protective legislation struggle.

Labour women were very much a part of this movement away from feminism. At the national level, co-operation with middle-class feminist groups in lobbying campaigns and public demonstrations dried up almost completely. In 1935, Labour Party women passed a resolution calling on the party to disaffiliate the Open Door Council on the grounds that it was 'directly opposed to the interests of industrial women workers and trade union principles'.[96] Relations with the NUSEC whose position after 1927 on the issue of sex-based protective legislation was not far from that of labour women, were also strained and they too gradually faded away. Most of the prominent labour women on the executive committee resigned between 1927 and 1931.[97] Requests from the NUSEC for joint efforts

in the cause of equal franchise, maternal welfare and fair unemployment compensation for married women workers received a
very cold response from the SJC.[98] NUSEC members and labour
women both worked in the distressed areas to help victims of
unemployment but they were careful not to cross class and political
lines.

The protective legislation fight isolated labour women from
feminist influences in their own ranks. The ILP, which had been an
important source of feminist inspiration since its foundation, disaffiliated from the Labour Party in 1932. Although the main reason was
the ILP's demand for the right to an independent vote in Parliament
which the party refused to give, the protective legislation fight also
played a part in souring relations between the two labour parties.
Marion Phillips had publicly and harshly criticized Dorothy Jewson,
a prominent ILPer, for not supporting the party position on the issue
at the International Labour and Socialist meeting in September 1929.
Both Miss Jewson and Dora Russell were disappointed by the
attitude of Labour women leaders and after disaffiliation, they ceased
to work with them. The loss was considerable. ILP women had led
the way in the major struggles of the twenties for birth control, family
allowances and a distinct women's voice in the party. As for working-
class feminists like Selina Cooper, Jennie Baker, Annot Robinson,
Emma Sproson, Mrs White and others, the task of reconciling their
socialism and their feminism became much harder after the industrial
legislation struggle. Selina went indestructably on, moving closer to
the Communist Party in the thirties, but most of the others left
political life. They were literally a dying breed.[99]

The struggle over industrial protection for women also had
important political consequences for middle-class feminist organizations. Above all, it demonstrated the ineffectiveness of 'non-party'
status. It was clear that women were as deeply divided along class
and political lines as men, and their feminist views, where they
existed, reflected these divisions. With the exception of a tiny minority
of egalitarians, labour women had remained loyal to their party's
policy on the issue of sex-based protective legislation and women
wage-earners had been unresponsive to the propaganda efforts of the
Open Door Council. Organized middle-class feminists themselves
found it difficult to remain neutral in their attitudes towards the
established parties. They had a natural affinity for the Liberal Party
but unfortunately, the Liberals as a weak third party in a two-party

system, could not offer them access to policy-making. The protective legislation fight further alienated the only other party that might have been sympathetic to some of their goals – the Labour Party. Ideologically and organizationally divided and without a political base, middle-class feminists either threw their energies into a widening range of diverse issues and causes or moved outside national politics to the international arena.

CONCLUSIONS

If there was any one reason for the deterioration in the relations between labour women and middle-class feminists in the twenties, it was the absorption of women after 1918 into a political party structure broadly based on social and economic class divisions. Shared gender concerns could not compete with the growing strength of class and party loyalty. The prewar feminist/socialist alliance left an ideological legacy that in the immediate postwar years appeared to cross class and political barriers. This legacy found expression in the almost identical agendas of new feminists and labour women. But the appearance of a common programme proved illusory. The values that framed and shaped the agendas were increasingly related to class.

This is not to suggest that rank-and-file labour women either had no interest in women centred issues or abandoned them out of loyalty to the party. On the contrary, they continued to define their political role in gender terms, claiming the right to put the 'woman's point of view' in the party and to work for reform in the interests of working-class women as mothers, wives and wage workers. The most significant characteristic of labour women's gender focus, one that the party structure encouraged, was that it was confined to working-class women. It contained no recognition that all women had similar needs and concerns. Since the war, labour women had been inclined to see middle-class women as beneficiaries of the employing and profiteering class and therefore out of sympathy with workers and their problems. Labour Party warnings may have deepened this mistrust but for a generation of activists with little or no contact with middle-class reformers, such warnings were probably unnecessary. The older generation of labour women who had absorbed feminist ideas as part of the suffrage campaign lost ground to the much more numerous postwar generation. Their voice had its effect in sustaining the fight for reforms like birth control and family allowances within the party, but could not prevail when it came to relations with middle-class feminists outside the party.

Middle-class feminists had a similar class bias which contributed to their worsening relations with labour. At its core was an antipathy to the mass working-class party based on the conviction that organized working-class males were a bastion of unenlightened, reactionary and anti-feminist ideas. As if to confirm their opinion, the Labour Party consistently failed to live up to its commitment to sexual equality or to carry out its promises to enact women-centred reforms, concentrating instead on male-oriented industrial and social legislation. Feminists increasingly assumed that labour women, especially their leaders, spoke on behalf of the male-dominated party rather than as representatives of working-class women. Neo-malthusian allusions to 'inferior racial elements' hint at darker prejudices while the defence in the name of economic freedom of the right of mine owners to work women and children like beasts dragging heavy tubs of coal along cramped mineshafts suggests a well developed ability to divide the female population into 'them' and 'us.'

The fight over protective legislation makes no sense outside the context of this atmosphere of mutual class suspicion generated within the framework of class politics. The difference of opinion with the largest feminist group, the NUSEC, was slight after 1927 and the Open Door Council, in spite of its aggressiveness, clever strategies and voluminous propaganda was a very small organization compared to the Labour Party. Nor did the issue itself seem to evoke much interest among either Labour women or women wage-earners. The struggle was decisive precisely because of the propaganda which brought previously concealed class hostility into open political and public discourse. Local Labour women might not remember precisely why the Open Door Council objected to the Party's 1924 Factory Act, but they could not forget that Elizabeth Abbott had challenged Marion Phillips to a public debate on the wireless. They might not read the letters in *The Times*, but they could not avoid the endless arguments, justifications and explanations that appeared in *Labour Woman* in the years from 1924 to 1931. They were left with the strong impression that middle-class feminists who claimed to be interested in the welfare of working women, were opposed to the Labour Party and were criticizing the movement in public. Thus 'feminism' became associated with an anti-labour position.

The comparison with the similar conflict over protective legislation in the United States confirms the greater signficance of class and political concerns in the British case. The similarity of the arguments educated middle-class feminists and women labour leaders used in both countries indicates the common ideological and cultural roots of the two movements. The greater prominence given to the class and political differences between the two sides in Britain owed much to the existence of the Labour Party which identified the advocates of protective legislation not with a particular social feminist perspective as in the United States but with a working-class political organization.

The split between labour and feminism drove labour women towards a change of language and policy. As feminism became unacceptable as word or creed, Labour Party women hesitated to continue advocating policies specifically for women in women-centred language. Without a gender identification, they had to fall back on the position male leaders and Marion Phillips had outlined for them at the time of the 1918 merger – one of theoretical equality masking a secondary status. Once they abandoned their claim to distinct gender power, the only acceptable position for them was as supporting players, fundraising, canvassing and holding social events in the local parties. After about 1932, it is hard to find women in the national party. No longer seeking to represent women's special needs, they disappeared from view.

CHAPTER 5

'Helping others' – women in local labour politics, 1919–1939

Most of the working-class women who joined a labour or socialist organization in the interwar years made their political contribution close to home. The need to fit their politics into the hours between 'dinner and tea' usually confined them to the local labour community. In their Labour Party women's section, Guild or ILP branch, national party business had to compete for their attention with more familiar and pressing local issues. Local personalities and power structures shaped their political lives far more decisively than the national leadership. Very few working-class labour women stood as parliamentary candidates in this decade but hundreds won election to local councils and boards of guardians and secured appointment to the magistrates' bench.

Women developed a different relationship with the male majority at the local level than they had with the leaders in the national organizations. As we have seen, the Labour Party's National Executive Committee and the Co-operative Union strongly resisted the idea of women members acting as a distinct group in the national party. They feared that such a clear gender demarcation would provoke 'sex antagonism' and destroy party unity. Locally, a predominately segregated organizational structure encouraged a division of political responsibility along gender lines that was broadly acceptable to both sexes. Although Labour Party men and women frequently disagreed on where the line between their 'spheres' should be drawn, 'separate-but-equal' gender roles came closer to realization in local parties than nationally in this period.

Municipal government was another area where 'separate spheres' appears to have helped rather than hindered working-class women's political interests. Only a handful of exceptional women were elected to Parliament in the interwar years and all of them were careful to avoid any exclusive identification with women's issues. The national electorate evidently considered the majority of women candidates unsuited to parliamentary business, assuming perhaps that finance, the economy and foreign affairs called for masculine expertise. In contrast, local government voters seemed prepared to recognize working-class women's household and family experience as proper qualification for related areas of local administration such as the care of children, the elderly and the poor. In local government too, women had to fight to widen a very narrow, male definition of their public responsibilities, but those who recorded their experiences, felt that they eventually achieved the status of respected colleagues.

WOMEN IN LOCAL LABOUR ORGANIZATIONS

Working-class women who wanted to join the political labour movement in the twenties and thirties had a number of organizations to choose from. No matter which one they joined first, a Labour League of Youth or the Independent Labour Party (ILP), the overwhelming majority eventually came into the Labour Party. The party's national network of constituency parties and women's sections, begun in 1918, expanded rapidly in the twenties, making it the most accessible of local labour organizations. But conviction as much as convenience drew women to the party. Even before 1924 when Labour demonstrated its ability to gain control of government, labour women recognized it as 'the best hope for the working class' and the most likely means of securing social justice.[1]

There was a great deal of fluidity in the membership of local labour and socialist organizations in the twenties. Dual or multiple membership was common. More than half of the women who joined the Labour Party, for example, also joined the Women's Co-operative Guild. As one activist expressed it, 'when you belonged to one, you belonged to the other'. Membership of the Guild went from around 30,000 in 1918 to 83,000 in 1929.[2] If women joined the Labour Party because they believed it had the power to make changes, they joined the Guild because it was more concerned with the specific needs of working-class women. The Guild did not confine its interests to co-operation and the 'woman with the shopping basket'. It was deeply committed to women-centred social welfare reforms including birth control, nursery schools and improved maternity and child-care services. Above all, true to the ideas of Margaret Llewelyn Davies, it encouraged its members to see themselves as housewives who were also 'thinking, self-determining persons'.[3]

In the interwar years, the local labour community in some areas of the country included the ILP and the Communist Party. Until Labour banned the communists in 1925 and the ILP disaffiliated in 1932, joint membership with the Labour Party was common among men and women alike. Neither of the more ideological parties attracted a large following however. In their peak years from 1926 to 1928, the ILP had no more than 38,000 members, most of them in Scotland and the industrial north, and the Communist Party just over 10,000. Women made up about a fifth of ILP membership but were only a fifteenth of the communists.[4]

For women, the political decision about which organization to join involved a choice between separate or integrated organizations. The Labour Party constitution of 1918 allowed women members to attend the regular constituency party meetings or their own separate sections, or both. The first generation of Labour Party women showed a strong preference for their own meetings and the number of women's sections grew from a handful to 2,000 in the course of the decade.[5] Women in the Guild were equally dedicated to their separate status. They resisted all the Co-operative Union's attempts to push them into the mixed guilds. The ILP and the Communist Party offered the alternative of sexually integrated branches. In the early twenties both parties tried to establish a network of local women's groups modelled on those of the Labour Party but they were never popular with the more active of their women members. Unlike the large majority of women who joined the Labour Party and the Women's Co-operative Guild, the core activists who chose the ILP or the Communist Party consciously rejected gender segregation.

All the labour and socialist organizations were officially committed to sexual equality in their ranks. In practice, however, the principle was subject to different interpretations. The women in the Labour Party and the Guild who were organized separately from men, generally took it to mean equal but different. They argued that women had their own political interests and areas of expertise and they expected these to receive the same consideration in the party as men's concerns. In the smaller, integrated organizations, however, women members were determined to establish equality without gender discrimination of any sort. They opposed special treatment for women on the grounds that it perpetuated the sexual inequalities in capitalist society.

ILP and Communist women were inclined to be scornful of their segregated sisters, accusing them of being little more than 'house-wives' and 'tea-makers', for the male membership. In a study of women in the Communist Party, Sue Bruley found these charges amply justified in the case of that party's women's groups. While the women in the mixed local communist parties shared all political activities with their male comrades, those who met separately assumed a largely domestic and supporting role. She implied that this was also the case for Labour and Guild women. Their segregation created female 'ghettoes' shut off from the main arenas of political power, decision-making and direct action.[6] Since this charge assigns an insignificant political role to a large percentage of organized labour women, it merits investigation.

First, it is important to note the enormous range of conditions in local Labour parties which could affect the status of women members. In mining communities, where gender roles were strictly differen-tiated, Labour Party women were more likely to confine themselves to supportive, domestic responsibilities than they did, for example, in textile towns where gender roles were less rigidly defined. Labour parties in towns with a varied economic base generally showed more flexibility in the way men and women divided the work of the constituency while those with a middle-class leadership, men or women, seemed to prefer gender integration to separate women's sections. Whether the constituency was a safe Labour seat, marginal, or hard-to-win affected the policies and strategies of local parties and their attitudes towards women members and candidates. Above all, the personalities of local leaders set the standards in gender relations and often the level of party activity as well. Time and again, one can see dramatic changes in the level of effective co-operation between the sexes coinciding with the arrival or departure of leading personalities.

Generalizing with care, it is certainly true that a distinct gender division of responsibility emerged in the constituency Labour parties from their foundation – one that bore more than a passing resem-blance to the traditional gender roles in the working-class family. The women's sections did most of the fundraising. They organized the bazaars, jumble sales and potato pie suppers that helped to pay the party's rent and election expenses. They ran the social events –

the children's Christmas party, the socials, picnics and seaside outings that brought labour families together. They did the bulk of the routine work of election management, canvassing in the afternoons, manning the party's headquarters and the polling stations on election day. On the other hand, the members who attended regular party meetings, most of whom were men, dealt with the political business of the constituency. They selected the candidates for parliamentary and local government, discussed party policy, conducted elections, decided on the resolutions and delegates they wished to send to the annual party conferences and maintained links with the local trades and municipal councils.

The same gender division was common in men's and women's political agendas. They worked together on specific issues and campaigns but each sex maintained separate areas of interest and activity. Labour women were ardent peace activists, joining the men in support of the ILP-inspired No More War group but organizing their own demonstrations and marches. They took responsibility for keeping a close eye on the local schools to make sure they were not teaching 'militarist values'.[7] Women's sections were active in the national birth control and maternal and child welfare campaigns plus a host of local issues from sanitation to education, related to their interests as housewives and mothers. The male-dominated constituency parties spent more time on party political matters than social welfare reforms. Their main concerns in the interwar years were fighting elections, spreading the Labour message and trying to follow the party line on relations with the local communist party. Work-related issues like unemployment, national insurance and the dole were on the agenda in many constituencies after the recession that began in 1921 and deepened into depression in 1929.

There is no indication in their writings or speeches that Labour women regarded their work in the sections as inferior to that of the mixed ward or constituency meetings because of its domestic and social aspects. They seem to have taken pride in their ability to use their skills in cooking, sewing and catering for the benfit of the labour movement. Dorothy Russell from Cheshire admitted that 'women seemed to have the domestic jobs to do' but made no apology for it. She said how proud she was to have made tea for the Dean of Canterbury at a meeting in support of the unemployed.[8] Another rank and file activist, Mrs Ford from Tottenham, remembered with pride the year when the section raised the money to pay the rent on their meeting hall by making lavender bags, baking cakes to raffle and holding jumble sales. She recalled taking up her living-room carpet to turn the room into the ward's election headquarters where the women addressed envelopes and made endless cups of tea. Yet when asked if men and women shared constituency work, she declared: 'Oh yes, there had never been any difference between men and women in the Labour Party.'[9]

Such a gender division did not exist so obviously in the ILP or the Communist Party. Because they were small and intensely propagandist, they needed to make full use of every member's time and skills regardless of gender. Men and women worked together in all areas of local party activity from distributing literature and serving on committees to organizing striking industrial workers and speaking on street corners. All this shared activity generated an atmosphere of equality that was extremely satisfying to many of the women members. 'Whoever could do the job, did it in the CP', explained Hettie Bower, a London member. Nellie Logan wrote: 'We were in it together – no time to think of what sex one was – we were human beings wanting a better deal.'[10]

There was no gender separation of issues in the ILP either. Issues of concern to women were a part of the common agendas of local branches. In keeping with its prewar record of support for feminist causes, the party endorsed equal pay, a system of family allowances, birth control advice to be given at local maternity and child welfare clinics and nursery schools. In contrast, the Communist Party virtually ignored women's social welfare needs. As Hilda Nicholas from the Bristol Communist Party pointed out: 'The party was just not interested in social reform.'[11] The accepted view was that women's oppression was based on their class, not their gender and would therefore only be changed by the proletarian revolution. Reports of the comprehensive services Soviet Russia provided for its working women and their children gave credibility to this idea. Sue Bruley found that the cadre activists in the Communist Party deliberately avoided any association with specifically women's issues for fear of differentiating themselves from their male comrades. According to Bruley, 'they took on the persona of pseudo-men. Like the men, they associated women in general with the home, so they did not consider the possibility of women's issues that might relate to themselves.'[12]

Neither Labour Party nor Guild women shared this view. They

saw no contradiction between giving special attention to women's needs and an equal partnership with men in the organization. Convinced that each sex had its own contribution to make to the common cause of labour, they tried to ensure that women's concerns received equal consideration and implementation in the constituency. Lily Watson described confronting male members in her constituency party over equal voting rights and support for the women's social programme. 'I remember going to a meeting and some of the men saying we women should not vote as we had a women's section. We said we had joined the Labour Party not the women's section and we got the vote.' On another occasion, the women suggested having social evenings. ' We had managed to get a hall. The men said, no, we were political. We said socialism meant social and got our way.'[13]

Minutes of Labour Party women's sections from towns and cities across the country show women making a sustained effort to secure separate-but-equal rights. One of the most contentious issues in several of the local parties was the reluctance of the male-controlled executive committees to accept women candidates for local government office. This was an area where women were placing themselves in direct competition with men. Council seats were generally regarded as stepping stones to parliamentary seats and were therefore hotly contested.

The sections repeatedly pressed the claims of women candidates. The Windsor Labour Party women's section asked the party for 'special consideration to be given to the claims of women to be represented' on the Town Council.[14] In Stockport, the women discussed municipal candidates and 'our secretary was instructed to write the executive committee asking why names sent from our section never receive any further consideration '.[15] In Manchester, in 1932, the minutes record that 'the delegates were unanimously of the opinion that women candidates are not welcomed by the Party officials'.[16] In York, on 14 March 1933, the women's section discussed the same question: 'The members felt that our women do not get the prominence they are entitled to and in view of that we should consistently forward nominations for the panel if only to let the Party know that we are a live section.'[17] In 1925, Doncaster women's section sent a resolution to Labour Party headquarters asking for an explanation as to why ' a woman candidate was not run in one of the last four by-elections'.[18]

In some sections, women's struggle to establish equality of gender interests was an on-going battle. In Willesden, North London, the section sent a letter of protest in March 1926 to the West Willesden Labour Party complaining that they were not kept informed about nominations for local elections. They asked for an explanation. In May, they pressed for the section to be represented on the Council of Action set up to co-ordinate local efforts in the General Strike. In June, they pushed the party to send a delegate to the Labour Party Annual conference, promising to pay a portion of the expenses. Getting no response, they went 'en masse' to 'thrash this thing out' with the Party. In October 1926, they called on Marion Phillips, the Party's Chief Woman Officer, to come and explain to them the exact nature of their relationship with the constituency party, 'seeing that we cannot get proper recognition'. Perhaps as a result of this meeting, they sent another letter of protest to West Willesden in November on the subject of 'equality of the sexes'. In January 1927, they objected to the nomination of a Mr Baggett for a vacancy on the Board of Guardians in Stonebridge Ward and suggested that a woman be nominated.[19]

In a number of constituencies, the women's section acted as the conscience of the party, prodding it to act according to its principles over matters that fell within their sphere of concern. Any sign that the local party was acting indecisively on the peace issue, for example, brought forth a strong rebuke from the women's section. In York, it appears that the party considered sending Labour representatives to a 'Military Sunday' demonstration. The party had, after all, supported the war and many members were veterans. The women's section sent the following resolution: 'That this meeting regards the Military Sunday demonstration as propaganda to promote and preserve a mentality in the glorification of militarism and war and are of the opinion that the participation of Labour representatives would be contrary to the desire of the Party to work for the abolition of the loathsome business of war.'[20] The sections were also very active in the 'Hands Off China' campaign which was organized in response to the British government's decision to send military and naval reinforcements to protect its trading interests after the invasion of Central China by Nationalist forces in 1927. Several women's sections, including Willesden, asked their parties to form local 'Hands Off China' committees.[21]

The characterization of women in the Labour Party as 'ghettoized' or as housewives playing a purely supportive and domestic role has to be reconsidered in the light of this evidence. Although Labour women did not fight with the men in the party over who should make the tea, they did struggle for recognition of their right to have their voices heard in constituency affairs and in local government. Far from being isolated, the women in the sections worked to sustain contacts not just between themselves and male activists, but between all sections of the labour community, including ILPers and trade unionists, through social events. Wood Green was one of many sections that had joint socials with the trades council and the ILP. The Stockport section wrote to the party executive committee after the general election in November 1928 suggesting 'a social reunion to bind all sections of the Labour movement together'.[22]

Women's sections and Co-operative Guilds also took responsibility for educating the next generation of labour men and women in the principles of the movement. They did a great deal of work with children and young adults. The Guild ran co-operative classes for children ages four to fourteen and offered scholarships to young co-operative employees to provide them with further education. The women's sections maintained close ties with the local Labour colleges and Workers' Education Association (WEA) groups, and supported similar scholarships. Both organizations involved children in their political as well as their social activities. A favourite method of teaching internationalism and peace was to organize processions with children dressed in national costumes representing countries around the globe. Such activities spread the message of socialism and helped to give working-class children who rarely moved outside their own neighbourhoods an awareness of their place within a wider world.[23]

In some areas, Labour and Co-operative women had a more impressive record of participation in direct action politics than men. They were involved in the campaigns for peace and the care of maternity over a number of years. The streets were still a major arena for local party politics in the interwar years, especially in working-class neighbourhoods, so the women in the sections did their campaigning through organized marches, demonstrations and street-corner meetings. Labour women also took to the streets 'with babies and banners' every year for Women's Week, held at the beginning of June. The most notable of these processions was held in Durham where in 1925, 25,000 women, many of them with their children, marched through the town with bands and floats. Newcastle mustered 5,000, South Yorkshire 3,500 and Middlesex 3,000 in the same year.[24]

Labour women were particularly vigorous in their work for the unemployed. The Doncaster section successfully petitioned the Council to provide shelter, seating and lavatory accommodation for the women who had to line up for hours in all weathers outside the Employment Exchange.[25] The North Tottenham section held meetings outside the Exchange to call attention to the injustice and indignities of a system that forced men and women, unemployed through no fault of their own, to beg the Relieving Officers for money to prevent their families from starving. Individual women members joined the National Unemployed Workers' Movement (NUWM) and learnt to plead the cases of unemployed men and women before the officers. They became experts in manipulating the system for the benefit of the unemployed. Mrs Mitchell was one of these and she explained that the secret of their success was that they were 'always demonstrating. Everytime they brought anything in, we were up in arms; we rallied in our thousands.'[26]

Labour women's activities in the General Strike of May 1926 are further evidence both of their capacity for direct action and their sense of close involvement in the workers' struggle. Women's sections demanded representation on the local Councils of Action that maintained communication between local strikers during the nine days of the strike. They ran soup kitchens and organized a series of concerts by choirs of Welsh miners. On their own account they raised 300,000 pounds for boots and clothing for miners' families, a phenomenal sum to come from the working class in a time of recession and a general strike. Marge Evans went onto the ships in the Bristol docks to sell miners' lamps. She adopted a miner's child for several months. Bertha Grieveson collected money at the dock gates in Chatham and helped in the organization of the adoption scheme in her neighbourhood. In South Wales, labour women organized meetings of up to 10,000 miners' wives. Mrs Mitchell described a scene in Tottenham during the strike that confirms the role of women generally in community direct-action politics:

And there was a report went out on the grapevine that a tram was coming down the hill. And the women from round Tewkesbury and being a Monday afternoon, they were mostly washing and left their washing tubs; they were wiping their arms on their coarse aprons to overturn that tram when it got to the bottom of the hill. And they flew up from all around the back, the women ready to rush out and turn the tram over if it came down the hill ...[27]

Labour women's record of gender-distinct political activism in the twenties compares well with the more integrated activities of women in the ILP and the Communist Party. But whether separatism or integration better served the interests of women's equality in organized working-class politics is not easy to determine. Differences in size, ideology and constitution between the three organizations make a direct comparison difficult and women's own strong commitment to their choice reduced the chances for an objective assessment of the issue.

Equality based on an absence of sex discrimination was probably most successful in the ILP which had by far the best record of supporting women's issues and sponsoring women candidates for local government office. However, even though ILP respondents for this study said they valued the sense of comradeship in local branches, they admitted that women were less likely than men to hold leadership positions. ILP branches showed the same reluctance to send women delegates to their national conferences as local Labour parties. The result in Florence Widdowson's phrase was 'a man-made conference and a man-made NAC (National Administrative Council)'.[28] The ILP's failure to attract larger numbers of working-class women owed something to the fact that its mixed meetings intimidated them. The ILP gained a reputation among them for being, as Elizabeth Wheeler expressed it, 'only a few intellectuals'. Furthermore, as the decade progressed, the ILP, left in the centre between the Communist Party on the left and the mass Labour Party on the right, was less and less able to assert political influence in the broader movement. This was an important factor in the Labour Party's refusal to adopt either birth control or family allowances.

Gender equality in the Communist Party had similarly mixed results. It was certainly personally rewarding for women activists. Their skills were fully used; they were always 'in the thick of things'; they were able to further their education and a surprising number of them had the opportunity to go to the Soviet Union. However, by disavowing in the name of equality, the political significance of women's roles as housewives and mothers and refusing their support to the women's groups, the cadre women communists encouraged the party in its treatment of women as of secondary importance in the class struggle. Even if the Comintern can be blamed for the party playing little or no part in the major women's social reform campaigns of the twenties, its slow reaction to the wave of strikes by women workers in the early thirties has to be attributed in part to the reluctance of women members to press for special attention to their own sex.

Feminist historians have generally taken the view that the convention of 'separate spheres' has been very damaging for women. However, Guild and Labour women were able to make the idea that they were 'equal but different' serve their political purposes well in several important respects. Separate organization undoubtedly helped bring working-class women into the Labour Party. Several of the activists mentioned that new women members often lacked self-confidence in a public situation – 'they had to be encouraged'. Women's sections enabled them to acquire a political education and develop their skills, especially the one they all seemed to dread – public speaking – in a supportive environment. Women who might have stayed silent and confined themselves to making the tea in a mixed organization, became effective activists in the sections or guild branches.

Labour women were also able to benefit from their special responsibility for fundraising and election management. The men in the constituency recognized the vital importance of these services to the continuation and success of the local party. They supported women's claims to better representation at national conferences on the basis of their valuable contributions. Mr G. T. Garrett admitted to the 1929 conference that his District Labour Party was 'dependent on the women' for its financial support. Mr F. A. Broad from the Edmonton Labour Party agreed. He said that 'locally, we raise and spend in the work of the Movement perhaps ten times the amount that is handled through the central organizations and the bulk of that money is raised by the women'. He added that 'nine-tenths of my canvassing is done by women'. Councillor Alex Griffin from Edge Hill acknowledged the impact of the women in his constituency. 'I say, quite frankly that it is the women of Liverpool who have broken down Tory rule in Liverpool once and for all.'[29] Local parties were women's only ally in their struggles to increase their power at the national level.

Labour women's concentration on serving the interests of the working-class family, of women and children in particular, gave them an area of political expertise to claim as their own. It was a large area, covering international peace, consumer affairs, health, education and social welfare and anything relating to women's citizenship. They were able to use this platform to justify their claim to be represented on any deputation, local government committee, or public office where such issues might be discussed. On the basis of this gender-specific programme, women were co-opted in large numbers onto local authority education and maternity and child welfare committees. There was nothing disreputable about co-option. It enabled working-class Labour women to gain experience in public administration and often paved the way to their subsequent election.

The extent to which Labour men were prepared to recognize and support the women's claim seems to have varied from party to party and from individual to individual. In some cases, Willesden, for example, women members had to assert their right to fair representation repeatedly especially where men and women were in direct competition as candidates for elected office. In other parties, the more active and determined Labour women who ran for office or put forward their names as candidates enjoyed the full support of their male colleagues.

As long as no male interest was threatened, Labour men appear to have been comfortable with the idea that matters relating to the working-class family were properly the responsibility of women members. They could agree with Francis Graves from the *Windsor Express* that: 'Much of the work of public authorities is concerned with matters on which women are likely to have better informed minds than men – the care of children, housing and many matters of health ... ' They often referred to 'the women's side of the movement' and the 'women's standpoint'.[30] They praised Labour women on such grounds as, 'she was a consistent champion of women's interests' and 'a fearless champion of women and the weak'.[31] This acceptance no doubt helped to produce gender accord and an effective working partnership in some local parties and co-operative societies.

In terms of policy-making power, women came up against barriers in their local organizations, whether they tried to make themselves indistinguishable from men or quite distinct from them. Labour women were rarely chosen as delegates to the Annual Party Conferences where policy decisions were made, especially after 1929 when most parties were allowed only one delegate. They often struggled in vain to get their male comrades' support for more controversial women's issues such as birth control. Those who attended mixed ward meetings might be elected secretary or treasurer but they were frequently the only women representatives on executive committees. In the Communist Party and the ILP, women became organizers, propagandists and even local party secretaries, but they were similarly excluded from the upper ranks of power. The sense of comradeship and lack of discrimination that women communists felt personally, was at odds with the disdain which the party showed towards working-class women generally. Received notions of sex equality made little progress against deeply held beliefs that politics was men's business and women's contribution was a matter of expediency. Women were almost always an organizational, not a political, concern.

The question of power and effectiveness, however, is one of definition. According to the male definition, fundraising, canvassing and keeping the labour community together through social events were merely support services not 'real' politics. Yet they were very effective in sustaining the financial viability and evangelical spirit of the local party. Women's political activities tended to focus more on the wider working-class community rather than internal party affairs. Peace marches, street meetings, work with the unemployed, birth control clinics, children's classes and processions, even jumble sales were community events. It is reasonable to believe that these efforts contributed to the membership and electoral strength of both the Labour and Co-operative Parties, but it is impossible to take an accurate measurement.

Public recognition of women's contribution to local labour politics came in the form of election to a local council or poor law board or appointment to the bench. Local government was the most accessible, perhaps the only, political arena in which labour women were able to exercise power through collective decision-making and achieve tangible results from the process. The 500 or so, Guild, Labour or ILP women who became councillors or magistrates in the twenties were pioneers, the first of their class to walk into imposing council chambers and court rooms where most of the seats were occupied by middle-class men. It is time to see how they fared and what they were able to achieve.

LABOUR WOMEN IN LOCAL GOVERNMENT

Following the national pattern in the extension of the popular franchise, British women won the right to participate in local government in stages and by social class. The first public office opened to women in 1870 was on school boards but it was limited to middle-class women and withdrawn in 1902 when the local authorities took over school administration. In 1907, women were declared eligible to sit on borough and county councils, but a property qualification effectively disbarred those from the working class. The one elective office that was open to working-class women before the war was that of poor law guardian and from 1894 to 1914, over a hundred Co-operative Guild, Labour League and ILP women ran successfully for this office. Finally, in 1914, before the national suffrage grant, women achieved equality in the local franchise and eligibility for all local government offices. In 1919, they won the right to serve as jurors and justices of the peace.

Labour women were quick to recognize how much they had to gain from local government representation. Following the Liberal Party's introduction of state welfare measures in 1908 and its efforts to rationalize overlapping local authorities, county and municipal councils collected a wide range of powers.[32] By 1920, a medium-sized borough like Chatham, in addition to such essential services as highways, public utilities, transport and sewage, was also responsible for municipal housing, education and public health services. The latter included overseeing fever and lying-in hospitals, asylums, and maternity and child welfare clinics. Since many of these were areas of administration that clearly affected the working-class woman voter more directly than male constituents, labour women could argue the need for women's interests to be fairly represented by their own sex.

Municipal councils also had wide discretionary powers in areas of social reform which labour women were very eager to secure for their local communities. The first state welfare measures passed by Liberal governments before and just after the First World War were permissive not mandatory. They depended on support from local councils for their implementation. Councils received the authority in 1908 to introduce schemes for free milk, meals and medical care for needy school children. The 1918 Education Act allowed them to establish nursery schools and give working-class children access to secondary education by building new schools and offering more scholarships and maintenance grants. Under the terms of the Maternity and Child Welfare Act, councils could provide free clinics for mothers and babies, and the services of qualified doctors, mid-wives and health visitors. Local councils had the power to insist on equal pay for municipal employees, including schoolteachers, and resist popular pressures to force women teachers to retire on marriage. These were strong incentives for labour women to fight hard for council seats, especially since, without determined pressure by Labour groups, Conservative councillors were inclined to ignore reform measures in the interests of saving the ratepayers' money.

With the same reforming goals in mind, labour women hoped to increase their representation on the boards of poor law guardians. The boards were responsible for the indigent poor. Most of these were working-class elderly people, but unmarried mothers and their babies, destitute widows and abandoned wives, vagrants and tramps, orphans and mentally retarded children were just as likely to be workhouse inmates. Conditions in the workhouses were often dickensian; dirt, infection, malnutrition, regimentation and a gen-erally punitive spirit prevailed. The helpless inmates were entirely at the mercy of the guardians who controlled the kind of care in terms of diet, clothing, training and discipline they received.

Poor law guardians also determined the extent and amount of outdoor relief for the able-bodied poor. As unemployment grew from late 1920, the boards became the centres of political battles in many boroughs. Labour councillors insisted on giving relief to the un-employed at rates high enough to enable them to keep themselves and their families. Their Conservative counterparts were just as insistent on refusing it in the interests of the ratepayers and for fear it would encourage indolence in the working poor. In the borough of Poplar, the Labour-controlled council, which included five women members, went to prison in 1921 rather than lower the rate of out-relief to pay for London County Council services which did not directly benefit the poverty-stricken families of the unemployed.[33]

In view of the opportunities in local government for providing immediate and practical help for working-class families, it is not surprising to find Co-operative Guild branches and Labour Party women's sections in the twenties devoting a good deal of their time to educating their members in the work of councils and poor law boards and encouraging them to be candidates. Weekend schools offered courses in the subject and local women councillors were in constant demand to come to meetings and describe just what they did on their various committees and how they held their own with the male and often Conservative majority. As reported in local minutes, their talks give a good idea of how labour women activists themselves defined their role in local government and the grounds on which they made their appeal to the voters.

Labour women's approach to local government work was entirely consistent with their view of women's roles in the party. They argued that working-class women had special political and social concerns that were best understood and represented by women of their own class. As a member of the Chatham section put it: 'We ought to have a representative of our own to voice our thoughts and our own peculiar way of judging questions.'[34] Mrs Sands, a Manchester councillor, echoed this sentiment. She urged her section members to put themselves forward as municipal candidates because, 'it is women who understand women's wants and needs better than men'.[35] Labour women claimed expert knowledge that men did not have in areas such as maternity and child welfare, education, housing and household budgets. This expertise was 'grounded in the detail of their daily lives' and they felt that it qualified them for a place on the administrative bodies that dealt with these issues. Hannah Mitchell likened council work to household management: 'Just as the housewife has to cook, sew, clean and spend in the best interest of the family so has the Council to do most of these things in the interest of the citizens. It is well that women are present on such bodies.'[36]

At the same time, labour women argued against limiting their political contribution in local government to women's interests. They regarded this specialist concern as part of a wider vocation to improve living conditions for the working-class as a whole. They compared their position to that of a coal miner or engineer who might consider himself particularly well qualified to discuss matters relating to his industry but not disqualified from giving opinions on other issues. Talking about their work, labour women municipal councillors and guardians commonly emphasized the opportunity that local government service offered to help *all* members of their class who were in need. In a talk to the Bilston Labour Party section, a woman councillor said, 'it was the most fascinating work to think that you were helping others'.[37] A poor law guardian pointed out how vital it was for labour women to be present on the boards 'as they were able to get extra help for poor people'.[38]

This distinctive approach is evident in the accounts labour women gave of their contribution to various local government bodies. Jessie Stephen, for example, who was elected to the Bermondsey Board of Guardians in 1921, shared with most Labour guardians a determination to mitigate the harshness of the Victorian poor law and bring some dignity and comfort to working people left destitute after a life of labour. She insisted that poverty was not a crime, but the consequence of the economic system, and that workhouse inmates deserved to be treated with kindness and consideration. One of her first acts was to get rid of the rituals of deference which obliged old people to stand up when a guardian entered the room. 'Neither I nor my [Labour] colleagues, could stomach this kow-towing to elected representives and it must cease.' Finding the inmates eating on benches, she ordered proper chairs and tables and a greater variety of food.[39]

Along with this general concern for the welfare of working-class inmates, Jessie paid special attention to women's needs. She ended the practice of segregating unmarried mothers in the workhouse infirmary and subjecting them to lectures about their 'sinfulness'. She also asked that a woman be appointed to interview them. 'One of the men objected, telling us these sordid cases might cause pain to the delicate feelings of women members. I laughed outright. '"What you mean, sir, is that men prefer to wallow in the sordid details."'[40] Other labour women guardians worked hard to save children from the stigma and soul-destroying atmosphere of the workhouse by getting rid of the uniform and placing them in a family or in small, family-type units outside the workhouse so that they could attend regular schools. Labour and Guild women guardians also opposed all attempts to send workhouse boys into the navy or any branch of the armed services.[41]

Hannah Mitchell's career in local government, as a guardian before the war, a councillor from 1924 to 1935, and a justice of the peace from 1926 to 1946, shows a similar pattern. Like all Labour councillors, Hannah fought the Conservatives over giving out-relief to the unemployed, turning in fury on one councillor who proposed to cut the coal allowance in a winter of heavy unemployment. But as she explained to her constituents, her political interests were chiefly centred on the 'health and well-being of the people, particularly the women and children'.[42] As a member of the parks committee, she thought of the 'tired mothers who have trundled prams all

afternoon', who wanted to sit and rest and have a cup of tea before
going home. Her vision of the parks as places of rest and refreshment
clashed with that of her male colleagues who thought in terms of
'football, bowling greens and ... chairs set on concrete round the
bandstand'.[43] When she was on the baths committee, she initiated
the building of an 'up-to-date little wash-house' where housewives
could hire a deep tub, have plenty of hot water, hot-air dryers and
ironing tables to do their laundry. Because so many of the
neighbouring houses had no bathrooms, she saw that these were
added to the wash house.

Middle-class women reformers pioneered the domestication of
local council work at the end of the nineteenth century when
property qualifications kept working-class women out of the running
for places on boards of education, rural and urban district councils.
Labour women differed from their middle-class sisters in their
stronger party political affiliation and their ability to bring knowledge based on experience to a client population that was mostly
drawn from their own class. When Hannah Mitchell sat on the local
relief committee, she was able to support her arguments in favour of
giving relief with facts, not figures, about working-class household
budgets. 'I knew just how much food could be bought out of the
allowance, knew the cost of children's clothes and footwear, could tell
at a glance if the applicant was in ill health.'[44]

Another difference between labour and middle-class women in
local government lay in their attitudes towards outdoor relief.
Middle- class women, true to their liberal views usually supported
Conservative councillors in their reluctance to offer money payments
to the unemployed. They clung to the idea that out-relief would
undermine the independence, thrift and desire to work among
working people. Labour women knew from experience the disastrous
effects of unemployment on working-class families who rarely had
savings to fall back on. They took the view that state help was not
charity but payment owed to those workers who were ratepayers and
the victims of capitalist inefficiency or greed. The staunchness with
which Labour women guardians defended the rights of the unemployed to outdoor relief was no doubt another reason why, in
working-class communities, they were more likely to be elected than
middle-class women Liberals.[45]

The first Labour women justices approached their work on the
bench in much the same spirit as Labour women councillors and

guardians. They expected the understanding that came from being working-class housewives and mothers to give them superior insight into cases involving women and juvenile offenders. They refused to limit themselves to such cases, however, on the grounds that their political experience had prepared them to render judgment in any case that came before them. Like male justices, they only came to the bench after many years of public life. Hannah Mitchell wrote that her suffrage and ILP experience as well as her poor law work 'had taught me a lot about my fellow men and women'. She admitted that she generally thought of herself as 'counsel for women's defence' but found that she was 'quite often, whole-heartedly on the man's side'.[46] Mrs Scott, a Stockport Labour magistrate, resisted attempts by her fellow male justices to get her to step down during cases they deemed 'unpleasant' or 'unsuitable'. She said that she was appointed a magistrate to hear all cases and as long as male magistrates tried women in similar cases, she would stay and do her duty.[47]

How did the men who served with labour women on poor law boards, local councils and as fellow magistrates respond to the way women defined their role? Individual responses varied but in general, men were prepared to accept, even welcome, women's contribution in areas that were an extension of their traditional domestic roles. However, they were often reluctant to allow them to move out of this strictly limited sphere. On poor law boards, for example, male guardians encouraged women colleagues to deal only with matters relating to female and child inmates. They assigned them to visit boarded-out children and investigate women's claims for out-relief. They left any practical or domestic aspects of workhouse administration to women while keeping policy decisions, especially those relating to the rates and general finances, to themselves.[48]

On local councils, women rarely had representation on committees dealing with planning, finance, municipal trading, licensing, highways or transportation. They nearly always sat on those concerned with education, housing, public amenities and maternal and child welfare. When there were too few elected women councillors to serve on these committees, the council co-opted women rather than having male councillors undertake jobs that fell within women's sphere. One example of this careful gender division of responsibility appears in the minutes of the Tottenham Urban District Council maternity and child welfare committee. In 1921, there were three women and nine men on the committee. The 'lady members' were asked to form a sub-committee 'to deal with the question of new overalls for the health visitors and dressing gowns for the ante-natal clinics'.[49]

A comment in the *Chatham Observer* in June 1920 suggests the fairly narrow framework within which popular opinion expected women to function in local government. 'When women were put onto public bodies they had to use the finest tact and be content to just fill in the gaps where men were lacking.'[50] If this was what male councillors expected, they were doomed to disappointment. The verbatim accounts of council meetings in local papers in the early twenties, indicate that some women were prepared to challenge male expectations of appropriate behaviour for women councillors. According to a report of a meeting of the Barking Urban District Council in June 1920, for example, a woman alderman, Mrs Perrett, criticized one of the male councillors for 'wasting the Council's time with trivial matters'. Councillor Osborne apparently resented the attack. He implied that women councillors should play the game according to the existing male rules: 'If Alderman Mrs Perrett does not want to stay with the gentlemen, she knows what to do... She must understand that when she takes a man's place, she takes a man's responsibility.' Mrs Perrett replied that she had taken a woman's place not a man's to which Councillor Osborne issued the solemn reminder: 'You are among men.'[51]

Women's entry into the council chamber also gave a gender aspect to traditional male rivalry over coveted positions as committee chairmen. In Gillingham, the male-dominated Town Council decided to depose a Labour woman alderman, Mrs Parr, who had been the chairman of the maternity and child welfare committee for four years and replace her with a male Conservative. Mrs Parr's statement on losing her job says a good deal about gender relations in local government in this period. She began by stating Labour women's view that 'a woman chairman was able to give advice and help in certain matters which a man could not do'. She gave an example of a pregnant woman from the North of England who had come to her for help in getting pre-natal care and making hospital arrangements. She continued: 'Personally, I don't want to push this business of the chairmanship any further. I say that as Alderman Thomsett had got my job, let him get on with it but I shall never turn people away from my door when they want my advice.' It seems that part of the strategy to bring about her removal was to charge her with neglecting her 'home duties' in order to take part in public affairs.

She answered the charge in its own terms: 'She would like to inform her critics that she took up public work at the express wish of her husband.'[52]

As Mrs Parr's statement shows, labour women accepted the gender division of responsibility in local government and tried to use it to their advantage. The grounds on which they took a stand in disputes with their male colleagues mostly concerned equal opportunity for women candidates in committee assignments and support from Labour colleagues for reform measures that women wished to see implemented. A typical example comes from the Jarrow division of the Hebburn Labour Party in 1928. The women members raised the question of the 'treatment of our lady councillors at the local council meeting'. They complained that some male co-opted members were moved onto a special committee for the reorganization of the schools and 'our lady councillors ignored'. The same local Labour Party received a letter from the women's section two years later 'protesting against the members of the Council who did not vote for Mrs Peterkin for the Public Assistance Committee'. A group meeting was called to settle the matter.[53]

Women in local government, in Ruth Wild's words, 'had to fight to get [their] point of view across'.[54] Hannah Mitchell who sensed 'a strong undercurrent of anti-feminism' on the public bodies with which she was associated, was a consistent advocate of women's interests. On one occasion she tried to convince her male colleagues on the relief committee, that it was unfair to deny out-relief to a sick or injured charwoman on the grounds that she could get 'light work'. She wrote: 'I could never get my male colleagues to see that no one would employ a woman to dust china.'[55] Mrs. Kathleen Chambers from Bradford's west ward, 'persistently demanded equality of conditions for all women municipal employees with their male colleagues, whether they [were] doctors, teachers, women police or manual workers'.[56] Mrs Kitchener from Tottenham met opposition from other council members when she demanded electric light and bathrooms for council houses.[57] Mrs Grundy from Shipley in Yorkshire tried to get an assurance from the chairman of the baths committee that women would get turkish baths at the same price as men.[58] On issues, large and small, women in local government struggled to get consideration for women's needs in a larger framework of justice for their class.

Local voters endorsed the notion of 'separate spheres' by electing women candidates more readily to poor law boards where domestic and nurturing skills had a very obvious place, than to city and town councils which addressed themselves to the business community and covered a wider range of administrative areas. It is hard to tell whether the concept was an asset or a liability but it seems unlikely that labour women would have increased their representation quite as much without relating their area of expertise to specific tasks in local government.

Precise figures of the number of labour women in local government in the twenties are hard to find because the Labour Party did not break down their election statistics by gender. The party made substantial gains in the course of the decade. In 1919, it had a net gain of 412 seats and captured its first county borough in Bradford along with twelve London metropolitan boroughs. Labour increased its local government representation every year from 1923 to1929 by which time it controlled fifteen county boroughs, thirteen municipal and fourteen metropolitan boroughs. Just how many of the new Labour seats were held by women is unclear but all sources indicate that they were a significant part of the Party's rapid and sustained growth in municipal government.[59]

The Guild kept records of Co-operative women in local government. Their figures show that in 1920–1, there were 65 women on town, urban district and county councils. In 1928, the number had risen to 120. As the Labour Party had at least three times as many women members and an efficient local party system, one can treble that figure for Labour women. The Women's Co-operative Guild had 190 poor law guardians in 1920 and 283 in 1928 bringing the total of Labour and Co-operative guardians to about 800. The number of Guild magistrates rose from 12 in 1920 to 125 in 1928.[60] Among the labour men and women respondents in this study, close to a third of the women had been local borough councillors compared to just under one half of the men.

Local government was the front line of working-class women's advance into public life. There were never more than nine Labour women Members of Parliament in the twenties and most of these were middle class, single, and anxious to appear indistinguishable from the men of their party. They realized that if they allowed themselves to be identified only with women's or family issues, they would make little headway in Parliament. In local government, Labour women elected officials were also a minority even on Labour-controlled councils, but they were often present in sufficient numbers to act and be treated as a distinct group. This helps to explain why 'our lady councillors' were able to accomplish so much. They obliged male majorities, Labour and Conservative alike, to recognize the specific set of interests they represented and the particular skills they possessed. They were fortunate that these skills and interests seemed appropriate to the nature of local government work, especially to that of poor law boards.

Labour women's achievements in local government were related to their goal of improving the conditions of life and the opportunities available to working-class families. They were practical and small-scale reforms which merited a side column in the local newspaper but which had an immediate, ameliorative effect on the lives of local people. Hannah Mitchell's wash house was just one example of a number of local amenities from public lavatories and swimming baths to hospitals, baby clinics, playgrounds and libraries that were a prominent part of the legacy of Labour women councillors. Mrs Fawcett from York persuaded the council to purchase a 'Babies Home' and Mrs Jessie Clarke from Barking campaigned successfully for a new method of dust collection in her town, to stop dustmen having to walk through row houses to pick up household refuse. Mrs Chard from Uxbridge was responsible for the town's first day nursery.[61] Mrs Kitchener won her battle to have bathrooms put into Tottenham's council houses.

When there were labour women on local councils, working-class children were likely to benefit from improved health care and educational opportunities. Labour women councillors put baby clinics, school medical inspection, free milk and meals, more nursery and secondary schools high on the list of their political priorities. The 'Geddes axe' that cut government grants to local authorities for social services like these after 1921, and unsympathetic majorities on local councils hindered women's efforts, but they were persistent and prepared to take a series of small steps towards their goals. Working-class women benefited too, from councillors who understood their problems and worked to solve them in very practical ways. Maternity services improved in the twenties and so did the standard of municipal housing.

Labour women guardians made a difference to the quality of life for workhouse inmates, bringing some comfort and dignity to the last years of the elderly poor and giving the children a much better chance in life. They brought human sympathy and class empathy to the task. They insisted that workhouse girls have the same amount of schooling and job training as boys. They were firm and consistent advocates of out-relief payments to allow the unemployed to feed their families and always supported the Labour group in their stand on this issue.

Such achievements have had scant recognition in the histories of the Labour Party. Small-scale and scattered as they were, they make an impressive showing when compared with the social reform record of the national Labour Party in this period. Minority status frustrated the party's efforts to introduce any of the reforms that were to lay the foundation for the co-operative commonwealth. John Wheatley's 1924 Housing Act stands as the party's only significant contribution to this endeavour. It is not too much to claim that whatever was done to improve the lives of working people in the twenties was primarily the work of labour councillors and among these, women were most closely identified with reform issues.

CONCLUSIONS

Women made their most significant contribution to the political labour movement of the twenties at the local, not the national, level. At bottom, this was because the majority of rank-and-file labour activists, men and women, as well as working-class voters were more comfortable with the idea of gender-distinct politics based on traditional gender roles, than with the notion of women's participation on equal and competitive terms. National leaders argued that any division along gender lines would destroy party unity and did all they could to circumvent it in the constitution and on national conference agendas. Local parties reached different conclusions. Most of the new women members chose separate organization. The division of political responsibility along gender lines that developed was in keeping with their definition of a separate-but-equal role. Male members seem to have found this arrangement less threatening than one in which women competed directly with them for power in the constituency. Gender-distinct politics gave women the opportunity to pursue their own reform programmes and win election to local government office.

The contention that gender segregation in the Labour Party and the Women's Co-operative Guild reduced women to auxiliary players, mere 'cakemakers' to the male majority is not supported by the evidence, at least not for the twenties. Their activities in fundraising, canvassing and organizing social events were vital to the survival of the local parties and there is no reason to consider them of less political significance than choosing candidates or sending resolutions to party conferences. Labour women were strongly represented in a range of 'direct action' political campaigns from peace and birth control to work for the unemployed and in support of the General Strike. They challenged the male-controlled local parties whenever they felt that their rights to equal representation and to party support for their reform programmes were being ignored.

On balance, it appears that the separate-but-equal policy to which Labour Party and Co-operative Guild women adhered was as effective, in terms of integrating women into the political labour movement, as the egalitarian approach taken by women in the ILP and the Communist Party. In neither case were women able to break into the upper echelons of power, either as a group or as individuals. Shared political responsibility and close camaraderie in local ILP and Communist Party branches did not translate into policy-making power for women members any more than the segregated organization in the Labour Party and the Guild. Socialist ideals could not overcome deep-rooted male fears of women's autonomy or the sense that women were unsuited to certain areas of political life by reason of their gender and inexperience.

Labour and Guild women used the idea of 'separate spheres' most effectively to win seats on local government bodies. They claimed that their domestic and maternal experience made them ideally qualified for work that dealt with working-class women and children, the elderly, the young, the sick and the destitute. The voters, most of whom were working-class, appear to have accepted this claim as one criteria in their choice of a candidate. Male councillors and guardians were also willing to co-operate with female colleagues on the basis of a strict division of gender responsibility. In practice, such a rigid division was unworkable and as women's representation and experience increased, they were able to establish a more flexible sharing of responsibility without sacrificing their special interest in the needs of working-class women and children.

Rank-and file-women members took pride in the contribution they made to the labour movement through their local parties and on local government bodies. They felt personally enriched and thought they had helped others of their class. The record supports this evaluation. The women's sections sustained the local parties. They helped to link Labour's political organization to its working-class constituents through a range of public activities. They made the party more attractive to working-class housewives and thus widened its constituency base. They were unofficial ambassadors for the party each time they gave advice to neighbours on how to make unemployment claims, how to get medical benefits and how to survive the means' test.

Labour women on local government bodies improved the quality of life for untold numbers of their class who were always on the verge of being overwhelmed by the problems associated with urban poverty. A wash house not only reduced the amount of time spent on the weekly wash, it relieved domestic tension by removing piles of damp clothes from tiny kitchens. A maintenance grant to enable a working-class child to have a secondary education not only enhanced the life of that child but the lives of his or her future family members also. Political histories do not usually evaluate this kind of local, piecemeal, social change. As a result, women's contribution to labour politics has been missed. When the organizational focus is placed on the local community, the family and the individual, new definitions of political effectiveness emerge.

CHAPTER 6

'Doing our bit to see the people are not dragged down' – class struggle in the thirties

After 1931, women's status ceased to be an issue in interwar labour politics. Labour Party women made no further claims for policy-making power at the national level. The change of tactic may have been a reaction to the failure of their struggle for autonomy in the party and their break with organized feminism in the preceding decade, but the crisis atmosphere of the thirties was an additional factor in discouraging them from reviving the debate. Economic depression, reactionary governments and the spread of fascism threatened the very survival of their class and party, appealing to their deepest political instinct to protect the down-trodden and pushing their struggle for rights as party women into the background.

Although they abandoned their efforts to persuade the national party leaders to give women's interests equal weight with men's, Labour women continued to address the social welfare needs of working-class women. Unlike their campaigns in the twenties for birth control and family allowances, however, those of the thirties posed no threat to male authority or party unity. Labour Party leaders generally supported their efforts to defend working-class women and children against the effects of economic depression and government cutbacks. Labour women in their turn, threw their support behind their party's efforts to prevent the National Government making the most vulnerable sections of the population the scapegoats for the failures of capitalism.

Other developments contributed to the disappearance of open gender conflict in the Labour Party. The division of political responsibility along gender lines which created tension at the national level in the twenties became blurred in the thirties. In the immediate postwar decade, social welfare and peace were very much women's issues. In the thirties, mass unemployment and fascist aggression made them central concerns for the whole party. Dissent, always alive and well in the Labour Party, lost its gender component as male and female party members responded similarly to domestic and international crises. For the first time, Labour Party women took a position alongside the men on the right or left wing of the party over such issues as the United Front, non-intervention in Spain and rearmament. As the gender gap closed, there was a shift towards greater sexual integration in the local constituency parties. The thirties generation of women members showed less enthusiasm than their predecessors for separate organization. While the number of individual women members rose, the women's sections suffered a relative decline.

Labour women signaled their move away from a focus on gender-specific policies by abruptly dropping from their speeches and writings all references to women's special interests and the necessity for their voices to be heard in the movement. When they argued for their reform programme, they used the language of class and directed their appeals and their criticism at hostile governments or greedy capitalists rather than at the men of their party. In an obvious departure from twenties' policy, they deliberately avoided partici-pation in women-related campaigns, such as legal abortion, that were likely to be contentious. Younger members introduced a new concept into their arguments for women's rights, that of democratic citizenship, in reaction to the spread of authoritarianism in interwar political discourse.

When Labour Party women stopped asking for separate-but-equal status, they had to settle for the inequalities laid down in the 1918 constitution and its later revisions. The more integrated they became, the less visible they were. In the thirties the national records suggest an all-male party with a handful of exceptional women. Yet, many women respondents in this study described the thirties, with all their hardships as the highpoint of their political lives. In those years, Labour men and women marched together against the hated Means Test; they joined arms to make barriers against Mosley's black shirts; they raised money for Spanish republicans and collected signatures for the Peace Ballot. They recognized the class enemy at home and abroad and knew the justice of their cause.

GENDER ISSUES DISAPPEAR FROM THE RECORDS OF THE LABOUR PARTY

As we saw in earlier chapters, Labour Party women in the twenties kept the question of gender relations alive through a series of challenges to the male leadership. On three occasions between 1919 and 1931, they tried to persuade the party to change the constitution to give them greater autonomy.[1] Just as often, they asked for the right to elect their National Executive Committee representatives themselves at their own conference. They called for resolutions passed at their conferences to go directly onto the national agenda where they would have a chance of becoming party policy. At every opportunity, they drew the attention of the party to their need for more representatives on all policy-making bodies. In addition to these demands for access to policy-making power, organized women pressed for the adoption of radical social welfare measures to ease the burdens upon working-class wives and mothers. These activities stimulated discussion of women's role in the national labour organization and produced open conflict between the sexes.

The thirties present a startling contrast. Labour women's demands for greater autonomy came to an abrupt end. Twice in the decade, in 1933 and 1936, the Labour Party proposed changes to its constitution. Labour women ignored these opportunities to press their earlier claims. Their silence is all the more remarkable because on both occasions, other groups within the party, the Labour League of Youth and the local constituency parties, made the same demand for direct and increased representation on the NEC as women had done earlier. During the debate on the constitutional changes at the 1937 annual conference, the only woman who spoke, a Mrs E. Packenham representing Chelthenham East Labour Party, supported the constituency parties' claim and did not mention the women in the party at all. Nor did Labour women protest when the party decided that out of the four 'divisions' into which the conference delegates were divided, trade unions, socialist affiliates, local constituency parties and women, only women had no right to the 'direct and separate election of executive committee members'.[2]

Labour Party women seemed more prepared in the thirties than in the twenties to accept a limited role in national party politics. In 1929, in order to make its annual conference smaller and more efficient, the party had passed a constitutional amendment decreeing that local parties could send a second delegate only if they had 2,500 women members, instead of 500 as before. The result was a drastic reduction in the already small number of women attending the party's main policy-making body. In the thirties, with few exceptions, the only women to address the party conferences were those on the NEC and the SJC (Standing Joint Committee of Industrial Women's Organizations) who had no responsibility to put the point of view of the rank-and-file. Yet in the whole decade, only one women's section submitted a resolution to the women's conference proposing that they urge the party to return to the old rule of 500 women members as a condition for a second delegate. The vote was 542 to 165 in favour of the motion but almost 500 women delegates either deliberately abstained or did not bother to vote on the issue.[3]

One incident, in particular, seems to indicate that by the early thirties, Labour Party women had already turned their attention away from the struggle for more power at the national level. After the 1927 National Women's Conference, the business committee discussed the need to provide funding to enable more working-class women to run as parliamentary candidates. Since few Labour women candidates were eligible for union funds, the committee decided to look for alternative sources of financial support. They asked the NEC to consider the matter, but after lengthy negotiations the executive declared that it was prevented by the constitution from acting as a 'promoting' body for candidates and even if this were changed, women candidates could not expect preferential treatment.[4] Realizing that Labour women would have to help themselves, the SJC in 1930 asked the sections to find out if their members were willing to make a small annual contribution towards the election expenses of women parliamentary candidates. The replies indicated very little support for the scheme among the rank-and-file. After two months, only 165 of the 2,045 questionnaires had been returned and of these only 96 were in favour of the levy.[5] The SJC raised the matter again in 1935, but the sections were still not prepared to support the fund so they gave up the attempt.[6]

The shift away from a gender perspective can be detected in Labour women's speeches and writings in the thirties. Women who spoke at conferences or wrote to *Labour Woman* in the twenties made a point of stating that they were putting the 'women's point of view'. Without ever losing sight of their class and party affiliation, they couched their opinions about housing, education, pensions, rent, the cost of living and peace in women-centred terms. They named the study of housing that they conducted just after the war 'The Working *Woman's* House'; one of their major concerns in education was to ensure that girls had equal opportunities with boys; pension discussions focused on war widows and deserted wives; rents and the cost of living were viewed primarily from the perspective of the working-class housewife and peace was an aspect of maternalism. A speech by Mrs Hood, a Justice of the Peace and Guild member, to the 1927 National Women's Conference epitomized the 'gender' spirit of the twenties: 'Women are consumed with a holy discontent with their surroundings. They realize that men have failed them with regard to housing, education, employment, pensions, war and even the laws of the country are most unjust to its women citizens who are rising in revolt.'[7]

The focus of discussion on the same political issues in the thirties was class, not gender. Interest in the way these questions affected working-class women and children remained but it was rarely the central theme. Labour women spoke as members of a class under attack by reactionary forces representing capitalism at home and abroad. In the housing debate, they criticized the National and Conservative governments for removing rent controls, failing to provide affordable homes for working people and allowing private contractors to build sub-standard houses. The pensions issue also provided an opportunity for an attack on the government. Edna Hanes from Leeds, arguing in 1937 for a universal old-age pension at sixty years, said: 'When we consider the huge amount of money spent on re-armament, we are of the opinion that it is not too much to ask that this amount should be spent on pensions for the well-being of the people of the country.'[8]

When they talked about education in the thirties, Labour and Guild women revealed the depth of their distrust of a government that they described as deliberately standing in the way of educational opportunity for working-class children. They protested vehemently against the 1932 cuts in grants to education authorities and denounced the 1935 Education Act for extending the school-leaving age to fifteen but failing to include maintenance provisions. They were particularly incensed by a clause in the act allowing children to leave school at fourteen for 'beneficial employment' or 'home duties', since it clearly discriminated against working-class children. Dorothy Elliott had no illusions about the philosophy behind the legislation. She said: 'They [the House of Lords] wanted to keep the workers' children in the mines and feeding machines instead of having an opportunity for proper education.'[9] Leah Manning's comments were on similar lines:

The powers that be did not mind when working class children were taught a few things, such as, a little arithmetic, a little scripture, a little writing, and taught to be content with the station wherein God had pleased to call them. But when their children were given an opportunity of a secondary education and going through to the University, they regarded them as rivals who would take the bread out of the mouths of their own children.[10]

Arguments based on class considerations also prevailed in the speeches Labour Party women made at their 1938 conference on the subject of rising food prices. The impact upon women and children was mentioned but only in the context of what they described as a deliberate attack by a capitalist government upon working-class living standards. The first speaker, Mrs Mound (West Willesden Women's Section), condemned the government's food policy 'which has neglected consumers' interests and deliberately raised wholesale prices by tariffs, quotas, etc, so that good food is unobtainable by the majority of the workers'. Mrs Mackereth (Railway Women's Guild) named old age pensioners and the unemployed as well as mothers and children as victims of the National Government's policy of 'giving subsidies so readily while the working classes were being drained so badly'. Mrs Wallhead-Nichol (Welwyn Garden City Women's Section) urged that 'a perpetual vigilance should be kept on the set of gangsters who were now in Government. Huge profits were being made while the working classes were being squeezed dry.'[11]

Labour women made a similar change of emphasis in their discussions of the peace issue which was consistently on their agendas throughout the interwar period. In the twenties, they stressed women's special responsibility for preserving peace, arguing that, as mothers, they provided the cannon fodder for war. They talked of World War I as a male folly in which voteless women played no part and argued that now women had political power there would be no more wars. From 1932, as international tensions mounted, Labour Party women made less and less use of these maternalist arguments. They were more likely to identify themselves with the workers of all countries who were once again being drawn into war by capitalist governments.[12] Mrs Horrabin spoke at the National Women's Conference in 1932 after the Japanese invasion of Russia. She said: 'War was the only way out of capitalism's difficulties at the present time. There was danger for the workers of every country because the working class of every country wanted work and if it was war work, it was hard to tell them to resist that work. She wanted the workers to say that, even if it meant starvation, they would not work on munitions.'[13] Mrs Paton of the Rushcliffe women's section declared: 'She felt the platform had not realised how some of the women felt about the possibility of war on Russia – in order that the capitalist countries might destroy the germ of socialism that was being sustained there.'[14]

The results of this withdrawal from the earlier self-conscious assertion of gender rights and the women's point of view were two-fold. 'Sex antagonism' as Labour men liked to call it, disappeared from party discourse. Male Labour leaders resumed their prewar habit of expressing 'gratitude' every year for the splendid services that the women in the party performed, with special reference to their fundraising and canvassing. Labour women stopped questioning the party's commitment to the equality of the sexes. Indeed the subject of gender equality in the party was never raised. It had become a non-issue. The price of gender cohesion, however, was a loss of gender identity for Labour women and their virtual elimination from policy-making power nationally. In this sense, they fulfilled the expectations of the male leadership since they first entered the party in 1918. They were loyal party workers, concentrating on issues of interest to women voters without challenging male control of the policy-making structure.

A NEW APPROACH TO GENDER ISSUES

The programme of reforms in the interests of working-class women which Labour Party women adopted in the thirties showed a change of approach to gender relations in the party. It was a move away from such issues as birth control and family allowances which championed women's interests and challenged male authority, and towards reforms intended to defend working-class women against the policies of a hostile government. Labour women looked upon the campaigns against the unfair treatment of unemployed married women and the high rate of maternal mortality as part of the larger class struggle not as a means of incorporating women's needs into the Labour Party programme. They sought the party's endorsement for their agenda and conspicuously avoided issues likely to cause conflict with the male majority.

The anomalies fight is a particularly good example of the way Labour women avoided open conflict with their own party. The 1931 Anomalies Act was passed under the Labour government by the Minister of Labour, Margaret Bondfield. It was an attempt to cut down on fraudulent claims for unemployment benefit and was targeted at married women who claimed benefit even though they had no plans to return to insured work. (Insured work for women was factory or office work since domestic servants were not eligible for unemployment insurance.) Bondfield later explained that she framed the act in response to 'complaints ... made by the neighbours of such women that they had been heard to boast in the district that they had no intention of going back to work'. She insisted that preventing such abuses was 'beneficial to the workers'.[15] Whatever the intent, the act proved to be the means of victimizing married women workers in the depression years. In the first eleven working days after its introduction in October 1931, 71,567 married women out of the 81,716 cases under review, lost their unemployment benefit. Over the decade, the number of disallowed married women totalled more than a quarter of a million.[16]

The anomalies regulations seemed ideally suited for making married women sacrificial lambs in the effort to cut the cost of social services. They specified that to qualify for unemployment benefit, married women had to prove that they had worked in an insured occupation since marriage and had the intention and prospects of finding similar insured work in their home district. This created a number of nightmarish no-win situations for the married woman worker. If she showed that she had made every effort to obtain insurable work, as she was bound to do, her failure in the short term was cited as evidence that she had no prospect of ultimate success and she was disallowed. The married woman who found an insured job outside her district could be disallowed for taking it under the anomalies regulations and disallowed for not taking it under the unemployment insurance regulations. In contrast to other workers in insured occupations, married women could be disallowed when laid off, on the grounds that they could not reasonably expect to get work in their old trade and in their district. Such blatant injustice produced wide discrepancies in the decisions of the umpires which added another element of unfairness and uncertainty to these regulations.

Labour women protested the unfair treatment of married women under the Anomalies Act for the rest of the decade. They did not, however, blame Margaret Bondfield or the Labour Party for passing the act in the first place. They placed the responsibility squarely on the shoulders of Bondfield's successor, the Conservative, Sir Henry Betterton, on the grounds that he had framed the regulations of the act in such a way as to make legitimately unemployed married women workers ineligible for benefit. It was left to ILP women to point out the flaws in this argument. Mrs Lane faulted Bondfield for having based her legislation on 'stories from gossiping neighbours' and for failing to foresee, even when the Labour Party was clearly on the verge of collapse, that in the hands of a reactionary government, the Anomalies Act would be used as a weapon against the workers.[17] Miss Annie Hambley added her criticism. She asked, 'could it not have been left to the Tories and Liberals to bring to notice these alleged abuses? Did the Labour Government think that the un-employed would exploit their own Insurance Fund?'[18] Labour women at the conference objected to the ILP attack on their first woman cabinet member and reiterated their view that the National Government was solely responsible for the disastrous effects of the anomalies legislation.

Married women's right to work was another issue on which Labour women appeared to change their focus in the thirties. In the twenties the subject provoked a clear difference of opinion among the rank-and-file between those who supported married women's place in the labour market on the grounds of equal rights, and those who opposed it because it meant taking jobs away from male and single women workers. The Labour Party supported the principle from a trade union perspective. They recognized that if the right to engage in paid work was ever based on need, as was suggested in the treatment of married women, trade union bargaining would become superfluous. Thus there were strong gender elements to the debate.

In contrast, the frame of reference for the discussion of married women's right to work in the thirties was the hostile forces outside the labour movement. Instead of focusing on rival gender claims to wage work, the Labour Party and Labour women made the issue part of a broader critique of the capitalist system and the National Government. Putting the official party position, the SJC argued that the attack on married women's right to work was the capitalists' attempt to find a scapegoat for the breakdown of their economic system. In their report on *Women in Industry*, May 1935, the committee stated: 'Discrimination against married women or any other particular section of workers is no cure for the injustices of a profit-making economic order.'[19]

As well as a shift in the official party line on the question of married women's right to work, similar changes of perspective emerged in the attitudes of the rank-and-file. In 1934, Mary Sutherland, successor to Marion Phillips as Chief Woman Officer, invited *Labour Woman* readers to write an essay expressing their views on the subject of married women and paid work. Over a hundred responded and of these, three out of four were in support of married women's right to work. Among those opposing, most agreed that married women might work if their husbands were unemployed or earning very low wages.[20] In the handful of published essays, the writers were more inclined to attribute the problem to the capitalist system than to male prejudice or married women workers' selfishness. Mrs E. E. Mann from Enfield wrote: 'It must be very bitter for men to see married women working while they themselves are unemployed with children to keep but they must not blame the women for what is the fault of the system. To impose retrogressive restrictions on any section of society will not mend matters.'[21] Mrs Margaret Tarr from Hornchurch addressed those who opposed married women's right to work in these terms: 'We should look deeper and condemn the whole system which in the control of education, employment, wage rates, scientific research and every kind of enterprise, disregards the humanity of the individual and seeks only victories for its profit making processes.'[22]

The Labour women essay writers who were among the majority in support of married women's right to work in 1934, used another argument that was significantly different from any the supporters had made in the previous decade. They emphasized the importance of safeguarding the freedom of the individual to make choices about his or her life. Mrs Tarr, for example, referred her opponents to the principles for which the Labour Party stood: 'The Labour Party demonstrates its belief in the liberty and freedom of the individual and Labour women would do well to ponder it.' She insisted that a married woman should have 'the liberty of the individual to carve out her own career'.[23] Miss H. M. Rowe from Stretford, declared that to deny the right of married women to keep their jobs is to 'take away from them that precious gift of freedom of choice over one's actions that distinguishes the freeman from a slave'. She drew a direct connection between the treatment of married women in Britain and what was happening to women in the fascist countries. 'Those countries like Italy and Germany which are loudest in denying women's fundamental right to a job, whatever her state, are the very places where freedom of thought and action of all individuals are curtailed'.[24]

The difference between this line of reasoning and that of egalitarian feminists was subtle but significant. Both groups talked of the denial of a married woman's right to wage work as a violation of the principle of individual rights, but while feminists of the twenties had equal gender rights in mind, the essay writers in the thirties were referring to democratic rights. They made the connection between married women's right to work and the threat to democratic freedom posed by fascism at home and in Europe. As Miss Rowe explained: 'Once the principle of freedom for one is denied for whatever reason, expediency or economic distress, what is there to prevent it from being taken away from another?'[25]

The writers who disagreed with the majority in opposing married women's right to work also used dissimilar arguments to those of their predecessors a decade before. They did not argue that married women workers who had employed husbands were somehow denying a livelihood to another working-class family or depriving a single woman of a job. Instead they implied that women who stayed at home were able to be 'better citizens' than those who went out to work. Not only could they provide a more comfortable and supportive environment for husbands and children but they could devote their leisure time to public service and labour politics.[26]

How far these rank-and-file authors represented the views of most Labour Party women is difficult to determine. The fact that all of them came from the south of England may account for their relative lack of concern about poverty. They did not express any fear that married women's work was taking too much out of a diminishing wages 'pie' and was therefore an act of selfishness unless it could be justified on the basis of need. Supporters and opponents alike seemed more anxious to respond to the question of married women workers' neglect of home and family than their unfairness to male primary providers. Two of the supporters stated that married women who had developed skills in a job or profession were better-off hiring someone else to care for their children than giving up their jobs to become discontented housewives.

At one level, the letters in *Labour Woman* in 1934 about married women's right to work seem to reflect a change in popular attitudes towards gender roles. The new popular women's journals, *Woman*, *Woman's Own* and *Woman and Home* that began to appear soon after the mid-decade give some insight into the change. They described the 'new woman' of the thirties as neither the 'sweet, domestic stay-at-home' nor the 'fierce feminist' but a 'cool, efficient and determinedly attractive person' who was trying to live two lives at once as wage-earner and sweetheart, citizen and home-maker.[27] This new woman did not challenge men either at work or at home. She was 'less aggressively feminist than independently feminine'. A writer for *Woman* in 1937 declared that the 'suffrage feminist who fought like a tigress for emancipation, for the vote, for education and for many other things' was an 'old-fashioned figure, unsympathetically remembered by all but a very few'. The thirties woman seemed to bear a strong resemblance to the nineteen eighties woman, trying to be 'all things to all men'.[28]

The attitudes described were no doubt associated with working-class women's new roles as producers and consumers in the chemical, electrical and food-processing industries of the thirties. The women's journals advertised a host of new products from cosmetics and domestic appliances to processed foods, sporting and leisure equipment, that were all unavailable to even better-off working-class families in the twenties. They addressed the young, single women who worked in the new industries as factory or office workers, the housewives who could afford to buy the new products for themselves and their families and the growing numbers of married women who tried to combine a job and a family. Excluded from this modern, consumer society were unemployed women industrial workers in the North of England and the wives of the unemployed in the 'economically distressed' areas.

Married women's right to work had always been accepted in Lancashire and Yorkshire textile towns where it was the common practice among mill workers. From the mid-thirties, it appears that southern women were coming closer to their northern sisters in their attitude towards this controversial subject. However, it is likely that the uneven economic growth that divided the stagnating industrial north from the expanding southeast in the thirties, created even greater differences of perspective between working-class women in the two regions. More evidence than has been produced here is needed to support this thesis but it does suggest that there were economic and cultural as well as political forces leading to a breakdown of the gender division in the Labour Party and the development of different sorts of tensions that crossed gender lines.[29]

Labour women's third major campaign of the thirties was also related to the economic depression. They determined to halt the alarming rise in maternal mortality and morbidity. The care of motherhood, like peace, was a consistent concern of labour women's organizations from their foundation. Before the war, the struggle centred on getting the Liberal government to set up maternity and child welfare clinics; in the twenties it became a fight with their own party to provide working-class women with access to free birth control information and devices. The maternal mortality campaign was in a sense a return to the prewar strategy. With the Labour Party out of office and without much hope of an imminent return, women activists made the issue part of a broader Labour effort to defend working-class living standards against a hostile government.

Maternal mortality received considerable official attention in the interwar years. Between 1918 and 1937 there were five Ministry of Health reports on the subject, showing a concern for healthy maternity as vital to population growth and military strength. In 1928, the Ministry set up a departmental Committee on Maternal Mortality and Morbidity, chaired by Gertrude Tuckwell, which conducted a series of investigations into the causes of death in childbirth. In 1929, a group of fourteen doctors looked at 2,000 cases and reported that at least half were preventable with as many as 616 due to puerperal sepsis. Two years later, a second study found that the maternal mortality rate was rising during the depression years. The committee reported that the 3,000 deaths in 1930 represented a rate of 4.40 per 1,000 safe deliveries, compared to 4.33 in 1929.[30]

The results of these studies received wide publicity among all labour women. Speaker after speaker at national women's conferences quoted the awful figure of 3,000 childbirth deaths as evidence of the ever-present dangers of women's primary occupation. They argued that existing maternity services were failing to ensure that poor women received proper medical attention during pregnancy, birth and post-partum recovery. In 1931, they organized a deputation to the Labour Minister of Health, Arthur Greenwood, asking for a National Maternity Service which would place all areas of maternal and child care under the control of state welfare agencies. Arthur Greenwood promised his support for the scheme and sent a circular to local authorities to determine the state of existing services. This was as far as the Labour Government went and Alderman Rose Davies criticized the minister at the National Conference of Labour Women in 1931 for failing to fulfill his promise.[31] Up to this point the campaign seemed very similar to those for birth control and family allowances in the twenties where Labour women expected their party to give 'equal time' to their special needs.

After the fall of the Labour government in late 1931, Labour women changed their campaign strategy. Faced with a government that was intent on cutting, not expanding, existing maternity services, plans for a state- run maternity scheme were clearly out of the question. They needed a strategy that would get the support of the whole labour movement and convince the National Government that their cutbacks were undermining maternity and thus endangering the nation. From 1932, they began to emphasize malnutrition due to unemployment and low wages as a primary cause of maternal deaths and illness.

Malnutrition was at the centre of the political debate between the National Government led by Labour's ex-leader Ramsey McDonald and the Labour Party, for the greater part of the decade. The party claimed that cuts in unemployment benefit and social services meant that working- class families could not get enough of the essential foods to sustain normal health and vigour. Ramsey MacDonald admitted in a broadcast to the nation in August 1931 that, 'unemployment benefit is not a living wage; it was never meant to be one', yet the government vigorously denied the connection between the cuts and malnutrition among unemployed workers. The Minister of Health argued that if malnutrition existed, it was due to the ignorance of working-class housewives who failed to recognize the benefits of 'cold water and carrots' and bought poor quality food for their families.[32]

By focusing on malnutrition as the cause of maternal mortality, Labour and Guild women killed several birds with one stone. They connected what was essentially a women's concern to the key issue in their party's political struggle against the National Government – the treatment of the unemployed. At the same time, they reminded the government that denying milk to expectant and nursing mothers, cutting back on maternity services, reducing unemployment benefit and maintaining the Means Test, all weakened the nation because they contributed to the death and illness of mothers. Although this may not have hastened the restoration of benefits, it most certainly influenced the Minister of Health's decision to carefully monitor childbirth mortality rates.

From 1933 to 1938, Labour women made the rise in maternal mortality part of a general indictment of National Government policy towards the working class. The Standing Joint Committee report in 1933 accusing the government of *Creating a C3 [impoverished] Nation* included a section calling for an investigation into the effects of poor nutrition on maternal health in areas of high unemployment. The report suggested that in homes where families were struggling to survive on inadequate unemployment benefit, pregnant women often gave away their food to husbands and children. As a result they became rundown and more susceptible to infection or other problems during child birth.[33] Gathering further evidence for its case, the SJC noted in 1936 that 'some medical officers of health reported an increase of malnutrition among mothers and school children and a number have definitely associated maternal deaths and ill-health with prolonged poverty'.[34] The Labour Women's Conference of that year passed a resolution proposed by Mrs Bocking from Scunthorpe Women's Section calling upon the government not only to improve medical and nursing care for expectant mothers but to 'increase family income by fifteen shillings a week for three months before and six months after childbirth'. This would enable pregnant women to eat properly and thus reduce maternal mortality.[35]

The decision of Labour women leaders to highlight the role of malnutrition in maternal mortality helped to integrate their agenda into the mainstream policy of the party. That it was a conscious political decision seems clear because, from a medical point of view, the argument was on rather shaky ground. When Dr Edith Summerskill, a practising physician and Labour parliamentary candidate, spoke about the causes of childbirth deaths at the National Conference of Labour women in 1936, she insisted that malnutrition was at most, only a contributory cause. She blamed careless medical practitioners, inadequate maternity services and abortion. 'She wanted delegates to remember that twelve percent of all the women who died did so following an abortion and thirty-seven percent died following some infection.'[36]

Dr Summerskill was the only Labour woman delegate to refer to abortion in the many discussions on maternal mortality held in the course of the decade. Silence about such a well-known cause of maternal death and injury during a campaign to prevent it, is perplexing; silence among informed women who had fought for birth control with determination and enthusiasm only a few years before, even more so.

Abortion provides the most telling example of Labour women's avoidance of issues likely to cause gender conflict in the party during the crisis years of the thirties. Judging by their previous reform record, there was every reason for them to make therapeutic abortion a major campaign issue. In the thirties, abortion came out of the shadows and entered public discourse. Concern about declining population which prompted the government's maternal mortality studies inevitably called attention to abortion-related deaths. The spread of birth control and maternal and child welfare clinics exposed working-class women's reproductive lives to official and professional scrutiny. Birth control advocates, in spite of their efforts to distance themselves from abortion, found themselves bombarded with requests for help from working-class women who were desperate to end unwanted pregnancies.[37] From mid-decade, reformers in the legal and medical professions, eugenicists and middle-class feminists, each with rather a different perspective, began to organize to change the 1861 law that made abortion a felony punishable by life imprisonment.[38]

Labour women must have been aware of the growing public interest in abortion and they could hardly have avoided seeing the connection between this issue and birth control, for which they fought so long and hard in the twenties. Like birth control, abortion was a practice to which women of all classes resorted, yet one where class discrimination clearly prevailed. Women who could afford to pay for the service were able to secure abortions secretly from sympathetic doctors or from medically unqualified abortionists in a wide network of private clinics. By the thirties, the operation was relatively safe because of developments in antiseptics and the technology of curettage.[39] Working-class women, on the other hand, had to rely on neighbours who 'helped out' in these situations or failing that, on self-induced abortion. Both methods involved a higher incidence of death and injury than among better-off women. Labour women had argued for birth control on the grounds that poor women should not be denied access to potentially life-saving and life-enhancing information readily available to middle-class women who could afford to pay for it. The same argument applied with even greater force to abortion.

There were other reasons for Labour women to connect abortion with birth control. Working-class women were just as much in need of safe and legal abortion as of effective methods of family limitation. Indeed, it appears that significant numbers made no distinction between the two, using abortion as a fall-back method of fertility control. They took pills and other abortifacients, widely advertised in the popular press, to 'bring on' or 'regulate' their menstrual period when they found they had been 'caught'. Barbara Brookes comments on this practice in her study, 'Abortion in England, 1919–1939'. She cites reports by middle- class feminists who served as lay workers in maternity and child welfare clinics in the interwar years. Janet Chance, who worked at the Walworth Women's Welfare Centre, noted among the older women who attended, a pronounced 'negative eugenic tendency'. The women 'habitually brought on miscarriages by the use of drugs and other ways, invariably with injury to themselves as individuals and as mothers'.[40] Charis Frankenburg and Mary Stocks made similar observations based on their work in a Salford clinic. They found that attempted abortion was 'almost a convention among working-class women as soon as they realized they were "caught" again'.[41]

A further encouragement for Labour Party women to take up the abortion issue was the willingness of middle-class socialist feminists to help organize the campaign as they had done so effectively in the case of birth control. In 1936, a group of them formed the Abortion Law Reform Association (ALRA) with the stated purpose of articulating working-class women's need for legal abortion. The ALRA bore a close resemblance to the Workers' Birth Control Group. It had many of the same leaders including Dora Russell, Frieda Laski, Bertha Lorsignol, Dorothy Thurtle and Stella Browne. It was a single issue organization like the WBCG and there is little doubt that it was well equipped in skills and experience to run a campaign to unify the work of local Labour women activists. The leaders of the ALRA organized a conference in London in May 1936, making sure that 'working women would be well represented and given time to speak'. The report of the conference gives a rare glimpse into working-class women's feelings on the subject of abortion, A Mrs Williams from

Leeds asserted that 'the [anti-abortion] law was no deterrent to working mothers of the industrial north to whom an unwanted pregnancy meant the cessation of a "very necessary income."' Another working woman made a speech to the effect that abortion should be available to women who did not want to raise children to be cannon fodder.[42]

These links between the abortion and birth control issues were apparently not enough to encourage Labour women to take up the cause. Their silence and inaction were in marked contrast to the response of other women's organizations. Most of the middle-class feminist organizations joined the campaign. In 1935, the National Council of Women urged the government to appoint a committee to inquire into the incidence of abortion with a view to reforming the law. It followed up this request the following year with a deputation to the Minister of Health. The National Union of Societies for Equal Citizenship (NUSEC), adopted a resolution calling for abortion law reform in 1935.[43]

It could be argued that the involvement of middle-class feminist groups was the reason why Labour Party women preferred not to participate in the abortion campaign. Relations between the two classes of organized women remained strained in the thirties with little or no co-operation even on issues like maternal mortality in which both were active. Feminism was discredited among women in the political labour movement. However, Labour women had the closest of ties to the Women's Co-operative Guild which was the first of any women's organization to demand a change in the anti-abortion laws. Delegates to the 1934 Co-operative Women's Congress passed the following strongly worded resolution by a vote of 1,340 to 20:

In view of the persistently high maternal death rate and the evils arising from the illegal practice of abortion, this Congress calls upon the Government to revise the abortion laws of 1861 by bringing them into harmony with modern conditions and ideas, thereby making of abortion a legal operation that can be carried out under the same conditions as any other surgical operation. It further asks that women now suffering from imprisonment for breaking these antiquated laws, be amnestied.[44]

The evidence suggests that Labour's women leaders deliberately avoided bringing the issue of abortion before the rank-and-file. An organization called the Socialist Medical Association submitted a resolution calling for reform of the abortion law to the 1934 Annual

Labour Party Conference. The NEC referred it to the SJC which discussed it on 14 March 1935. They decided to check the credentials of the Socialist Medical Association presumably to see if it was connected to the Communist Party and that was the first and last time the SJC discussed the subject. It was never brought to the attention of women conference delegates.[45] Equally clear, however, is the absence of a grass-roots demand for abortion reform from the women's sections. The subject does not appear once in the available section minutes.[46]

Why did Labour Party women ignore an opportunity to work for a reform that went hand in hand with their interest in birth control and would help to save the lives of the women of their class? The most obvious explanation is that they remembered the unsuccessful outcome of the long drawn-out birth control struggle and hesitated to repeat it. It was, to say the least, unlikely that the party would support another reform certain to provoke determined resistance from Roman Catholic members. However, the weight of the evidence implies that this was not the only reason. Labour women did not pursue controversial reforms specifically for women in the thirties because they were too busy responding to the crises that threatened to overwhelm their people and their party. The testimony of local women activists from the interwar years shows that they shared two fundamental political values. The first was a desire to help the weak and the oppressed of their class and the other to preserve peace. The crises of the thirties represented a direct appeal to these values, displacing the priority given earlier to women-centred reforms.

Neither leaders nor rank-and-file Labour women appear to have been aware of a decisive change of political direction in the thirties. They did not decide at a public meeting or a conference that they would stop trying to get more policy-making power for women in the party and stay clear of the abortion issue because it would alienate their male comrades. The decision was unexpressed because in a sense it was an involuntary response to external forces beyond their control. The need for party unity that had seemed merely an excuse for the party not to meet its obligations to women members in the twenties, did not have to be explained when a hostile government threatened to take away the means of livelihood from three million unemployed workers and their families. Labour women rushed to the barricades to struggle side by side with the men of their embattled party against the forces of reaction at home and across the Channel.

COMING TO THE AID OF THE PARTY

The issues of the thirties that generated something akin to the emotional fervour and energy of the birth control struggle in the twenties, were not specific to women but embraced the entire working class. The Means Test, which was introduced in August 1931 to cut the cost of supporting the long-term unemployed, united the men and women of the party in revolt against its cruelty and injustice. The Means Test burned itself into the consciousness of the twentieth-century British working class just as the 1834 Poor Law had done for earlier generations.

What made the Means Test such a rallying point for Labour men and women was that it applied to the working-class household not just the individual unemployed worker. Under the terms of the Unemployment Insurance Act of 1931, unemployed workers who had used up their twenty-six weeks of insured benefit, were subject to a means test to establish eligibility for 'transitional benefit', before they fell into pauperism. The Means Test required the unemployed worker to declare all family income, including savings in the Post Office or the Co-operative Society, old age and disability pensions or wages drawn by other members of the household, and even children's free school milk and meals. Investigating officers would visit the claimant's home and interrogate neighbours to check that he or she was not concealing anything.[47] The amount of transitional benefit, which could never exceed the already low insured benefit rates, was then calculated on the basis of the total resources of the household. Family destitution was thus the prerequisite for a benefit that was always less than a living wage.

It is not hard to see why Labour Party activists of both sexes regarded the Means Test as punishment meted out by one class to another rather than as part of the common sacrifice in a time of national crisis. The government assigned the administration of the Means Test to the poor law authorities, first the Public Assistance Committees (PACs), whose members were selected by the mostly Conservative County Councils and then a government-appointed Unemployment Assistance Board. Workers found themselves reduced to the level of paupers for becoming unemployed through no fault of their own. The Poor Law still carried a heavy weight of social stigma. Skilled workers in particular, the engineers, miners and textile workers who had never imagined having to resort to the Poor

Law during their earning years, felt the humiliation and injustice of their position.

The Means Test also pitted the interests of earners against non-earners in any one family. A common pattern was for older male or female industrial workers to be unemployed while their teenage children worked in dead-end jobs. The children's wages would be deducted from the parents' benefit leaving them dependent on the goodwill of their teenagers for survival. This painful situation led to splits in many working-class families with teenage children leaving home so as not to incur the burden of supporting their parents.[48]

Labour women resented such degrading and unjust treatment of their class as much as the men. Their speeches on the subject were almost identical in sentiment and wording. Resolutions demanding the abolition of the Means Test flooded into the National Conference of Labour women as well as the Annual Party Conference in 1932. In a composite resolution drawn up from the hundreds received from women's sections, Miss Manicom of the Transport and General Workers Union moved the following: 'This conference of Labour women protests against the pauperisation and humiliation of the unemployed and the additional burden thrown upon the rates by the hard administration of the Means Test.'[49] Mr A. E. Eyton of the Amalgamated Electrical Workers moving a similar resolution at the Party conference, asked rhetorically: 'Has anything known in the history of our land done so much to break up family life and unity as the Means Test? Prostitutes had been made by the hundreds as a result of unemployment and the transitional benefit inhumanity.'[50] Mrs Dollar of the London Labour Party referred to the misery caused by the harsh application of the Means Test in St Pancras. She felt it was time, 'the working-class were awake to their responsibilities and she appealed to the delegates [at the women's conference] to go out and do their bit and see that the people were not dragged down'.[51] Ben Tillett called upon the delegates at the Party conference to 'go out on to the street corners' to tell the people that the Means Test was 'causing the destruction of family life'.[52]

Labour men and women followed this advice and took their message about the 'intolerable evil and cruel injustice' of the Means Tests out into the streets. Local constituency parties, especially those in the depressed industrial areas, organized marches and demonstrations. The Nelson Labour Party's march was led by the Mayor and among other leading Labour figures, Selina Cooper, then well into her sixties. Addressing the crowd gathered at the recreation ground, she described the Means Test as, 'deliberately designed by the National Government to crush the workers into complete subjection'.[53] Local Labour parties also picketed the public assistance committees, demanding a more humane interpretation of the regulations governing transitional benefit. Labour-controlled boards of guardians, now acting as sub-committees under the control of the PACs, were so vehemently opposed to the punitive approach to the unemployed that some refused to administer the Means Test at all. The National Government had allowed for this possibility and recalcitrant boards of elected guardians were replaced by a non-elected government commission.[54]

Another issue that brought Labour Party men and women together in a joint campaign was the Spanish Civil War. By 1936, the Labour Party leadership was grappling with the problem of how to respond to the threat of fascism at home and in Europe. Franco's armed attack on his country's legitimate republican government presented the Party with a very difficult decision. There was a strong sentiment among the rank-and-file in favour of opposing the government's policy of non-intervention especially when it became clear that Hitler and Mussolini were giving arms to Franco. However, the party feared that active intervention by Britain and France on the side of republican Spain would bring a full-scale European war. The Labour leadership supported non-intervention until 1937 when it declared the necessity to allow Spain to buy arms for its protection against the fascist aggressors. Rank-and-file members who wanted to help the Spanish republicans but were opposed to war resolved their ambivalence by organizing to send non-military aid to the embattled republic in what became in the words of one historian, 'the biggest movement of international solidarity in British history'.[55]

More than a thousand 'Aid to Spain' or 'Spanish Relief' committees were formed, often with a mixed membership, men and women, representatives from every Labour, co-operative, socialist or communist organization, working and middle class. The committees organized public meetings, collected food and clothing, arranged for medical aid and raised money. Almost every women's section, local Labour Party and Women's Co-operative Guild was involved in the campaign in some way. Women knitted gloves, socks, balaklavas and woolly jumpers. Labour families took in Basque children orphaned by the war. Labour women like Nellie Jackson from Yorkshire spoke on public platforms alongside prominent Labour or ILP speakers and were proud to see their eloquence rewarded with contributions to the cause.[56] A few Communist Party and Labour women went out with the male volunteers to play their part in the war itself, and some of these did not return.[57]

The Means Test and the Spanish Civil War created a sense of unity and enthusiasm in the organized labour movement that made gender differences seem irrelevant. Neither the Means Test inquisitors nor fascist bombs discriminated between the sexes in their attack on working people. Both issues were self-evident examples of class oppression. They generated a sense of moral outrage in the labour movement, among men and women alike. In the twenties, the mainstream party implied that Labour women's ethical approach to politics was inappropriate for a mass party intent on gaining parliamentary power. In the thirties, rank-and-file members of both sexes found it the only proper response to political events that presented themselves in clear moral terms.[58]

The crises of the thirties prompted some women leaders in the Labour Party to argue that issues previously considered strictly a part of 'the women's side' were more properly the concern of the entire labour movement. While Labour women had always wanted the party to pay attention to matters of special significance to women, they had not, until the thirties, shown any willingness to abandon the gender division of political responsibility even at the national level. In 1936, Barbara Ayrton Gould and Ellen Wilkinson urged the party to take a leadership role in the Hunger Marches instead of leaving it to the communist-run National Unemployed Workers' Movement (NUWM). Ayrton-Gould took the opportunity to warn the party of the dangers of continuing to assume that hunger and malnutrition were matters best left to the women to deal with. She said:

It is more than time that this great Movement took up these questions as a whole. You have left the question of malnutrition chiefly to women. Feeding is not peculiarly a woman's job, it is the job of everybody. It is the job of the whole nation. The government have been much cleverer than you are. They know what they are doing...They know that half-starved people do not revolt, neither do they fight Fascism, neither do they build up a socialist state...

She ended: 'Let us join together in a great crusade to stop the misery of millions starving in the midst of plenty.'[59]

DISSENT ACROSS GENDER LINES

Just as the gender division of political interests that had developed in the twenties became blurred in response to the crises of the thirties, dissent also lost its gender component. Labour Party women began to identify with the left or the right of the movement and to line up on one side or the other on the issues that divided the party as a whole, just like the men. In some instances, local sections took their cue from the constituency party; in others, the sections decided their own position based on the convictions of the majority or of the most emphatic. Some dissidents seem to have moved around until they found a section or another organization that was more compatible with their point of view.[60]

The most contentious question for the Labour Party in the latter half of the thirties was how to respond to the communist proposal for a united front against fascism. From 1934 to 1935, the Communist Party began to call on all socialist and working-class organizations to unite against fascism and work to form a popular front of anti-fascists from all classes. In pursuit of this policy, the Communists reapplied for affiliation to the Labour Party in 1934. The party rejected the application by 1,728,000 votes to 592,000 and refused to have anything to do with the United Front.[61] The Socialist League, formed in 1932 with members from the disaffiliated ILP and the Labour left wing, organized a Unity Campaign to pressure the party into changing its policy.[62] The NEC responded with an orgy of expulsions and disaffiliations of individuals and organizations with any connection to the Communist Party or the United Front.

In the twenties, Labour women had taken no part at all in the lengthy debates over relations with the Communists. In the thirties, the women's sections were as involved as the local parties and trades councils in the dispute over the United Front. Women's organizers reported 'trouble with communist activities and United Front agitation' in sections all over the country. In Denbigh, North Wales, the organizer, Mrs Andrews, faced questions from the members of the section who wanted to know if it was all right for communist women from Colwyn Bay to address them. They pointed out that 'several of the younger members were rallying around the communist leader' and some had joined communist cells in Bangor and Holyhead. The chairman of the Neath section complained of 'much trouble' with communists and United Front supporters. She had been obliged to outlaw communist speakers from the section. Mrs Andrews noted 'strong support for the Unity Campaign' in the section at Ebbw Vale, Nye Bevan's constituency. In West Rhondda she was told, 'some of the members had been influenced by their husbands and were using the section for communist propaganda on the matter of the United Front'.[63]

The story was the same in other parts of the country. The Yorkshire organizer found 'communistically minded folk' infiltrating the section in Sheffield Park. A member of the section put a motion for the 'immediate return of the Socialist League into affiliation', which 'had it gone to the vote would have carried', but the secretary managed to hold off the vote while she sought guidance from the local Labour member of Parliament.[64] Mrs Annie Townley, organizer in southwest England, found it hard to explain to some sections just why they could have nothing to do with organizations that appeared to represent the best interests of their class. Finding that many members of the Westbury section had joined the proscribed Left Book Club and were attending meetings in Bristol and Bath with Victor Gollancz and Harry Pollitt as speakers, she wrote: 'So we go on, having more and more difficulties to contend with as it is difficult to say they ought not to have joined the Left Book Club. I made clear just what the party decisions meant and appealed to the women to concentrate on our own work.'[65]

Evidently, many Labour women were not interested in concentrating on their 'own work' if that meant confining themselves to canvassing, fundraising and a separate agenda. They felt just as strongly as their male comrades on the question of the United Front and those who disagreed with the party's policy resented the efforts of section officers to make them 'obey orders'. A Mrs F. Johnson from Mexborough, Yorkshire, for example, wrote to the District Organizer in July 1937, to complain that the secretary of her section had refused to allow discussion of an offer by a representative of the Left Book Club to come and explain the aims of the organization. The only reason the secretary gave for her action was that the women's sections had been 'instructed to have nothing to do with the Left Book Club'. Mrs Johnson thought it 'deplorable and undemocratic that Labour women should be instructed what and what not to read'.[66] Her letter eventually reached Mary Sutherland, the Chief Woman Officer, who declared that the section had acted properly and Mrs Johnson must accept the decision. In August, the Mexborough secretary wrote to tell Mary Sutherland that Mrs Johnson had left, adding, 'you will be pleased to learn that we have no "left wing elements" in the section now'.[67]

Mrs Johnson's public expression of resentment at the party's witchhunt of the Left is a good indication of the extent to which Labour Party women were participants in the mainstream political debate between the left and the right. Mr G. R. Strauss from North Lambeth, a Socialist Leaguer echoed Mrs Johnson's complaints about the undemocratic methods of party officials at the Annual Conference in 1937. He asked why only members on the left of the movement were denied the right of association with comrades outside the party. He mentioned party leaders who regularly sat on the same platform as Winston Churchill who was certainly less of a friend to labour than Harry Pollitt. He had a message for the NEC: 'I believe that the delegates would like to convey to the NEC a request that they do not waste their energies in nosing about the local Labour parties up and down the country to try to find something active and militant, and then calling it communist and setting upon it.' He called the Unity Campaign a 'manifestation of the discontent among the rank-and-file with the inaction and compromise of the leaders in all important matters that were taking place'.[68] 'The-rank and-file' no longer referred just to men.

The positions that women took during their conference debate on the Popular Front in 1938 were strikingly similar to those of Labour men at the annual party conferences. The opponents of the Front objected strongly not so much to the association with the Communist Party as to the idea of compromising the Labour Party's socialist programme by allying with the Liberals. Mrs S. E. Barker stressed that 'there was no fundamental difference between Toryism and Liberalism' since both were capitalist parties. Support for the Popular Front meant 'being asked to associate with a wing of capitalist organisation to defeat the latest form of capitalism which was Fascism'.[69] Mrs Auld agreed with her that the 'Liberal Party wanted the Movement to throw over years of work to give the Liberals publicity and power.'[70] Herbert Morrison made a similar complaint about the Popular Front at the Annual Party Conference the year before. In his view the Communist Party was asking Labour, 'in the cause of progressive unity', to hand over some of its hard-won seats to the Liberals 'whom [we] have been fighting for years to destroy'.[71]

Labour men and women who supported the Popular Front, also used the same arguments in defending their position. They emphasized that the struggle the labour movement faced was not between capitalism and socialism but between fascism and democracy. If they did not defend democracy first, British socialists would suffer the same fate as their German, Italian and Spanish comrades. Mrs R. Morris reminded the delegates to the Labour Women's Conference in 1938 of the terrible danger fascism posed to the young. 'Youth would have to fight, and more than that, would have to suffer whether it liked it or not, because it would live under a Fascist dictatorship.'[72] In a speech to the annual conference in 1936, Alex Gossip of the Amalgamated Furnishing Trades Association, made a similar impassioned plea to the delegates to join the Popular Front to defend democracy. The victory of fascism would mean ' the destruction of our trade union movement, the destruction of our co-operative societies, the destruction of everything the working class has built up'.[73]

The left wing also argued for the United Front as a way of defeating the National Government which they regarded as 'a Fascist government, every bit as much as those in Germany and Italy'. At the Women's Conference in 1938, Miss Alexander, representing the National Union of Shop Assistants, denounced Chamberlain and the National Government as 'the enemies of democracy'. She said: 'A Popular Front could get rid of the National Government now, once and for all.' Mrs Duncan from the Cambell Women's Section in Barking agreed. She reminded the delegates that 'all the protest meetings and demonstrations that had been held against Chamberlain had not succeeded in turning him out'. She argued that a popular front government in Britain would go a long way to improving the condition of the working class, pointing to the example of France where Leon Blum's government had secured increased wages and shorter hours for workers.[74] Mr C. A. Adolph representing the National Union of Distributive and Allied Workers (NUDAW) at the Party conference made a similar point. There were certain reform policies that all progressive parties could agree upon. 'On the question of war and peace, of democracy, of the demand for a forty-hour week and holidays with pay, it is possible to work with the widest possible sections of the movement.'[75]

Local Labour parties with left-wing majorities appear to have ignored the party ban and worked with proscribed left-wing organizations in a number of United Front activities. The male and female members justified their actions by citing the Labour Party's belated and limited support for Spanish republicans and its refusal to take part in organizing the hungry and unemployed. The Communist Party had filled the gap and initiated many of the programmes making the strongest appeal to their socialist ideals. Labour and Guild women played a big part in providing meals for hunger marchers who were organized by the communist-led National Unemployed Workers Movement (NUWM). They joined in local demonstrations with communist and ILP members against the Means Test and spoke with them on public platforms on issues like 'Aid to Spain'. A few of the more prominent Labour women, including Selina Cooper, Jennie Lee, and Ellen Wilkinson, were active in the international Women's Committee Against War and Fascism alongside middle-class feminists like Vera Brittain and Dr Maud Royden. The committee described itself as non-sectarian and non-party but was actually controlled by the Communist Party.[76] Labour women who engaged in united front activities such as these suffered the same treatment as men. The party expelled individuals – Jessie Stephen was one – and disaffiliated recalcitrant sections like Wood Green.[77]

The other issue that divided both men and women in the party in the second half of the decade but at an even deeper emotional level was that of war and peace. From 1918, the party maintained a firm commitment to 'the abolition of war through the League of Nations and the strengthening of the collective peace system by expanding and clarifying the undertaking not to resort to war'.[78] Labour's policy seems to have reflected the general sentiment in the country. According to the Peace Ballot, which the Labour Party helped to conduct in 1936, over eleven million people supported Britain's membership in the League. Over ten million were in favour of disarmament by international agreement and only half, six million, supported the use of military sanctions to stop violence.[79] From 1935, however, with each international crisis beginning with Mussolini's invasion of Abyssinia in August, Hitler's remilitarization of the Rhineland in March 1936, the Spanish Civil War, 1936–9 and the Nazi Anschluss with Austria in February 1938, the Labour Party moved towards accepting rearmament, even under a pro-fascist national government.

This was one issue where a gender division might have prevailed.

In the twenties, the mainstream party had been content to leave its women members to uphold the moral centre of the party's commitment to peace. Women were the great peace crusaders of the postwar decade, active in the No More War movement and ever-vigilant watch dogs against militarism. The women in the sections inscribed 'Peace' on their banners, spoke of it as an essential part of their socialism and made it the outstanding characteristic of their political identity in the party. There was equally strong pacifist sentiment among the men in the party but the party's decision to support war in 1914 and its parliamentary goals, always implied that it would sacrifice its peace principles for the national interest, traditionally defined. However, as fascist aggression mounted, especially in Spain, any gender distinction in the Labour Party on the peace issue disappeared. Labour women divided in much the same way as the rest of the movement.

A minority of Labour men and women, centred in the local parties, maintained a totally pacifist position and argued strongly against the Labour Party's decision to support sanctions against Mussolini in 1935 and re-armament in 1937. George Lansbury, Dr Salter, Lord Ponsonby and Lucy Cox represented this pacifist point of view at national party conferences. They argued that wars had accomplished nothing in the past and any military efforts to stop fascism would only mean the slaughter of innocent working men, women and children. Lucy Cox said that if she were going to write a letter to her unborn son, she would say that 1914–18 had proved beyond doubt that 'war can never be ended by war and that nothing worthwhile in this world can be safeguarded by war'.[80] Lansbury resigned the leadership of the party when it voted for sanctions in 1935.

Delegates to the women's conference in 1938 used very similar pacifist arguments to oppose the party's decision on rearmament. Councillor Iris Condon from the West Bermondsey Women's Section urged the delegates to stand firm in their opposition to war and preparation for war. 'They would never stop militarism by supporting militarism or by building a superior armed force. Armaments would be used to massacre workers whether under collective security or any other way.' She said that the pacifist policy for constructive peace was to get the British government to summon a world conference to discuss the 'economic troubles which were at the root of the threats to peace'.[81] Mrs Philpot from the South Ward Women's Section, Croydon, said that her section 'believed in the absolute and utter futility of war and that war was wrong in any circumstances and that the greatest cause of poverty in the country was the way the country was supporting the present race in armaments'. Minnie Pallister added, 'Peace would never be got by crushing one person or one nation.'[82]

The Women's Co-operative Guild also maintained its pacifist commitment up to and beyond the outbreak of war. Unlike Labour women, Guild members still used the terminology of the twenties in emphasizing working-class women's special responsibility for the preservation of peace. In 1933, some Guild members in local branches had the inspired idea of wearing white instead of red poppies on armistice day as a symbol of their rejection of war and support for peace. The white poppy campaign was a great success and spread quickly through the branches. The Guild kept open house for communist and ILP as well as Labour women and thus no doubt helped to sustain the pacifist minority in the broader labour and co-operative movement. It is hard to tell to what extent Labour women who changed their minds on the peace issue felt obliged to leave the Guild.

Those Labour Party men and women who recognized, however reluctantly, that fascist aggression could only be stopped by armed force divided into two groups roughly corresponding to the right and left wings in the Party. The official Labour Party policy the right wing supported was based on the assessment that continental fascism was an immediate and powerful threat to the country's national security which the Labour Party as a prospective government could not afford to ignore. With the model of the Spanish bombing before them, they had to support rearmament then and there under whatever political circumstances prevailed.

Such a policy represented a significant shift for Labour Party women after years of commitment to peace and abhorrence of war. For the majority who decided to follow the party's lead and accept rearmament, the Spanish Civil War seems to have been the catalyst. Mrs Gould who put the resolution supporting the party's rearmament policy to the women's conference in 1938, told the delegates that she had just returned from Spain. She had been horrified by the sight of civilians, women and children, being killed by fascist bombs from Italy and Germany. 'She had been a Pacifist all her life and never did she think that the time would come when she would back arms and fighting, but in a world of mad dogs – a world that was becoming more and more a Fascist world – Labour women must stand behind the Labour Party in demanding that there should be arms to defend democracy and arms to go to Spain.'[83]

The Labour Party made it easier for men and women in the party to accept what amounted to a total about-face on the peace issue by making almost no change in its rhetoric. In 1938, the Party still talked of peace through 'collective security' and of 'uniting all peace-loving nations on the basis of the League Covenant in order to defend peace by a common stand against aggression' long after it had become apparent that the League was unable to play any such role.[84] After the Party had agreed to support rearmament, it continued to describe its foreign policy as a 'constructive peace policy...which will call a halt to the armaments race, secure as speedily as possible the abolition of air armaments, check the drift to war and lay the foundation of real co-operation among nations'.[85] Men and women who spoke in favour of rearmament used the same 'peace' terminology. This raises the question of the real strength of support among the rank-and-file for the decision that underlay the rhetoric, to support a war on the terms and conditions set by a government hostile to the working class.

The party's left wing, led by Sir Stafford Cripps and the Socialist League, recognized that armed force would be needed to stop fascism but rejected rearmament while the National Government was in power. They argued that rearming under the capitalist National Government would leave Labour with no control over recruitment, the conditions of wartime industry or the conduct of the war. There were Labour women who agreed with this view. Mrs Brooks of the Association of Women Clerks and Secretaries said that 'if the rearmament programme were supported, they had no guarantee at all that the armaments would be used for the defense of democracy. On the contrary, every indication showed that they would be used for the furtherance of Fascism'. Mrs Boltz, North Lambeth Women's section, thought the Labour Party had sold the workers short by allowing arms to a government that was clearly in sympathy with the fascist dictators. Mrs Audrey Hunt warned that having conceded arms, Labour would be supporting private armaments manufacturers, an undemocratic army and conscription, all of which it had declared were against its principles.[86]

Participation in internal dissent may be the true measure of integration. If this is the case, the external threats to Labour from the

National Government and fascism provided the opportunity for women to enter the mainstream of the Labour Party. It is worth noting, however, the continued existence of a gender division in the national organization. Men and women debated the same issues separately at different conferences and while the men's debates resulted in the formation of policy decisions, the women's did not. If the women's conference had voted overwhelmingly in favour of support for the United Front and opposition to rearmament, it would have made no difference whatsoever to party policy. Women's integration into the mainstream debates at the national level was therefore not matched by a position of power. Something different seemed to be happening at the local party level in the thirties, however, where there were signs of a breakdown of gender segregation.

GENDER INTEGRATION IN LOCAL LABOUR PARTIES

In 1932, on the death of Marion Phillips, the organization sub-committee of the Labour Party produced a report on the current status of women. The Report suggested that it might be time to abolish separate women's sections and integrate women fully into the movement. It argued that the new generation of party women had a very different attitude towards gender relations than the preceding one. The earlier generation had tended to be 'sex-conscious' and inclined to 'sex antagonism' because of its association with the suffrage campaign. Lacking this background, the new generation was more interested in 'political comradeship' than gender conflict. Moreover, advances in education and changing social mores had tended to lessen the gap between the sexes. Young women who served their political apprenticeship with like-minded young men in the Labour League of Youth were disinclined to join separate women's sections when it was time to graduate to the local parties. The report noted a 'growing disposition to cease separate sex activities and join together in all phases of Party work'.[87]

Although the report shows how completely the national party had failed to understand the aspirations of its women members in the twenties, it was correct in its assessment that the women's sections were losing support in the thirties. The sections declined in numbers even after 1932 when women's overall membership began to recover from the drop caused by the party's 1931 disaster. In 1932, there were 1,704 sections and a total women's membership of 154,000. In 1935, the membership had risen to 172,910 but the sections declined to 1,604. By 1938, the number of sections had fallen to 1,601 while the membership was up to 178, 121.[88]

Women's organizers reported in the thirties on the struggles of sections to survive when reduced to a handful of members. Mrs Gibb, the organizer for the North-West of England, commented on the sad state of the Colne Federation of Labour Women: 'Generally, there are few new faces at this meeting. This division seems to make no headway and certainly while there are good loyal women, they do not bring along new members.'[89] The York section which had flourished in the twenties with up to a hundred women attending meetings found its numbers reduced to less than ten in 1932-4.[90] Some sections like those in Bradford and Crook closed down for a year or two in the early thirties. At the height of the economic and political crisis in 1931, the Crook section passed the following resolution: 'Resolved that for a period or until the women's section can muster a reasonable number of women together we remain with the men's section.'[91] The Bradford section never restarted because of 'a very strong opinion among some men that there was not a case for a women's section'.[92] Organizers mentioned some specific regional problems affecting the women's sections. In one instance, the opening of a rubber works in Melksham, Wiltshire making gas masks in preparation for war, employed quite a few of the married women section members. The section tried to solve the problem by arranging alternate meetings, in the daytime for young mothers and in the evenings for those who worked, but membership fell anyway.[93] More often, the organizers complained of apathy and indifference and sections that were 'in a rut'.

In some cases, the problem of declining numbers was due to an aging membership. The Chief Woman Officer admitted that the sections did not attract younger women in sufficient numbers so that the majority of members were middle-aged and older. In 1936, she wrote: 'It is generally true to say that the great majority of our members, at least those who attend our meetings and carry on the work of the party are "not so young."'[94] Some new sections were started on the growing council housing estates with a membership of younger married women with small children but it is hard to tell how successful they were. Women organizers seemed more inclined to beat their breasts over 'problem' sections than to congratulate themselves on the successes.

In the depressed areas, poverty was one of the most significant causes of declining membership in the women's sections. Lack of funds limited the activities of the sections and in some cases closed their doors altogether. Mrs A. G. Bennett, the President of a women's section in Pennydarren, South Wales, whose members were 'terribly poor on account of long years of unemployment', explained how the section had to compete with middle-class charitable organizations giving away food and clothing. She wrote asking Mary Sutherland to send clothing so that the section could offer 'something tangible to women who would otherwise join the Quakers or go to the social service centres'. She said her members were looking forward to the conference in Treharris where Miss Sutherland was to speak but she did not think that many would be able to attend because they did not have the money for the bus fare of one and sixpence and 'some of them have not the clothes to go in'. She ended on a note of bitterness, 'and to think this government allowing out the meagre pittance for our people, and really good people, to live on and they are allowing for Princess Elizabeth 25,000 pounds a year. It's enough to make the people revolt'.[95]

Poverty undermined the sections in other ways. Male-dominated constituency parties were hostile towards existing sections and discouraged the formation of new ones because they did not want women's fundraising activities diverted from the main party. Lack of funds meant that women could not afford to send delegates to the women's conferences or to the advisory council meetings; they could not raise money for outings or social events or buy *Labour Woman*.[96] Under these circumstances, the sections tended to lose touch with the rest of the movement and become bored with the restricted range of activities and the constant preoccupation with raising money to pay the rent for their meeting place.

Although these difficulties meant that the women's sections declined in numbers and lost some of their appeal, they continued to be the majority experience for women in the Labour Party. This was because most Labour women were still married and at home. They were too busy with family responsibilities to attend regular evening meetings and may well have felt more comfortable among their own sex. What is different about the thirties, however, is the growing numbers of mostly younger women who, as the party's 1932 report suggested, found sex segregation 'old-fashioned' and preferred to join the mixed ward and constituency parties.

Women activists in local Labour parties testified to a much closer working relationship with their male comrades in the thirties than they had enjoyed in the previous decade. In the twenties, women conducted their own campaigns for peace, birth control, nursery schools, school meals programmes and maternity and child care. They marched, demonstrated and lobbied for these causes on their own. In the thirties, women marched alongside the men to demonstrate their opposition to the Means Test and support for republican Spain. Margaret Mitchell from Tottenham remembered how her women's section joined the members of the North Tottenham party and the Tottenham Trades Council as well as local communists in mass rallies against the Means Test. 'See we were all up against this means test ... so we all used to rally and go down [to Bethnal Green] ... We had these big rallies up in London, Hyde Park, Trafalgar Square. Huge demonstrations we had.' She had been in Cable Street when Mosley and his Blackshirts tried to walk through the East End. 'We from Tottenham had a very good contingent fighting the Blackshirts.'[97]

There were social, economic and regional factors that encouraged women's closer integration into the local parties in the thirties. Smaller families, newer houses, convenience foods and labour-saving devices such as indoor plumbing and the gas or electric stove, no doubt made it easier for some working-class women to enjoy a full political life on similar terms to male members. From the mid-thirties, popular attitudes about appropriate roles for women changed somewhat so that participation in 'citizenship' activities became more acceptable even for working-class women. In this more permissive environment, women's mutual support was less important and integrated organization an increasingly popular choice. Above all, however, the crises of the thirties discouraged gender segregation in the political Labour movement. Labour men and women were drawn together to face the common enemy of reaction that threatened their living standards and the survival of their party.

CONCLUSIONS

Labour women responded to the crises of the thirties rather as they had done to the First World War. They waived their gender claims in favour of party unity and the common struggle against the forces of class oppression. Instead of asking for separate-but-equal status, as they had in the twenties, they accepted integration into the mainstream Party on the terms offered by the male majority, that is without attention to women's special interests or compensation for their numerical weakness in the trade unions. Although Labour Party women made progress in the twenties towards persuading local parties to accept the concept of their separate-but- equal status, they were soundly defeated at the national level. How well did they fare when they switched tactics in the thirties and moved towards a position that party leaders had urged upon them since 1918?

In terms of power within the national party, 'integration' resulted in some significant losses and few gains. The tenuous links between rank- and-file women and the policy-making apparatus of the party disappeared. Not only were there fewer women at the party's Annual Conferences, there were fewer women on the slate of parliamentary candidates and on the proliferating party committees.[98] The SJC tightened its control over local sections by limiting discussion at the women's conferences to reports that it had prepared with the prior approval of the NEC. This arrangement stifled local initiatives. None of the thirties campaigns began as the birth control campaign had done in response to a concerted demand from the local sections. Even more than her predecessor, Mary Sutherland kept a tight lid on any hint of rank-and-file deviation from the party line.

In the absence of pressure from women members, the party could safely ignore women as a distinct group. As a result they ceased to exist in NEC deliberations or policy formulation. The Labour League of Youth took their place as the thorn in the party's side.[99] The women's conference was little more than a 'talking shop' where women delegates were reduced to commenting on decisions already made or about to be made by the male-dominated party conference. Women's decisions were reported to the conference but without the element of challenge that existed in the twenties, they rarely generated any debate there. Women's intense involvement in all-party issues like unemployment and the Means Test, the Spanish Civil War, the United Front and rearmament certainly brought them into the partry mainstream but in the role of a Greek chorus with the main action taking place elsewhere.

The one gain for women in the national party was receiving party support for their women's welfare programme, most notably on the Anomalies Act and maternal mortality both of which were included in the party manifesto, *For Peace and Socialism,* and in legislation introduced by the parliamentary party. Of course, these were strong sticks with which to beat the government and as the party was not in power, it was not called upon to fulfill its promises. However, there is no doubt that the party recognized, if slowly, that 'women's issues' in the area of social reform belonged in the mainstream of party policy. They made good use, for example, of the Cost of Living study the women's sections conducted in 1937–8 to challenge the government's stubborn contention that unemployment benefit, if wisely spent, was enough to provide adequate nutrition for the unemployed worker and his family.

The gains from integration were more apparent in local than national politics. Labour women may have lost interest in exercising power in the national party, but they did not give up the struggle for a larger share of responsibility and office-holding in their local constituency parties and in local government. Labour women continued to gain ground in elections to local councils and as appointees to the public assistance committees and the magistrates bench.[100] Local party minutes give the impression of much closer gender co-operation than in the twenties. More women seem to have held office in the ward or constituency parties, and political activities were more likely to involve both sexes. Men and women were allied either on the right or the left of the party, supporting or opposing the United Front and rearmament. They worked together to picket public assistance committees in protest against the Means Test, raise funds for republican Spain and gather signatures for the Peace Ballot. They held joint marches and demonstrations and spoke from the same public platforms.

G. D. H. Cole was under the impression that women's influence in local parties increased in the thirties and was manifested in the parties' tendency to adopt an ethical stance on the political issues of that troubled decade. He gave the example of two contradictory positions that were strongly represented in the local parties. Many constituencies opposed the party's support for rearmament under the National Government, using the argument women often made in the twenties, that war would only benefit capitalists and armaments profiteers at the expense of the workers. At the same time, the local parties were vociferous in demanding that the party support military aid to the Spanish republic to allow it to defend itself against the fascist aggressors. Although it could be argued that G. D. H. Cole, having detected political inconsistency decided that women must be to blame, it may still be true that Labour women encouraged their local parties to view political events as separate moral issues rather than matters to be considered within an overall policy of political expediency.[101]

Few, if any, Labour Party women publicly acknowledged that something had been lost in the move away from separate-but-equal and towards greater integration into the mainstream party. From a historical perspective, however, the transition brought to an end a unique experiment. Labour women rank-and-file members in the twenties had put forward an alternative model for a mass working-class party. It was one in which working-class women's special needs and interests as wage workers, housewives and mothers would have equal weight in the party's conference debates and policy decisions with those of men. It included the idea of a parallel power structure consisting of the sections and women's conferences. Labour Party leaders could not accept that women's concerns were equal in political importance to men's. Fearful of the political effects of gender conflict, they resisted Labour women's every attempt to establish their model.

Labour women did not appear to notice the end of their struggle for separate-but-equal status, probably because they were so busy defending the party and their class against the enemy outside. But in one sense at least, the change was unremarkable. They had never put their gender and class interests in two different baskets. Their gender concerns focused on giving working-class women and children the same opportunity for healthy and fully developed lives as those of the middle class. They did not change their philosophy in the thirties; it was more a matter of being pushed into a defensive position and losing the opportunity to pursue more radical gender policies.

Judging from Labour women's comments in interviews and in the questionnaire, they experienced a greater sense of comradeship with the men in their party in the thirties than they had done in the twenties precisely because the issues were unrelated to gender and presented themselves in such clear moral and class terms. Inspired by

the injustice and suffering the National and Conservative governments brought to their class and by the fascist threat to the
international labour movement, they felt the exhilaration of crusaders, united in a common struggle. As Mrs Mitchell put it: 'You
knew you were fighting in a just cause.'[102] They remembered
thinking that capitalism would not survive the disaster of the
depression and that socialism must triumph because it was so
eminently right and just. From the confusion of labour politics in the
nineteen eighties, they looked back to the thirties as a time when class
politics made sense and the vision of the co-operative commonwealth
was still clearly before them.

Conclusion

When the Labour Party introduced the Welfare State after the Second World War, Labour and Co-operative women had good reason to believe that they had made a significant contribution to this landmark legislation. In the quarter century since 1918 when they were first admitted as members, labour women made social welfare reform in the interests of working-class women and their families their special concern. For more than a decade they struggled to get party support for nursery schools, improved health care for mothers and babies, birth control, and family allowances. They had only limited success with this agenda in the interwar period but Labour's postwar programme seemed a vindication of their efforts. A closer look at the Welfare State, however, reveals hardly a trace of labour women's input. The Liberal economists, William Beveridge and John Maynard Keynes provided the models; Labour men debated them and the mostly male Members of Parliament gave them the force of law. Excluded from their party's decision-making process, labour women had no opportunity to contribute from their considerable knowledge and experience of social welfare reform to their party's postwar policies.

This study has explored the reasons why labour men and women were unable to create an effective working partnership in the interwar years which would have given women an equal share in policy-making. It finds that the failure was not simply a case of male prejudice or reluctance to share power, although both of these existed. It was much more a matter of the difficulty both sexes had in overcoming traditional views about appropriate gender roles. No matter how sincerely labour activists of both sexes professed their belief as socialists in sexual equality, when they came to decide upon women's place in labour politics they showed a deep-seated attachment to the idea of separate gender spheres. The sense of being comrades in a common struggle that rank-and-file members so often expressed, had a subtext of gender distinction and male dominance they were less willing to acknowledge. As a result, labour women had to serve their class and party within the limits of unacknowledged discrimination and lack of power.

As soon as women joined the Labour Party in 1918 they faced a crucial decision. They could either accept the party's offer of integration on terms that would have obliged them to compete for positions of power with the large industrial trade unions, or keep their own separate meetings and women-centred reform programme. Like their co-operative sisters, the majority chose to preserve a distinct women's presence in the party. They wanted to make their voices heard as the representatives of the special interests of working-class women and give those interests equal weight with men's in party policy. Their choice of separate-but-equal status seemed justified when it became clear in the early twenties that most new women members preferred their own sections and the male leaders who insisted on integration still expected women to confine their contribution to acceptably feminine concerns.

The possibilities as well as the limitations of women's separate-but-equal alternative to the patriarchal party appeared most clearly in the birth control campaign. The issue of working women's access to birth control appealed to labour women's strongly humanitarian and reforming instincts and fulfilled what they saw as their special role in working-class politics. They wanted working-class mothers liberated from life sentences of repeated pregnancies, physical suffering and anxiety, and their children freed from the restrictions that came from over-stretched family resources. Under the direction of the Workers' Birth Control Group, the campaign generated more support, enthusiasm and co-ordinated effort from organized labour women than any other social reform issue in the period. Even Catholic women members seem to have endorsed this reform. The campaign failed to get Labour Party backing but it won over some local councils and helped bring the issue to the attention of working-class men and women inside and outside the movement.

In the birth control campaign, labour women proved their ability to unite behind a political cause and pursue it with tenacity and resourcefulness. But the campaign also revealed the drawbacks to gender separation and male control in labour politics. Shut out of the deliberations and policy-making of the national party, labour women had few opportunities to develop the political skills of bargaining and compromise that might have encouraged them to evaluate their campaign in the context of overall party strategy. They seemed unaware that their birth control proposal could pose a threat to Labour's success at the polls in the time of crisis following the General Strike. Gender separation similarly handicapped male leaders. Immersed in their own political concerns, they treated women members' demands for greater autonomy and women-centered policies as acts of sabotage, instead of reform initiatives from dedicated comrades. They failed to recognize the value to the movement of the organization, propaganda and management skills labour women displayed so prominently in the birth control campaign.

Labour women's struggle to find their place in the national Labour Party and Co-operative movement in the interwar years can be aptly summed up in the phrase 'damned if you do and damned if you don't'. They experienced marginality and defeat when they adopted an acceptably women-centred programme and then asked the male leaders to give it equal weight with the men's agenda. They were no better off when they abandoned their women's focus in the crisis years of the thirties and joined the men in the fight against unemployment and fascism. They enjoyed the comradeship of shared activities, but once they stopped demanding more power, male leaders could safely ignore them. By 1932, only a few exceptional women such as Margaret Bondfield, Susan Lawrence and Ellen Wilkinson appear in the national records. Labour women, as a distinct group, had disappeared from view, leaving male trade unionists in undisputed control of party policy.

It might be tempting to conclude that Labour's failure to make use of the skills and talents of women members in the national party justifies those historians who have ignored women's presence in interwar labour politics altogether. But this book argues that despite women's lack of power, their mass membership had significant implications for British social democracy. The 'engendering' of Labour politics meant that after 1918, anything to do with the health and welfare of working-class women and children tended to be labelled a 'women's issue' and assigned to the 'women's side of the movement' where it had little hope of implementation. When they denied women the power to shape policy and strategy, Labour and Co-operative leaders turned their backs on a broad area of social reform aimed at improving the living conditions of their working-class constituents. The more the male-dominated movement narrowed its political responsibilities to 'masculine' interests in industry, finance, trade, internal party organization and electoral politics, the more remote it became from the changing social and economic concerns of working people. The sad irony for Labour women was that their decision to call for separate-but-equal status to make sure the interests of working-class women and children were included in the party platform, actually weakened their party's commitment to social welfare.

Labour women's conflict with middle-class feminists also left its mark on social democratic politics in Britain. As soon as women were able to join the major political parties, the prewar co-operation between organized working-class women and middle-class feminists came to an end. After 1918, the Labour Party and the various feminist groups grew suspicious of each other's political motives and showed no interest in renewing their prewar alliance. Women activists had to make what was in effect a binding choice between their class and gender interests. This division, like that between the sexes in the Labour Party, weakened the post-suffrage initiative for reforms in the interests of working-class women. The two classes of women reformers campaigned independently for the same welfare programmes and were equally ineffective. The acrimonious fight over protective legislation for women workers cemented the split, leaving labour women convinced that feminists were hostile to the workers' movement and feminists scornful of the patriarchal Labour Party. In 1918 British social democracy had an opportunity to embrace the cause of women. By the thirties, if not earlier, the moment had passed.

Labour women's disappointing record of achievement in the national organizations stands in clear contrast to what they were able to accomplish in local labour politics and municipal government. Separate-but-equal gender relations worked well in local parties where the separation of the sexes was less rigid and the imbalance of power less extreme than in the national party structure. The main thrust of women's activities in local parties and co-operative societies was to transform labour politics from an adult male preoccupation to a more inclusive family and neighbourhood concern. Children's classes and Christmas parties, family outings and choirs, jumble sales and peace marches may not fit the conventional definition of effective party politics but they brought labour families together, educated a new generation of socialists and built bridges between the party and the community.

Labour women made their most visible and enduring contribution to social democracy in local government. Here was one area where they could assert their gender identity and serve their class at the same time. Labour voters and male comrades alike found validity in labour women's claim to serve as municipal housekeepers, applying to local government the skills of economy, order, nurture and sympathy, learnt through years of 'making do and mending' as working-class housewives. Labour women guardians and councillors helped sustain Labour's reputation as a reforming party, caring for the needs of urban workers and their families. Women councillors concentrated on small-scale reforms such as wash houses, public baths, playgrounds, libraries, mother and baby clinics and secondary school scholarships which helped working-class families in practical and lasting ways. The first labour women mayors were elected in the interwar years, a clear sign that within a few years of acquiring citizenship, labour women had secured an honoured place in civic life.

The group of fifty women and fifty men who answered the questionnaire or gave interviews for this study suggested and confirmed these conclusions. Their testimony showed a pattern of shared class experience with areas of marked gender difference. They shared working-class family backgrounds ranging from impoverished to comfortable. A majority were first children, and almost half came from families where one or both parents had some connection to the labour movement. In spite of gender, regional, income and oc-cupational differences, they had remarkably similar values and ideas, identifying their political goals in the same broad terms of class amelioration. Women's experience most clearly diverged from men's when they went into the work force where men were likely to be actively involved in trade unions and women were not. Women's political awareness developed from parental teaching and exposure to poverty in their own and neighbours' families. Their time at work did little to change these early impressions. A majority of male respondents had the opposite experience; contacts made through the union and on the job were more likely to shape their political ideas than family members or neighbourhood conditions.

These similarities and differences had a direct bearing on gender relations in labour politics. Women's experiences encouraged them to think of themselves as social reformers and pay less attention to the dynamics of power politics. Men emphasized the struggle to achieve socialism through organization and elections. They wanted the amelioration of their class but were sometimes ambiguous about social welfare reforms which might undermine the work of trade unions. Women were less likely than men to serve as delegates to party conferences, hold local office or win election to municipal councils. When they did, their gender often defined the scope of their responsibilities and the committees on which they served. Women were more likely to describe their accomplishments in terms of improvements they had made to the lives of working-class families and men in length of service and offices held.

Labour women's interwar record of limited success in national party politics and enduring contributions at the grass-roots level was part of a much broader pattern of women's experience in democratic political systems in this period. It remains substantially true today. Men still control the major parties and voters of both sexes consistently demonstrate a reluctantance to endorse women as their national political representatives. This account of British women in working-class politics suggests that these habits of prejudice and exclusion have similar political costs when applied to gender as they do when applied to class or race. What British social democracy might have been if it had succeeded in integrating women's interests and skills into the national movement after 1918 is still waiting to be discovered.

Appendix

The sample of fifty women and fifty men who were labour activists in the interwar years was obtained through advertisements in the local newspapers of twenty-one English towns and cities from Bristol in the southwest to Durham in the northeast. Fifteen of the respondents had been interviewed by local history groups in Bradford, Tottenham and Wolverhampton and they kindly sent me the transcripts. Apart from these fifteen, all the respondents completed questionnaires and nine also gave interviews.

THE QUESTIONNAIRE

1. Please give your name, address, date and place of birth:

2. Tell me a little about your *mother*:
    (a) What was her occupation before marriage?
    (b) What paid work, if any, did she do while you were growing up?
    (c) Which of the following organizations, if any, did she belong to and how actively did she participate? (Give names and dates if possible): (i) a trade union, (ii) a women's guild or other women's organization, (iii) a church or chapel, (iv) a political party?
    (d) Would you describe your mother as any of the following: (i) a socialist, (ii) a feminist, (iii) a conservative, (iv) a person with a strong sense of social justice, (v) too busy bringing up a family to have time for politics?
    (e) Do you remember anything about your mother that you now realize may have influenced your political attitudes?

3. Tell me a little about your *father*:
    (a) What was his main occupation?
    (b) Was he unemployed for any length of time during his working life?
    (c) Which of the following organizations, if any, did he belong to and how actively did he participate? Mention any offices he held. Give names and dates if possible:
        (i) a trade union, (ii) a working men's club, (iii) a church or chapel, (iv) a political party?

(d) Would you describe your father as any of the following:
    (i)   a socialist, (ii) a dedicated trade unionist, (iii) a supporter of women's rights, (iv) a conservative, (v) a person with a strong sense of social justice, (vi) not interested in politics?
(e) Do you remember anything about your father that you now realise influenced your political attitudes?

4.   How would you describe your family's circumstances when you were growing up?
    (a) comfortable (able to afford a few non-necessities like a holiday and a piano),
    (b) adequate for the necessities of food, clothing and shelter,
    (c) a hard struggle for survival?

5.   What was your place in the family?
    (a) first child or first daughter (son)
    (b) somewhere in the middle
    (c) youngest child or youngest daughter (son)

6.   Name the schools you went to; indicate how long you attended each one:
    (a) elementary school/s,
    (b) secondary school/s.
    (c) how old were you when you left school and why did you leave?

7.   Tell me about your work.
    (a) What was your first paid job?
    (b) What has been your main occupation?
    (c) Did you expect to work only until you married? (W)
    (d) How much of your wage did you contribute to the family?

8.   Did you belong to a trade union?
    (a) Which union was it?
    (b) How long were you a member?
    (c) What offices, if any, did you hold?
    (d) Were there men (women) in the union and if so:
        (i)   did they attend meetings regularly?
        (ii)   did they hold office?
        (iii) what did they contribute to the union and its activities?

9.   What was your first experience of labour politics? (Give the date you joined.)
    (a) in the Labour League of Youth,
    (b) in the Co-operative Movement,
    (c) in the ILP,

(d) in the Labour Party (specify if you joined a women's section)
(e) in another organization?

9. What made you decide to join a labour organization?
   (a) Did your parents encourage you?
   (b) Did you go with a friend?
   (c) Did you join through your trade union?
   (d) Was there another reason? Please give it.

10. What did you hope to achieve by taking part in organized labour politics?

11. If you are or have been married, please tell me a little about your husband (wife).
   (a) What was his/her occupation?
   (b) Was he/she a trade unionist? (Give the name of the trade union).
   (c) Was he/she a member of the ILP, the Labour Party or any other socialist or labour or organization?
   (d) Did he/she encourage your political activities?
   (e) Did you take part in labour politics together?
   (f) If you had children, which one of you usually stayed home from meetings to care for the children? Did either one of you give up politics while the children were small?

11. Tell me about your membership in the Co-op, ILP, CP or Labour Party:
   (a) Name the organization(s) of which you were a member.
   (b) How long were you/have you been, an active member (please give dates.)
   (c) List the offices you have held with titles and dates, if you can.

12. Describe the relations between men and women in your local constituency party, co-operative society, ILP or CP branch *in the early days* (1919–45). Was it, (a) an equal partnership, (b) men dominant or (c) women dominant? (Name the organization you are talking about)

13. These are the jobs most commonly done in local labour organizations. Please mark them according to whether they were mostly done by men (M), by women (W), or by both sexes (MW) in your experience. Add your own comments if you have any:
   (a) proposing and speaking on resolutions and candidates
   (b) committee work,
   (c) canvassing,
   (d) fundraising,
   (e) organizing social events,
   (f) standing for local party or local government office,

(g) marches and demonstrations

(h) making the tea

14. If you were active in a local party with a separate women's section or a local co-op with a women's guild, how was the work divided between the men and the women?

15. Here is a list of political issues from the period 1919–1945. Please indicate which were the most important to you *at that time* by numbering them from 1 (most important) to 9 (least important).

(a) education to age 16 years for all children

(b) improved care for mothers and infants

(c) unemployment and the Means Test

(d) more and better housing

(e) national medical service

(f) the United Front and relations with the communist party

(g) birth control information for all who wanted it

(h) some form of family allowance

(i) equal pay.

If I have missed an issue that was especially important to you, please add it.

16. Did you ever serve as a representative of the Labour Party, the Co-operative Party or the ILP in local government? Please give dates.

(a) Were you on the Board of Guardians or a public assistance committee?

(b) Were you elected to the local county borough, municipal borough, urban district or other council?

(c) If you were a local councillor, which committees did you serve on?

(d) Which committees did Labour women councillors usually serve on?

(e) What did you feel you were able to accomplish for working people through local government service?

17. Describe the community where you lived and were active in politics anytime during the period: (1919–1945). Was it:

(a) mostly working class,

(b) working and middle classs,

(c) mostly middle class?

What were the main industries in the town?

Was their strong or weak support for the following:

(a) trade unionism,

(b) the co-operative store and activities,

(c) the local ILP,

(d) the Labour Party,

(e) the National Unemployed Workers' Movement?

Did the area elect:

(a) a Labour MP,
(b) a Labour council,
(c) any women councillors, in the interwar period?

18. Did you ever take part in any of the following? Give dates and any
     other details you can remember:
     (a) an industrial strike,
     (b) a march for peace,
     (c) a march for the hungry and unemployed,
     (d) a demonstration against high rents,
     (e) any other public political activity such as a demonstration, march
          or petition campaign?

19. Looking back to the 1920s and 1930s, can you explain why you and
     others became dedicated activists in the labour cause? Which of the
     following best describes (i) your own motivation (I) (ii) other women's
     (W) and (iii) other men's (M)?
     (a) ambition for a career in public life which would bring public
          recognition?
     (b) a desire to help the poor and needy?
     (c) a desire to support the interests of the working class?
     (d) a feeling of special responsibility to improve the conditions of the
          working class family, particulary as they related to women and
          children?

21. How successful do you think the Labour and Co-operative Parties
     were in those early days in giving women equal opportunity with men
     to attend national party conferences and stand as candidates for local
     and Parliamentary elections?
     (a) Very successful
     (b) Moderately successful
     (c) Unsuccessful

22. Please add any personal comments or reminiscences.

Notes

INTRODUCTION

1 *Labour Party Report of the Annual Conference* (published London) for 1922, 1925 and 1929 show women members' phenomenal growth. In 1922, there were 100,000 women in 800 sections; in 1925, 200,000 in 1,535 sections and in 1929, just over 250,000 in 1,867 sections.

2 Mrs Fawcett (National Federation of Women Workers) speech at the Labour Party Annual Conference, 1918. *Labour Party Report* (1918) p. 104.

3 *Labour Party Report* (1929) shows that Labour's electoral victory brought nine Labour women into Parliament. This was the high point for Labour women MPs in the interwar years.

4 H. Pelling, *The Origins of the Labour Party* (London: Macmillan, 1954), Ross McKibbon, *The Evolution of the Labour Party, 1910–1924* (Oxford University Press, 1974), K. D. Brown, ed., *The First Labour Party, 1906–1914* (London: Croom Helm, 1985), Ralph Miliband, *Parliamentary Socialism* (London: Merlin Press, 1975) – contain few if any references to women in the party.

5 Details of the sample of men and women activists are set out in the appendix.

1 'THE DOORS ARE OPEN' – WOMEN'S ENTRY INTO LABOUR POLITICS

1 Men's and women's trade union membership peaked around 1920. In that year, there were 1,342,000 women (as opposed to 437,000 in 1914 and 835,000 in 1925) and 7,006,000 men (3,708,000 in 1914 and 4,671,000 in 1925). Source: A. H. Halsey ed., *Trends in British Society since 1900* (London: Macmillan, 1972) p. 123.

2 Government regulation of working-class women in the First World War included separation allowances paid to soldiers' dependents; compulsory job registration; middle-class welfare supervisors; rent control; food rationing; compulsory medical inspection of women suspected of having venereal disease under the Contagious Diseases Act and war savings

committees which told working-class women how to manage their household budgets.

3 David Englander, *Landlord and Tenant in Urban Britain 1835–1918* (Oxford University Press, 1983) p. 208 describes women's participation in rent strikes in Glasgow.

4 *Labour Party Report* (1915) p. 15.

5 Labour's 1918 manifesto, *Labour and the New Social Order* (The Labour Press, 1918) included a section entitled, 'The Complete Emancipation of Women' promising women equal franchise and equal pay, p. 5.

6 Lily Watson, unpublished essay for the Workers' Education Association, 'How I will Vote' *c.* 1921.

7 Barbara Drake, *Women in Trade Unions* (London: Virago Press, 1984) pp. 120, 127.
Joanna Bornat, 'Lost Leaders: Women, Trade Unionism and the Case of the General Union of Textile Workers, 1875–1914' in Angela V. John ed., *Unequal Opportunities* (Oxford and New York: Basil Blackwell, 1986) p. 213.

8 Olive Banks, *Becoming a Feminist: the Social Origins of the First Wave of Feminism* (London: Wheatsheaf Books, 1986) p. 90.

9 Margaret Llewelyn Davies, 'The Alliance of Labour Forces', *The Labour Magazine* May 1921 (BLPES Archives, London School of Economics).

10 Marion Phillips ed., *Women and the Labour Party* (London: Headley Bros., [1918]) p. 11.

11 Margaret Llewelyn Davies, *The Labour Magazine* VII, 2, February 1922.

12 'Report of the Annual Conference of the Women's Labour League' in the *League Leaflet* (March 1913).

13 *Labour Woman* (June 1916) Branch Reports show the involvement of League women on various wartime committees. The Derby branch secretary reported members sitting on 'the war relief committee, the national women's committee, the Belgian relief committee, the local branch of the National Council against Conscription and on the board of the hostel providing dinners for necessitous mothers'.

14 The extent of the support given by the Workers' National Committee to organized labour women's concerns is clear from the J. S. Middleton Correspondence in the Labour Party Archives. (File Nos. 30/2 and 32/3 LP Archives.)

15 The Railway Women's Guild was founded in Crewe in 1900 as a women's support group for the Amalgamated Society of Railway Servants.
Philip Bagwell tells some of the story in *The Railwaymen: a History of the National Union of Railwaymen* (London: George, Allen and Unwin, 1963) pp. 227–8.

16 The available autobiographical and biographical evidence on prewar labour women activists suggests that cross-membership with suffrage organizations was common. Ada Chew, Selina Cooper, Hannah Mitchell, Emma Sproson, Annot Robinson, Helen Crawfurd, Jennie

Baker and Jessie Stephen were all ardent suffragists and members of either the WSPU, the NUWSS or the Women's Freedom League.

17 Branch Reports to the League Annual Conference of 1912; reported in *Labour Woman* (February 1913) p. 12.

18 James Ramsey MacDonald, *Labour Party* (1914) p. 91.

19 Margaret L. Davies, *The Women's Guild and the Co-operative Union Grant, a Plea for Freedom of Speech and Self-Government* (issued by the Central Committee: 1915) p. 8.

20 In 1910, the Women's Co-operative Guild was invited to put the point of view of working class women to the Royal Commission on Divorce. Its findings were published in a pamphlet *Working Class Women and Divorce* (London and New York: Garland Publishing, 1980).

21 *ibid. Statistics of the Enquiry* (pp. 42–3). It is interesting to note that 25 branches with 1,438 members who opposed divorce (presumably because they were Roman Catholic) expressed the opinion that 'while there is divorce, the grounds should be the same for men and women'.

22 *Labour Woman* (February 1913) p. 148.

23 David Marquand, *Ramsey MacDonald* (London: Jonathan Cape, 1977) p. 147.

24 Leslie Parker Hume, *The National Union of Women's Suffrage Societies, 1897–1914* (New York: Garland Publishing Inc., 1982) p. 149.

25 Kier Hardie speaking at the Annual Conference of the Labour Party in 1905 in support of his Women's Enfranchisement Bill. *Labour Party Report* (1905) p. 14.

26 David Howell, *British Workers and the ILP 1888–1906* (Manchester University Press, 1983) p. 334.

27 W. Neal (Bradford) Letter to the *Labour Leader* (2 April 1904).

28 Margaret Bondfield, *Labour Party Report* (1910) p. 76.

29 Katherine Glasier, *League Leaflet* (November 1912).

30 Leonard Woolf attended the Annual Guild Conference in 1915 and appointed the contrast between the hostility among ILP and Labour Party men divided over the war and the more tolerant attitude among the women. *Labour Leader* (6 July 1916).

31 Barbara Drake, *Women in Trade Unions* p. 106.

32 Mrs Margaret Mitchell, interviewed by Tottenham People's History (15 May 1980).

33 Winifred More, letter entitled 'Women in the Industrial World, a Fair Field', *Labour Women* (November 1920) p. 178.

34 Phillip Snowden, letter to the *Keighley News* (1 January 1895). Quoted in Colin Cross, *Phillip Snowden* (London: Bevrie & Rockcliffe, 1966) p. 26.

35 Ethel Snowden, *The Real Women's Party* (London: ILP Publications, 1918) p. 4.

36 The Representation of the People Act of 1918 enfranchised women of thirty and over who were themselves or were married to, local government electors. These had to be occupiers of land or premises with

a yearly value of five pounds. This excluded all occupiers of furnished tenancies such as domestic servants and resident shop assistants.

37 Margaret Llewelyn Davies, *The Vote At Last!* (London: Co-op. Printing Society, 1918) p. 1.
38 Marion Phillips, *Labour Women* (March 1918) p. 265.
39 Mrs Harrison Bell, *Labour Party Report* (1919) p. 144.
40 Lily Watson, North Shields, response to question, 'What do you think was women's special contribution to the Labour movement in this period?' Questionnaire (June 1986) p. 5a.
41 Lily Watson, unpublished essay for the Workers' Education Association, 'Should Flappers Have the Vote' (*c.* 1921).
42 Mrs Fawcett (National Federation of Women Workers) speech at the Labour Party Annual Conference, *Labour Party Report* (1918) p. 104.
43 Arthur Henderson, speech to the Labour Party Annual Conference, *Labour Party Report* (1918) p. 95.
44 *The Daily Herald* (31 March 1919) p. 1.
45 'The Complete Emancipation of Women' in *Labour and the New Social Order* (The Labour Party Press, 1918) p. 5.
46 Numbers of Labour women who were endorsed Labour Party candidates for municipal office are not available. In May 1920, the number of Labour women elected as municipal councillors was 70, county councillors, 7 and urban district councillors, 22. There were 206 Labour women guardians. *Labour Woman* (May 1920) p. 71.
47 *Labour Party Report* (1922) p. 155.
48 Margaret Llewelyn Davies quoted Mr Allen in *The Vote At Last!* p. 6.
49 *ibid.* p. 11.
50 Mary Longman, General Secretary of the WLL, letter to Mr Middleton, secretary of the Labour Party, dated 24 June 1915; reported in the Minutes of the Central London WLL (Labour Party Archives).
51 *Labour Party Report*, 1918 (Appendix 1); the constitution allowed but did not oblige constituency parties to send a woman delegate where the number of women members exceeded 500.
52 Women's Labour League, Executive Committee Minutes (12 October 1917).
53 Marion Phillips, in *Labour Woman* (November 1917) p. 218.
54 Report of the National Conference of Labour Women held at Nottingham in January 1918, *Labour Woman* (February 1918) p. 261.
55 *Labour Woman* (January 1918) p. 253.
56 *ibid.* (April 1918) p. 283.
57 Marion Phillips, ed., *Women and the Labour Party*, p. 13.
58 *Labour Party Report* (1921) gives the number of women in the party as 70,000 (p. 48).
59 *Women's Cooperative Guild Annual Report* (London and Manchester, 1919–20) p. 1.
60 *ibid.* p. 2.
61 *ibid.*

62 Report of the National Labour Women's Conference held at Southport in June 1919, *Labour Woman* (July 1919) p. 81.

63 Hannah Mitchell, *The Hard Way Up: The Autobiography of Hannah Mitchell, Suffragette and Rebel* (London: Virago Limited, 1977) p. 189.

64 Jill Liddington, *The Life and Times of a Respectable Rebel: Selina Cooper 1864–1946* (London: Virago Press, 1984) p. 293.

65 Mrs Ford, South Tottenham Labour Party, interviewed for the People's History of Tottenham (1 November 1977) transcript part II, p. 1.

66 National Conference of Labour Women, May 1921, reported in *Labour Woman* (June 1921) p. 91.

67 Annot Robinson, speech at the Labour Party Annual Conference in 1921, *Labour Party* (1921) p. 154.

68 Speeches by Mr E. Baker (Lambeth North CLP) and Mr H. Edwards (Heyward and Radcliffe Divisional LP) at the LP Annual Conference in 1921. *Labour Party Report* (1921) pp. 155–6.

69 Margaret Bondfield, speech to the LP Annual Conference 1921. *Labour Party Report* (1921) p. 154.

70 Arthur Henderson; *ibid.* p. 156.

71 York, Stockport and Wood Green (London) sections sent resolutions in support of the Manchester Women's Advisory Council's proposed amendments to the LP constitution in relation to the direct election of women to the NEC. Doncaster discussed it but reached no decision and West Willesden (London) minutes did not refer to the subject.

72 Julia Bush, *Behind the Lines; East London Labour 1914–91* (London: The Merlin Press, 1984) argues from the evidence of East London communities that wartime grievances and the increased power of the state produced a major change in the level of popular expectations among the working class.

73 James E. Cronin and Jonathan Schneer eds., *Social Conflict and Political Order in Modern Britain* (New York: Rutgers University Press, 1982) pp. 118–19. Cronin argues for women's prominence in militant political activity and in the local networks of activists who became the core of the new constituency parties in the Labour resurgence after the First World War.

74 *Daily Herald* 31 March 1919 p. 1 and 23 February 1921.

75 *ibid.* 6 May 1919.

76 *The Labour Leader*, vol. 48: 16 (27 November 1919) p. 1.

77 Letter from Margaret Daplyn, Honourary Secretary Leyton WCG, in the *Daily Herald* (13 April 1919) p. 8.

78 Letter from Mrs Escott, Blaenau, Gwent, Abitillery, the *Daily Herald* (13 April 1919) p. 8.

79 'Our Women Councillors, Mrs Noble', in *Labour Woman* (February 1920).

80 E. L. Poulton, speech to the LP Annual Conference 1921. *Labour Party Report* (1921) p. 194.

81 Lily Watson, 'How I will vote', unpublished essay for the WEA, 1921.

82 Mrs Ford, transcript of interview (1 November 1977) p. 3.
83 Mrs Jessie Lynch, a reported interview in *Tottenham Calling* (May 1958) p. 2 and A. J. Lynch, *Autobiography* (Ann Arbor: Microfilms, 1954) pp. 87–8.

2 'THEIR DEVOTION WAS ABOUT EQUAL'–WOMEN AND MEN IN INTERWAR WORKING-CLASS POLITICS

1 The standard histories of the Labour Party, H. R. Pelling, *A Short History of the Labour Party, 1906–1960* (London: Macmillan, 1965), Karl Brand, *A Short History of the Labour Party* (Stanford University Press, 1964) G. D. H. Cole, *A History of the Labour Party from 1914* (New York: Augustus M. Kelley, 1969), make no reference to the influx of women members after the First World War.

2 The autobiographies of working-class women active in some area of labour politics include: Hannah Mitchell, *The Hard Way Up*, Ada Nield Chew, *The Life and Writings of a Working Woman*, Margaret Bondfield, *A Life's Work*. The first two focus on the period of the suffrage struggle before the First World War so there is very little autobiographical material by women active in the interwar years.

3 Of the 50 women activists, 37 answered the questionnaire; 5 were interviewed by the author; 3 by the Bradford Heritage Recording Unit; 3 by the People's History of Tottenham and 2 by John Rowley, a lecturer at Dudley Technical College, Wolverhampton. Of the 50 men, 33 answered the questionnaire; 4 were interviewed by the author; 4 by the BHRU; 4 by the PHT and 4 by Edmund and Ruth Frow for their book, *The Communist Party in Manchester, 1920–1926* (Manchester: North West History Group, CPGB in conjunction with the Working-Class Movement Library, Manchester, n.d.). Lynda Straker interviewed Bas Barker and wrote his account in *Free But Not Easy* (Derbyshire County Council, 1989). Interviews and the questionnaire for women date from 1986; for men from 1990. A copy of the questionnaire is in Appendix A.

4 With overlaps, 68 were in the LP, 23 women were in the WCG, 12 in the ILP and 11 in the CPGB.

5 David Howell, *British Workers and the ILP*, p. 33.

6 Margaret Llewelyn Davies, quoted in J. Gaffin and D. Thoms, *Caring and Sharing: The Centenary History of the Co-operative Women's Guild* (Manchester: Co-operative Union Limited, 1983) p. 20.

7 E. G. Janosik, *Constituency Labour Parties in Britain* (New York: Praeger, 1968) offers a study of CLP leaders in Britain in the sixties, analysing them on the basis of their occupations with no reference to their parental families.

8 Margaret Llewelyn Davies, quoted in *Caring and Sharing* p. 20.

9 Respondents comments quoted in the text will not be footnoted unless they are taken from sources other than the questionnaire and interviews given by the author.

10 Bas Barker and Lynda Straker, *Free But Not Easy*, p. 4.
11 Mrs Ford (Tottenham). From an interview by the People's History of Tottenham (11 January 1977) transcript, p. 3.
12 Mrs Mitchell (Tottenham). From an interview by the People's History of Tottenham (n.d.) transcript p. 12.
13 Lucy Thirkhill (Bradford, Yorks.) Interviewed by the Bradford Heritage Recording Unit (April 1985) transcript A0023/03 p. 59.
14 Anna Dagnell (Liverpool) private letter to author accompanying the questionnaire and dated 25 June 1991.
15 Frank Jackson (Tottenham). Interviewed by the People's History of Tottenham (5 October 1978) transcript p. 1.
16 Alice Onions (Wolverhampton) from John J. Rowley, 'Reminiscences of Alice Onions', *West Midlands Studies* 16, 1983 pp. 30–3.
17 Frank Jackson (Tottenham) transcript p. 2.
18 Bas Barker and Lynda Straker, *Free But Not Easy*, p. 11.
19 Mrs Margaret Mitchell (Tottenham). Interviewed by the People's History of Tottenham, transcript p. 2.
20 Jessie Stephen, 'Submission Is For Slaves' (unpublished autobiography: MSS Ruskin College, Oxford) p. 8.
21 In 1914 there were 357,956 women in trade unions which was approximately 6.3 per cent of the female work force. (Barbara Drake, *Women in Trade Unions*, Table 1.) There were only 30,000 in the Women's Co-operative Guild and 5,000 in the Women's Labour League.
22 Ruth and Edmund Frow talked to Stanley Boulton and Arthur Sheldon and included their short biographies in, *The Communist Party in Manchester, 1920–1926* pp. 51 and 68.
23 Bas Barker and Lynda Straker, *Free But Not Easy* p. 5.
24 During interviews, respondents were often interrupted by neighbours seeking their advice on issues ranging from pensions and rents to the repair obligations of the local council.
25 Lily Watson (North Shields), letter accompanying questionnaire, July 1986.
26 Tom Riley (Tottenham). Interviewed by the People's History of Tottenham (16 December 1978) transcript p. 4.
27 Alec Lipner (Tottenham). Interviewed by the People's History of Tottenham (13 April 1978) transcript p. 1.
28 Mrs Mitchell (Tottenham). Interviewed by the People's History of Tottenham, transcript p. 21.
29 Jessie Stephen, *Submission is for Slaves* p. 14.
30 Gladys Draper (London), interviewed for *Link* (May 1981) 34: 8.
31 Bas Barker and Lynda Straker, *Free But Not Easy* p. 30.
32 *ibid.* p. 31.
33 William Herbert (Tottenham). Interviewed by the People's History of Tottenham (n.d.) transcript p. 4.
34 Arthur Dutton (pseudonym) Bradford. Interviewed by Bradford Heritage Recording Unit (n.d.) transcript p. A0012/02/27.

35 Alec Lipner (Tottenham) transcript p. 13.
36 Frank Jackson (Tottenham) transcript p. 4.
37 Nellie Whitely (Bradford). Interviewed by Bradford Heritage Recording Unit transcript p. A0067/02/24.
38 Golda Barr, interview for *Link* by Jane Mace (April 1981) 35: 8.
39 Violet Fletcher (Wolverhampton). Interviewed by John Rowley (28 September 1982) transcript p. 4.
40 Kier Hardie, *The ILP After Twenty Years* (London: ILP Publications, 1912) p. 6.
41 Violet Fletcher (Wolverhampton) transcript p. 2.
42 Mrs Ford (Tottenham) transcript p. 3.
43 Nellie Whiteley (Bradford). Interview by the Bradford Heritage Recording Unit (BHRU) p. A0067/02/55.
44 Bas Barker and Lynda Straker, *Free But Not Easy*, pp. 33–8.
45 Arthur Dutton (pseudonym) Bradford. Interview by Bradford Heritage Recording Unit transcript p. A0012/02/23.

3 '…BUT THE SEATS ARE RESERVED FOR MEN' – THE GENDER STRUGGLES OF THE TWENTIES

1 Drastic cuts in public expenditure and in the social services were proposed by Sir Eric Geddes in February 1922. The 'Geddes Axe' fell on education, school meals and milk, maternity and child welfare and housing.
Marion Phillips and Margaret Bondfield both referred to a backlash against women. In 1923, Miss Phillips is quoted as saying: 'There is a feeling against women…the reaction against the freedom they have gained is very marked… There is a general feeling that women got too far on.' (Richard W. Hogue, ed., *British Labour Speaks*, (New York: Boni & Liveright, 1925) p. 125).
2 Ralph Miliband, *Parliamentary Socialism*, p. 148.
3 Labour women's numerical growth in the twenties was phenomenal. In 1922, there were 100,000 women in 800 sections; in 1925, approximately 200,000 in 1,535 sections and in 1927, 300,000. (National Agent's report in the *Labour Party Report* for 1922, 1925 and 1927).
4 The Labour Party supported the women's programme for nursery schools and their campaign against maternal mortality. The 1929 manifesto, *Labour and the Nation* p. 34, included a commitment to both of these reforms.
5 A. Caroline Sewell, letter to the Editor in *The Labour Woman* (November 1913) p. 114.
6 Margaret Llewelyn Davies, ed., *Maternity: Letters from Working Women* (London: Virago Press, 1978); first published in 1915.
7 *ibid.* Letter 62, pp. 89–90.
8 *ibid.* Letter 100, p. 129.
9 *ibid.* Letters 25 (p. 52); 32 (p. 59); 69 (p. 93); 91 (p. 115).

10 Jeffrey Weeks, *Sex, Politics and Society: The Regulation of Sexuality since 1800* (New York: Longman, 1981) p. 88.
11 Robert Roberts, *The Classic Slum* (Manchester: Pelican Books, 1973) pp. 200–1.
12 Mrs Ford (Tottenham South Labour Party). Interviewed by the People's History of Tottenham (1 November 1977) transcript p. 4.
13 Women's Co-operative Guild, Central Committee Minutes, 25 January 1923.
14 Ruth Hall, ed., *Dear Dr Stopes* (London: Penguin Books, 1981) pp. 11–46.
15 Peter Fryer, *The Birth Controllers* (New York: Stein & Day Publishers, 1966) p. 257.
16 Women's Co-operative Guild, *Annual Report* (1922–3) p. 22.
17 National Conference of Labour Women, Annual Report in *Labour Woman* (June 1923).
18 Dora Russell, *The Tamarisk Tree*, Vol 1 (London: Virago Press, 1977) p. 17.
19 Marion Phillips, 'Birth Control – A Plea for Careful Consideration', *Labour Woman* (March 1924) p. 34.
20 Dora Russell, *The Tamarisk Tree* p. 172.
21 Mrs Palmer, speech at the National Conference of Labour Women, 1924. Reported in *Labour Woman* (June 1924) p. 96.
22 Dora Russell, *The Tamarisk Tree*, p. 175.
23 Mrs Lane, speech at the NCLW, 1924. Reported in *Labour Woman* (June 1924) p. 96.
24 Mrs Spikey, Pontefract, speech to the NCLW, 1925. Reported in *Labour Woman* (June 1925) p. 123.
25 Mrs Jones of Greenwich, speech to the NCLW, 1924. Reported in *Woman* (June 1924) p. 96.
26 Mrs Lane, *ibid*.
27 Miss Quinn and Mrs Simpson, both Catholics, spoke at the NCLW in 1925. Reported in *Labour Woman* (July 1925) p. 123. There is no evidence in the local section minutes that birth control created outspoken clashes between Catholics and non-Catholics as divorce law reform had done in 1915.
28 Mrs Palmer, speech at the 1924 NLWC. Reported in *Labour Woman* (June 1924) p. 96.
29 Some Labour women had contact with middle-class birth-control organizations. Stella Browne was a socialist and she worked primarily with the New Generation League; Jennie Baker, whose personal campaign to bring birth-control information to working-class women began before the war, was a member of Marie Stopes' Society for Constructive Birth Control.
30 York Women's Section Minutes, 17 June–16 September 1924. (Held in the Archives of the York Public Library.)
31 Minutes of the Standing Joint Committee of Industrial Women's

Organizations, held Thursday, 18 June 1925 (NEC Minutes; BLPES) p. 271.

32 G. D. H. Cole, *History of the Labour Party* pp. 164–5.

33 *Labour Party Report* (Liverpool: 1925) p. 44.

34 The 'three-year rule' was passed at the 1925 Labour Party conference to prevent further discussion on the Communist Party's requests for affiliation. Minutes of a Joint Emergency Meeting of the NEC and the Standing Order committee (Liverpool, 25 September 1925).

35 I have been unable to find statistics giving the number of Roman Catholics in the Labour Party in the interwar years. Members were never asked their religious affiliation. Manchester and Salford and the Liverpool area had large Catholic working-class populations and other north-eastern towns and cities had some Catholics. My guess is that because women were spread all over the country they outnumbered Catholics but I cannot support my assumption with figures.

36 Ramsey MacDonald, NEC Minutes (25 November 1925). NEC Report, *Labour Woman* (October 1926).

37 Labour Party, NEC Minutes, 18 June 1925; 8 September 1925; 12 December 1925.

38 Richard Hoggart, *The Uses of Literacy* (London: Pelican Books, 1958) p. 76. Robert Roberts, *The Classic Slum*, p. 57. Jeffrey Weeks, *Sex, Politics and Society*, p. 167 discusses the 'Grundyism' that existed in the socialist movement alongside a sexual radicalism.

39 York Women's Section Minutes (17 June 1924). Gorton Women's Section minutes 15 January 1929.

40 Barbara Brookes, 'Women and Reproduction, 1860–1939', in Jane Lewis, ed., *Labour and Love: Women's Experience of Home and Family, 1850–1940* (Oxford: Basil Blackwell Press, 1986) pp. 149–67. She presents evidence that the preferred methods of birth control among the women attending clinics that opened in the twenties and thirties were coitus interruptus and the sheath. There were also significant numbers of self-induced abortions. However, Labour women no doubt believed the popular view among medical practitioners that the diaphragm was the safest and best form of female contraceptive – giving control to wives and not to husbands.

41 *Independent Labour Party National Administrative Conference* (London, 1926) p. 34.

42 Dora Russell, speech at the 1926 annual conference of the Labour Party. *Labour Party Report* (1926) p. 201.

43 Mr Horner, Miners' Federation, speech at the Annual Conference of the LP *Labour Party Report* (1926) p. 17.

44 Mrs Lawther, Blaydon District Labour Party, speech at the Annual Conference of the LP *Labour Party Report* (1927) p. 233.

45 Jill Liddington, *Selina Cooper*, p. 334.

46 Betty D. Vernon, *Ellen Wilkinson* (London: Croom Helm, 1982) p. 98. Ellen Wilkinson's opposition to Labour women's demand for birth

control to be given to working-class women at local clinics puzzled her biographer, Betty D. Vernon. She concluded that 'Ellen's aloofness [from the struggle] seems inexplicable except in terms of respect for Roman Catholic opinion in her constituency' but suggests, less convincingly, that she did not fully understand 'the link between poverty and over-population'.

47 Mrs Bamber (NUDAW), speech at the National Conference of Labour Women (Portsmouth, May 1928) *Report of the National Conference of Labour Women* (London, 1928) p. 27.

48 It is interesting to note that, under the editorship of Marion Phillips, *Labour Woman* made no reference to the Minister of Health's memo 153/MCW which represented the modest victory of the birth-control campaign.

49 Linda Ward, 'The Right to Choose: A Study of Women's Fight for Birth Control Provisions', unpublished Dissertation, No. A1673 (University of Bristol: 1981) p. 326.

50 Report on the Central Co-operative Women's Guild, Edmonton, in the *Tottenham and Edmonton Weekly Herald* (15 January 1926 p. 13 and 29 January 1926 p. 2).

51 Report of the Conference on the Giving of Information on Birth Control by Public Health Authorities, held 4 April 1930 (Archives of BLPES, London).

52 *ibid.* Mrs Powell, JP from Reigate described how she organized a group of working women who wanted birth-control information to be given at their local clinic. They drew up a resolution which was presented to the Town Council and 'though it was received with some little surprise, not a single man got up to say a word and it was passed unanimously'.
The *Bradford Pioneer* (9 January 1935) had an article about Councillor Marjorie McIntosh, the daughter of a local Bradford man well known in the Labour movement. She was a member of the Birmingham City Council and 'she won her spurs by a brilliant ten minute speech at the monthly Council meeting on the subject of birth control advice facilities at the public health clinics, which turned what looked like impending defeat into victory for the proposal'.

53 'How Shall Women Live?' in *Labour Woman* (November 1913) pp. 120–1.

54 'The Endowment of Mothers and Children' in *Labour Woman* (1 May 1922) p. 67.

55 Resolution on 'Mothers' Pensions' was defeated with 248 against and 184 in favour after arguments that they would cost 45 million pounds which a Labour Government would not be able to afford. *Labour Party Report* (1923) p. 113.

56 Marion Phillips explained Labour's idea of mothers' pensions as being 'to allow the mother to make a home for her children and to take her if she so desires out of the Labour market'. *Labour Woman* (February 1920) p. 34.

57 Mrs Hood speaking on mothers' pensions at the NCLW in Manchester in 1921. Reported in *Labour Woman* (June 1921) p. 96.
58 Marion Phillips, reporting on the Joint Committee on Mothers' Pensions at the NCLW in 1922. *Labour Woman* (June 1922) p. 94.
59 Eleanor Rathbone pioneered the idea of family endowment in her book, *Equal Pay and the Family*, published in 1917. In 1918, she established a small committee of feminist and Labour Party members called The Family Endowment Committee. President of the NUSEC from 1919, Eleanor Rathbone gradually converted the membership to a commitment to family allowances by linking them to equal pay. In 1924, she wrote *The Disinherited Family* the clearest statement of her views on the subject.
60 Mrs Banbury, speech at the NCLW in 1922. Reported in *Labour Woman* (June 1922) p. 96.
61 Mrs Clayton, Mrs Johnson and Jessie Stephen were all speakers in the debate over mothers' pensions at the NCLW in 1923. Reported in *Labour Woman* (June 1923) p. 92.
62 Marion Phillips reported the views of Labour women correspondents on the 'in-kind versus cash payments' debate in *Labour Woman* (June 1923) p. 92.
63 A Guild resolution on family endowment in 1921 called for mothers' pensions as an immediate measure but added: 'that financial provision for mothers and children as well as for widows can only be satisfactorily dealt with as part of a larger scheme for securing their economic independence by the adoption of the state bonus'. Women's Co-operative Guild *Annual Report* (1920–1) pp. 20–1.
64 Mrs Hood reported the comment by Emil Davies in her speech to the NCLW in 1922. Reported in *Labour Woman* (June 1922) p. 96.
65 Mrs Hooper, speaking at the LP conference. *Labour Party Report* (1923) p. 247.
66 *ibid.*
67 Jessie Stephen, *Labour Party Report* (1923) p. 247.
68 Miss Dorothy Evans (Chislehurst DLP) speech at the LP annual conference in 1925. *Labour Party Report* (1925) p. 192.
69 Mrs Rosalind Moore, *ibid.* p. 280.
70 H. N. Brailsford, *Socialism for Today* (London: ILP Publications, 1925) pp. 78–82.
71 Mrs Adamson, speech at the NCLW in Huddersfield in 1927. *Report of the NCLW* (May 1927) p. 43.
72 Minutes of the meeting of the Standing Joint Committee, 9 February 1928. Also reported in *Labour Woman* (June 1928) p. 82.
73 Mr John Bromley, MP, Locomotive Engineers and Firemen, speech at the LP Conference 1929 during the debate on family allowances. *Labour Party Report* (1929) pp. 164–5.
74 Arthur Henderson, *ibid.*

75 Rhys Davies, NUDAW, speech at the LP Conference, 1930. *Labour Party Report* (1930) p. 177.

76 Somerville Hastings, MP, *Labour Woman* (August 1930) p. 121.

77 Frances Edwards, letter to *Labour Woman* (September 1930) p. 137.

78 Mrs Read, *ibid.*

79 During the debate on the SJC's *Report on Equal Pay for Equal Work* (NCLW, 1930) pp. 42–54, the majority of Labour women trade unionists, including Ellen Wilkinson (NUDAW), Miss Dorothy Elliott (NUGW), Miss Evans (Association of Women Clerks and Secretaries) and Jennie Lee all linked family allowances to equal pay (p. 52).

80 Ernest Bevin, speech at the LP Conference in 1929, *Labour Party Report* (1929) p. 160.

81 Mrs Harrison Bell, speaking at the LP Conference in 1925. *Labour Party Report* (1925) p. 192.

82 Labour women's sections in Norwich, Manchester, Leeds, Durham, Birmingham, Reading, Mid-Bucks, Edmonton and Wood Green were among those sending resolutions to support changes in the constitution to make the women on the NEC directly responsible to the women's sections. *Report of the NCLW* for 1926–30.

83 Dorothy Jewson, *Report of the NCLW* (1928) pp. 61–4.

84 Minutes of the meeting of the NEC of the LP (26 and 27 March 1929) p. 256.

85 Mrs Thomson (Coventry), speech at the LP Conference, *Labour Party Report* (1929) p. 224.

86 Mr F. A. Broad, MP (Edmonton LP), *ibid.* p. 223.

87 Councillor Alex Griffin (Edge Hill DLP), *ibid.* p. 225.

88 Mr W. J. Setchell (Bermondsey and Rotherhythe Trades Councils), *ibid.* p. 222.

89 Mr G. T. Garrett, JP (Cambridgeshire Trades Council and DLP) *ibid.* p. 223.

90 Mrs Thomson, *ibid.* p. 224.

91 Susan Lawrence, *ibid.* pp. 225–6.

92 Mrs Johnson (Norwich WS) speaking at the NCLW in May 1930. *Report of the NCLW* (1930) p. 58.

93 Mrs Duncan Harris (Croyden WS) *ibid.* p. 60.

94 Marion Phillips, *ibid.* pp. 60–1.

95 J. S. Middleton, B. Ayrton Gould, G. R. Shephard, 'Report on Chief Woman Officer's Department', presented at a meeting of the Organization Sub-Committee (20 April 1932) pp. 262–8.

96 In 1929, there were almost 250,000 women members. Organized on the basis of one delegate for every 500 members, women would have had a substantial representation at party conferences and a significant block vote.

97 Stella Browne, quoted in Linda Ward, 'The Right to Choose', p. 150.

98 Labour Party Organizers' Reports for the early thirties contain many

examples of sections reduced to less than twenty members from earlier highs of one hundred or more.

4 'A SEX QUESTION OR A CLASS QUESTION?' – LABOUR WOMEN AND FEMINISM IN THE TWENTIES

1 The other joint campaigns were: divorce law reform; anti-sweating; national care of maternity; payment of maternity benefit directly to mothers.
2 Harold Smith, 'Sex versus Class: British Feminists and the Labour Movement, 1919–1929', *The Historian* Vol. XII (December 1985): 23.
3 *Labour Party Report* (1923) p. 60.
4 Executive Committee Minutes, NUSEC, 25 January 1923. (NUSEC records are in the Fawcett Library, London.)
5 *Labour Party Report* (1925) p. 295.
6 SJC issued a circular in 1921 advising organizations of working women in the Labour and Co-op. movements not to attach themselves to 'non party' women's organizations or to work with them. *Labour Party Report* (1922) p. 66.
7 Brian Harrison, *Prudent Revolutionaries* (Oxford: Clarendon Press, 1987) p. 107.
8 Kathleen Courtney, Charlotte Despard, Helen Pease, Katherine Glasier and Catherine Marshall were among the socialist feminists who left the NUWSS after the war to join the international peace movement or to become active in non-party work in the interests of the working class.
9 *NUSEC Annual Report* (London, 1919).
10 Harrison, *Prudent Revolutionaries*, p. 147.
11 Annual Report 1925, *Women's Leader* (May 1925) XVII No. 15.
12 Harrison, *Prudent Revolutionaries*, p. 107 mentions that Eleanor Rathbone's closest friends and associates were women Liberals.
13 Executive Committee Minutes, NUSEC (25 September 1924).
14 Selina Cooper in an undated letter to the Open Door Council wrote: 'As a working woman I am proud of the ODC because it says clearly what it wants and it is not prepared to stand aside at the will of social reformers who think other things more important.' (ODC records are in the Fawcett Library, London.)
15 Executive Committee Minutes, 1922–30, NUSEC.
16 *ibid.* 13 November 1924.
17 *Labour Party Report* (1925) p. 295.
18 Jill Liddington, *Selina Cooper* p. 292.
19 Mass Observation Archive, University of Sussex, 'Voluntary Associations' (Box 41) 18 November, 1937. The observer described the members as 'a type above the artisan, many of them with fur coats'.
20 Ellen Kendall, Questionnaire completed March 1985.
21 National Conference of Labour Women, June 1925. Report in *Labour Woman* (July 1925) p. 85.

22 *Labour Woman* (May 1916) p. 8.

23 The dismissals of married women employees by the London County Council and Susan Lawrence's championship of the women cleaners were discussed in *Labour Woman* (March 1922) p. 7.

24 Open Door International, Resolutions adopted for the Third Conference in Prague (July 1933) p. 5. (ODI archives are in the Fawcett Library, London.)

25 *NUSEC Annual Report* (1929) p. 1.

26 SJC pamphlet, 'The Employment of Married Women', published in *Labour Woman* (1 March 1922) p. 35.

27 War Cabinet Committee on Women in Industry interviews held on 4 October 1918. Mr F. H. Greenhalgh of the chemical industry reported: 'The men are beginning to contend that they ought to be paid higher wages and thus enable them to keep their wives and children at home.' Ministry of Labour File 5 (Public Record Office: London).

28 'The Employment of Married Women', in *Labour Woman* (March 1922) p. 35.

29 National Conference of Labour Women (June 1925) reported in *Labour Woman* (July 1925) p. 121.

30 *Report of the NCLW* (June 1932) pp. 107–8.

31 Report of the above conference in *Labour Woman* (July 1932) p. 105.

32 Dorothy Elliott, speaking at the National Conference of Labour Women in 1923. Report of the conference in *Labour Woman* (June 1923) p. 89.

33 Mrs Palmer, *ibid.*

34 The resolution was sent on 28 February 1923. It was printed in *Labour Woman* (March 1923) p. 32.

35 Annot Robinson (Manchester Central Women's Advisory Committee) speaking at the National Conference of Labour Women in 1923. Report in *Labour Woman* (June 1923) p. 89.

36 Emma Sproson (Wolverhampton Women's Section) speaking at the National Conference of Labour Women in 1925. Report in *Labour Woman* (July 1925) p. 121.

37 Monica Whately speaking at the National Conference of Labour Women in 1930. *Report of the NCLW* (June 1930) p. 48.

38 Dorothy Elliott, speaking to the National Conference of Labour Women in 1923. Report in *Labour Woman* (June 1923) p. 89.

39 Annot Robinson, *ibid.*

40 Jesse Stephen speaking to the National Conference of Labour Women, 1925. Report in *Labour Woman* (July 1925) p. 121.

41 Mrs Hammett, a Labour representative on the Manchester Board of Guardians used this phrase in a reply to Mrs E. D. Simon, an ex-Lady Mayoress of Manchester who was a strong supporter of married women's right to work. Article, 'Wives as Wage Earners' published in the *Manchester City News* (9 July 1927) p. 2.

42 Mrs Ward (Crewe Central) speaking to the National Conference of Labour Women in 1932. *Report of the NCLW* (June 1932) pp. 107–8.

43 Mrs Ball, a member of the Manchester Board of Guardians replying to Mrs E. D. Simon. *Manchester City News* (9 July 1927) p. 2.

44 Beatrice Webb wrote the Minority Report for the Committee on Women in Industry set up by the War Cabinet in 1918. *The Labour Gazette* (May 1919).

45 *ibid.*

46 *ibid.*

47 Labour Party, *Labour and the New Social Order* (London: 1918) p. 8.

48 Ellen Wilkinson, commenting on the 'Report on Equal Pay for Equal Work' at the National Labour Women's Conference in 1930. *Report of the NCLW* (June 1930) p. 43.

49 SJC publication, 'The Position of Wage-Earning Women', in *Labour Woman* (June 1924) p. 99.

50 Mrs Lee moved and Mrs Gaines seconded the resolution, York LP Women's Section Minutes (11 March 1930).

51 Ellen Wilkinson speaking to the National Conference of Labour Women in 1930 on equal pay. *Report of the NCLW* (June 1930) p. 43.

52 Dorothy Elliott, *ibid.* p. 44.

53 Harrison, *Prudent Revolutionaries*, p. 312.

54 Eva Hubback discussing 'new feminism' in *Time and Tide* (20 August 1926) p. 761.

55 Harrison, *Prudent Revolutionaries*, p. 110.

56 Mrs Claire Tamplin gave an address on birth control to the North Tottenham women's section on 20 January 1926. Recorded in the minutes taken from the Stirling House Group Labour Party Women's Sections.

57 Nancy Cott, *The Grounding of Modern Feminism* (New Haven: Yale University Press, 1987) p. 123.

58 Beatrice Webb, 'Minority Report on Women in Industry', Parliamentary Papers, 1919 (Cmd 135) p. 283.

59 *Report of the NUSEC* (1919) p. 2.

60 Sheila Lewenhak, *Women and Trade Unions*, London: Ernest Benn Ltd., 1977) p. 179.

61 *ibid.* p. 211 on the Two Shift system. Also *Labour Woman* (January 1930) pp. 6–7.

62 Lewenhak, *Women and Trade Unions*, p. 185. She mentions that 'only 4% of unemployed women as compared with 10% of unemployed men received benefit' and '34% of women's claims as compared to 15% made by men were disallowed'.

63 The Labour Party's Factory Act of 1924, in addition to the provisions listed in the text also included such welfare provisions as washing facilities and seating accommodation as well as improved light, warmth and ventilation. Details from *Labour Woman* (June 1923) p. 90.

64 The NUSEC Executive Committee Minutes (July 1924) p. 2.

65 Lewenhak, *Women and Trade Unions*, pp. 185–6; Nancy Cott, *Modern Feminism*, pp. 131–2.

66 Ellen Wilkinson, deputation to J. R. Clynes. Report in *Labour Woman* (January 1930) p. 7.

67 Vivien Hart, paper presented to the Sixth Berkshire Conference on the History of Women (June 1984): 'Defining the Alternatives: Class and Gender in Minimum Wage Policy', p. 14.

68 Mrs Wignall, speaking at the National Conference of Labour Women on the subject of protective legislation. *Report of the NCLW* (1930) p. 51.

69 *Report of the NUSEC* (1927–8) lists the reasons for the split over protective legislation. Eleanor Rathbone's policy won by only one vote.

70 Mrs E. M. White of the Radlett Constituency Party, Radlett Herts wrote a long letter to the *Daily Herald* on 14 February 1929, p. 4, criticizing Dorothy Elliott for supporting protective legislation while professing her support for sexual equality.

71 Dora Russell, speaking at the National Conference of Labour Women in 1930 explained that: 'Maternity legislation is not the same as protective legislation since it deals with women workers as mothers, not as women. *Report of the NCLW* (June 1930) p. 49.

72 Mrs Porteus put the ILP point of view on protective legislation. *ibid.* p. 48.

73 Open Door Council, 'Women and the Right to Work in the Mines' (London: 1928) ODI records, Fawcett Library.

74 ODI, Draft Proposal Second Conference, Stockholm (August 1931) p. 10.

75 ODI, Resolution Adopted Third Conference, Prague (July 1933).

76 Cott, *Modern Feminism*, p. 125.

77 Article, 'Pet Bogey of Exteme Feminism' *Labour Woman* (1 March 1929) p. 39 contains Labour women's protective legislation arguments and, according to Nancy Cott, they are similar to those used by the NCL and the American WTUL. Cott, *Modern Feminism*, p. 127.

78 Barbara Drake, 'Middle Class Women and Industrial Legislation' in *Labour Woman* (1 August 1924) p. 123 accused her middle-class opponents of a desire to return to *laissez-faire* capitalism as did the leaders of the NCL. Cott, *Modern Feminism*, p. 125.

79 Pauline Newman, quoted in Cott, *Modern Feminism*, p. 127.

80 Marion Phillips in *Labour Woman* (1 September 1929) p. 136.

81 Elisabeth Christman, quoted in Cott, *Modern Feminism*, p. 127.

82 Mrs Bell Richards in *Labour Woman* (1 February 1927) p. 21.

83 Ellen Wilkinson's private member's factory bill introduced in 1926 was lost.

84 Marion Phillips and Elizabeth Abbott of the ODC debated the issue of protective legislation in a BBC radio broadcast on 5 February 1929. Marion Phillips argued that equal pay was also protective legislation while Elizabeth Abbott asked why nurses could work at night if industrial workers could not.

85 The international bodies, including the International Socialist Organization, continued to support protective legislation for women. Some

modifications began to appear in the thirties. In 1933, the Montevideo Convention of the ILO deprecated any restrictions on shiftwork for women and removed distinctions for workers based on their sex. Lewenhak, *Women and Trade Unions*, p. 212.

86 The non-union women who spoke on the protective legislation issue tended to come from textile areas of Lancashire, like Mrs Wignall (cotton operative, Preston) and Mrs Aughton (Nelson Weavers' Association).

87 Barbara Drake, *Labour Woman* (1 August 1924) p. 123.

88 Article, 'Pet Bogey of Extreme Feminism' in *Labour Woman* (1 March 1929) p. 39.

89 Article, 'Equality, Real and Pretended' in *Labour Woman* (1 January 1929) p. 5.

90 Marion Phillips in *Labour Woman* (1 February 1927) p. 21.

91 Mrs Corner, speaking to the National Conference of Labour Women in 1930. *Report of the NCLW* (June 1930) p. 49.

92 Mrs Wignall, *ibid.* p. 51.

93 Monica Whately, *ibid.* p. 89.

94 Cott, *Modern Feminism*, p. 142.

95 *Report of the NCLW* (June 1930) p. 58.

96 Manchester Women's Advisory Council, resolution (January 1935).

97 According to the minutes, Barbara Ayrton Gould and Dorothy Jewson resigned from the NUSEC executive committee in January 1926. Selina stayed in touch until at least 1945 (Liddington, *Selina Cooper*, footnote 4, page 515). Monica Whately also stayed in the ODC, an affiliation that almost lost her her Parliamentary candidacy in 1931.

98 In 1929, in response to a request by the NUSEC to take part in a deputation to Ramsey McDonald on the question of birth control, the SJC secretary replied: 'She did not think that they could take part in a deputation of this kind.' NEC Minutes (14 March 1929).

99 Annot Robinson died in 1925; Emma Sproson in 1936; Jennie Baker does not appear in the records after 1929; clearly few of the suffragist generation continued to play an active political role into the thirties.

5 'HELPING OTHERS' – WOMEN IN LOCAL LABOUR POLITICS, 1919–1939

1 Lily Watson, unpublished essay for the Workers' Education Association, 1921, p. 3.

2 Women's Co-operative Guild, *Annual Report* for 1920–1, p. 16 and 1928–9, p. 16.

3 Margaret Llewelyn Davies, 'The Woman With the Basket' in *The Irish Economist* (February 1922) VII, 2, p. 14 (BLPES Archives: London).

4 ILP Membership 1927 (British Library of Politics, Economics and Society: ILP Collection) Microfiche #64).
CPGB figures from Susan Bruley, 'Socialism and Feminism Among

Women in the Communist Party 1920–1939, (PhD. dissertation Senate House, University of London: 1980) p. 132.

5 Report of the NCLW (1928) p. 12.
6 Susan Bruley, 'Socialism and Feminism Among Women in the Communist Party', p. 123.
7 Doncaster Women's Section, Minutes, 8 January 1923.
8 Dorothy Russell (Salford, Lancs.) questionnaire, November 1984.
9 Mrs Ford (Tottenham), interview transcript p. 2.
10 Hettie Bower (Hackney, North London) interview September 1986. Nellie Logan (Manchester) questionnaire, July 1986.
11 Hilda Nicholas (Bristol) interview, September 1986.
12 Susan Bruley, 'Socialism and Feminism Among Women in the Communist Party', p. 123.
13 Lily Watson, undated letter attached to questionnaire, July 1986.
14 Raymond South, *Heights and Depths: Labour in Windsor* (Hayes, Middx.: Colophon Press, 1985) p. 22.
15 Stockport Women's Section, Minutes, 19 November 1929.
16 Manchester Women's Advisory Council, Minutes, 17 January 1932.
17 York Women's Section Minutes, 14 March 1933.
18 Doncaster Women's Section, Minutes, 3 June 1925.
19 West Willesden Women's Section, Minutes, 8 March 1926, 14 June 1926, 4 October 1926, 8 November 1926, 22 February 1927.
20 York Women's Section, Minutes, 1 April 1924.
21 Stockport, Bilston (Manchester), Neward, Wood Green (London), York and Doncaster women's sections organized 'Hands Off China' committees in 1927.
22 Stockport Women's Section, Minutes, 1 November 1928.
23 Dorothy Berry (Rusholme, Manchester) recalled in a letter accompanying her questionnaire (May 1986), how she attended the Platt Lane Guild with her mother and went to co-op. children's classes. She also described the Guild's celebration of International Day. She dressed as a Belgian and presided over a mock meeting of co-operative presidents.
24 *Report of the NCLW* (1927) p. 17.
25 Jarrow Division of the Hebburn Labour Party, 14 April 1925. Report from the women's section.
26 Mrs Margaret Mitchell, first interview by People's History of Tottenham (15 May 1980) transcript p. 8.
27 *ibid.* second interview (21 May 1980) p. 12.
28 Florence Widdowson in *ILP Annual Conference Report* (1925) p. 107.
29 Mr G. T. Garrett (Cambridgeshire Trades Council and District Labour Party), Mr F. A. Broad, MP (Edmonston LP), Councillor Alex Griffin (Edge Hill DLP), all spoke at the Labour Party National Conference in 1929. *Labour Party Report* (1929) pp. 224–5.
30 Raymond South, *Heights and Depths*, pp. 22–3.
31 Extracts from descriptions of women Labour candidates taken from the ILP paper, *The Bradford Pioneer* (22 October 1926) p. 4.

32 Government decentralization was probably at its height in the twenties. The Local Government Act of 1929 was an attempt to reassert central control. The Boards of Guardians were replaced by Public Assistance Committees whose members were not directly elected but chosen by the largely Tory county councillors. The government also asserted its right to ignore the wishes of local elected representatives in cases where local spending exceeded the income from rates.

33 Noreen Branson, *Poplarism, 1919–1925* (London: Lawrence and Wishart, 1979) p. 6.

34 Gillingham Women Citizens in Council, report in the *Chatham, Rochester and Gillingham News* (26 January 1923) p. 4.

35 Bilston LP Women's Section, Minutes, 12 June 1929.

36 Hannah Mitchell, *Newton Heath Free Gazette* (5 March 1928) p. 2.

37 Bilston LP Women's Section, Minutes, 14 May 1930.

38 *ibid.* 8 April 1931.

39 Jessie Stephen, 'Submission is for Slaves', pp. 90–2.

40 *ibid.* p. 91.

41 Doncaster LP Women's Section, Minutes, 12 January 1923.

42 Hannah Mitchell, Manifesto, *To the Electors of Newton Heath Ward* [1932].

43 Geoffrey Mitchell ed., *The Hard Way Up: The Autobiography of Hannah Mitchell, Suffragette and Rebel* (London: Virago Press, 1977) p. 207.

44 *ibid.* p. 215.

45 Pat Hollis, *Ladies Elect: Women in English Local Government, 1865–1914* (Oxford: Clarendon Press, 1987) pp. 294–5.

46 Geoffrey Mitchell, *The Hard Way Up*, p. 235.

47 Margaret Llewelyn Davies, ed., *Life As We Have Known It* (New York: Norton Library, 1975) p. 98.

48 Bradford Board of Guardians, Minutes, 1919–1926. No women sat on the board's finance committee in this period.

49 Tottenham Urban District Council, Maternity and Child Welfare Committee Minutes, report for 1921.

50 *Chatham Observer*, 12 June 1920, p. 4.

51 *Barking Chronicle*, 7 January 1921, p. 1.

52 *Chatham, Rochester and Gillingham Observer*, 27 January 1939, p. 11.

53 Jarrow and Hebburn LP, Minutes 5 April 1928.

54 Ruth Wild (Pudsey, Yorks.) questionnaire, August 1986.

55 Geoffrey Mitchell, *The Hard Way Up*, p. 215.

56 Mrs Kathleen Chambers, reference in *The Bradford Pioneer*, 22 October 1926, p. 4.

57 *Tottenham Calling* (June 1950) Vol. 3, No. 5 p. 2.

58 *Bradford Pioneer* (22 October 1926) p. 4.

59 G. D. H. Cole, *History of the Labour Party*, pp. 447–8.

60 Women's Co-operative Guild, *Annual Report* for 1920–1 p. 16 and 1928–9 p. 16.

61 Mrs Fawcett, Mrs Jessie Clarke and Mrs Chard were all featured in a

series entitled, 'Our Women Councillors' in *Labour Woman* each month of 1920.

6 'DOING OUR BIT TO SEE THAT THE PEOPLE ARE NOT DRAGGED DOWN' – CLASS STRUGGLE IN THE THIRTIES

1 In 1919, Labour women in conference passed a resolution asking for the right to elect their own NEC representatives at their own conference. (National Conference of Labour Women Report: 1919, p. 32.) In 1929, they asked for their conference to be made an 'official conference of the Labour Party' with the right to submit three resolutions to the annual conference. (*Report of the NCLW*, 1929, p. 34.) In 1931, they repeated the 1929 request for a conference with power to participate in policy-making. (*Report of the NCLW*, 1931, pp. 31–2.)

2 *Labour Party Report* (1936) p. 49.

3 *Report of the NCLW* (1930) p. 61.

4 Labour Party, National Executive Committee Minutes, 26–7 February 1930.

5 General Purposes Committee of the Standing Joint Committee of Industrial and Political Organizations (SJC) Minutes, 8 May 1930.

6 SJC Minutes, 11 April 1935. An appeal for funds for women parliamentary candidates was sent to the sections in December 1934. By April 1935, only seven pounds, nineteen shillings had been received.

7 Mrs Hood, Chairman's Address, *Report of the NCLW* (1927) p. 3.

8 Edna Falkingham, speech to the Annual Labour Party Conference (*Labour Party Report*: 1937) p. 167.

9 Dorothy Elliott, speech to the NCLW, *Report of the NCLW* (1936) p. 47.

10 Leah Manning, speech to the NCLW, *Report of the NCLW* (1932) p. 65.

11 Cost of Living Debate, NCLW, *Report of the NCLW* (1938) pp. 92–3.

12 Men and women in the Labour Party continued to refer to the approaching European war in the late thirties in the same terms as the First World War, as a fight between capitalists for world markets.

13 Mrs Horrabin (Peterborough DLP), speech to the NCLW, *Report of the NCLW* (1932) p. 45.

14 Mrs Paton (Rushcliffe DLP), *ibid.*

15 Margaret Bondfield, speech to the NCLW, *Report of the NCLW* (1932) p. 60.

16 NCLW, *Report of the NCLW* (1932) p. 17.

17 Mrs Lane (ILP), speech to the NCLW, *Report of the NCLW* (1932) p. 61. ILP women staged a public demonstration against Margaret Bondfield at the conference, booing and hissing her. This was at the height of bad relations between the ILP and the LP over a number of issues, including protective legislation, and only months before the ILP dissaffiliation vote in November. The background of tension may explain why the

conference rallied to support Margaret Bondfield and refused to consider her responsible for the workings of the anomalies regulations.

18 Annie Hambley (ILP) *ibid.* p. 59.

19 SJC Report, *Married Women in Industry*, p. 40 (NEC Minutes, May 1935).

20 *Labour Woman* (March 1934) p. 39. Mary Sunderland announced that the competition on 'Should Married Women Take Paid Employment' had 'evoked a bigger response than any competition in the *Labour Woman.*'

21 Mrs E. E. Mann (Enfield) essay on 'Should Married Women Take Paid Employment', *Labour Woman* (April 1934) p. 56.

22 Mrs Margaret Tarr (Hornchurch) *ibid.*

23 *ibid.*

24 Miss H. M. Rowe (Stretford), *Labour Woman* (April 1934) p. 57.

25 *ibid.*

26 Mrs Gleadhill (Philadelphia), *ibid.*

27 Editorial, 'Woman – Where She Stands Today; What She Has Paid; Was it Worth It?' in *Woman* (5 June 1937) p. 7.

28 *ibid.*

29 There are occasional hints of regional tensions in the party records. At the 1936, Annual Conference, when Ellen Wilkinson appealed to the NEC to lead the Hunger Marches and organize the unemployed, Mrs Lucy Middleton, a prospective parliamentary candidate for Sutton, Plymouth, urged her to go and preach her message to the men and women voters in Epsom (a fast-growing suburb of London) and try to convince them of the plight of the unemployed. *Labour Party Report* (1936) p. 223.

30 Department Committee of the Ministry of Health, 'Report on Maternal Mortality', *Labour Woman* (October 1930) p. 155.

31 Alderman Rose Davies, speech to the NCLW, *Report of the NCLW* (1931) p. 101. She said: 'She wanted that big Conference of mothers to say to the Minister of Health (Labour minister, Arthur Greenwood) that he had done good work up till now, but mothers were dying and they wanted a speeding up with regard to the persons concerned so that they could see the beginning of a National Maternity Service.'

32 Mary Sutherland, 'Class Distinction in Health', *Labour Woman* (August 1936) p. 114.

33 SJC Report, 'Creating a C3 Nation', presented to the NCLW in 1933, *Report of the NCLW* (1933) p. 50.

34 SJC Report, 'Nutrition and Food Supplies – Does Malnutrition Exist?' Presented to the NCLW in 1936, *Report of the NCLW* (1936) p. 52.

35 Mrs Bocking (Scunthorpe WS), speech to the NCLW, *Report of the NCLW* (1936) p. 44.

36 Dr Edith Summerskill (Tottenham – Green Lanes WS); *ibid.*

37 Barbara Brookes, 'Abortion in England, 1919–1939', Ph.D. Dissertation, Bryn Mawr College: 1981 (printed by University Microfilms Internation 1987) p. 15. Brookes quotes from Marie Stopes, *Mother*

England – A Contemporary History (London: John Dale, Sons and Daniel-son, 1929) p. 183: 'I have had as many as twenty thousand requests for criminal abortion from women who did not even know it was criminal… In a given number of days one of our travelling clinics received only thirteen applications for scientific instructions in the control of conception, but eighty demands for criminal abortion.'

38 Brookes, 'Abortion in England', pp. 50–2. Progressive members of the medical profession wanted to stop the loss of life and the injury to women caused by the abortion laws. Eugenicists were interested in legal abortion as a way of stopping the breeding of the unfit.

39 Brookes, 'Abortion in England', p. 86.

40 *ibid.* p. 128.

41 *ibid.*

42 *ibid.* p. 136.

43 *ibid.* p. 135.

44 Women's Co-operative Guild *Annual Report* (Hartlepool, 1934) p. 23. The resolution calling for the legalisation of abortion was moved by the Blackhorse branch and seconded by Elmers End. It was passed by 1,340 votes to 20.

45 SJC Minutes (16 November 1934 and 14 March 1935). The latter entry read: 'The secretary reported that she had just received a statement on behalf of the Socialist Medical Association in relation to the resolution remitted to the Committee from the NEC of the Labour Party. She proposed to circulate it to the members of the Committee. It was further agreed that the Secretary should ascertain the membership of the Socialist Medical Association and its composition.'

46 There is no evidence of any interest in the abortion issue among the Party's women's sections. Available minutes contain no mention of the subject. One more reason for the lack of interest might be that many Labour women in the mid-thirties were beyond child-bearing age.

47 Sarah Seed, a respondent for this study who had been a Yorkshire woollen weaver, blacklisted after the 'More Looms Strike' in 1932, remembered the visit of the means test investigator to her home: 'I remember one time when he came in here and wanted to look at our Co-op savings book. We'd took some money out to pay a gas bill and, do you know, he wanted to see the gas bill to make sure. Ooh, I was that mad. I can get angry now just thinking about it.' The incident was reported in an article in the *Lancashire Evening Telegraph* (11 December 1984) p. 8.

48 Walter Greenwood's novel, *Love on the Dole* (London: Penguin Books, 1974) gives the best account of the effects of the Means Test on family life.

49 Miss Kate Manicom (Transport and General Workers' Union), speech to the NCLW, *Report of the NCLW* (1932) p. 57.

50 Mr A. E. Eyton (AEW), speech to the Annual Party Conference of the Labour Party. *Labour Party Report* (1932) p. 173.

51 Mrs Dollar (London Labour Party), speech to the NCLW, *Report of the NCLW* (1932) p. 58.
52 Ben Tillett, speech to the Annual Party Conference of the Labour Party. *Labour Party Report* (1932) p. 173.
53 Jill Liddington, *Selina Cooper*, p. 381.
54 *ibid.* p. 380.
55 Jim Fyrth, ed., *Britain, Fascism and the Popular Front* (London: Lawrence and Wishart, 1985) p. 19.
56 Nellie Jackson, a Labour woman activist from Shipley, East Yorkshire recalled how she and Jennie Lee spoke at a fundraising rally for the Spanish republicans in 1937 at the Keighley Mechanics Institute. They raised three hundred pounds at that one rally. (Questionnaire: November 1984.)
57 Sue Bruley, 'Women Against War and Fascism' in Jim Fyrth ed., *Britain, Fascism and the Popular Front*. Bruley points out that the first Briton to die in Spain was a woman, Felicia Brown, a member of the St Pancras branch of the CPGB. Altogether 100 other British women went to Spain including nurses sent by the Spanish Medical Aid Committee.
58 G. D. H. Cole made the suggestion that women influenced the local parties in the thirties with particular reference to their ethical stance on war. G. D. H. Cole, *History of the Labour Party*, p. 320.
59 Barbara Ayrton-Gould, speech to the Annual Conference of the Labour Party. *Labour Party Report* (1936) p. 223.
60 No statistics are available but the sample of Labour women activists suggests that the CPGB drew women from both the Labour Party and the ILP in the thirties because of its leadership role in organizing the unemployed and forming a united front. Nina Drongin from Chatham, Hetty Bower from North London and Hilda Nicholas from Bristol all moved over in the thirties. Selina Cooper also began to work with the CPGB in these years.
61 The Labour Party rejected the United Front at the annual conference in 1934, *Labour Party Report* (1934) p. 135, and again in 1937, *Labour Party Report* (1937) p. 156.
62 The Socialist League, led by Stafford Cripps and Aneurin Bevan opposed the Party on the united front, rearmament and aid to Spain. The women organizers' reports indicate that the League gained a following in some women's sections. Several submitted resolutions to the women's conference opposing the expulsion of its leaders.
63 Organizers' Reports (Labour Party Archives, Files 428, 446, 457, 459, 485 and 579). The reports are for 1937 and cover all eight regions: Scotland, Wales, Lancashire and the North-West, Yorkshire and the North-East, Midlands, South-West, South and London. Mrs Elizabeth Andrews was the organizer for Wales (File 485).
64 Mrs M. H. Gibb, organizer for Yorkshire (File 446).
65 Annie Townley, organizer for the South West, reported from Westbury, Wiltshire on 23 October 1937 (File 428).

66 The letter from Mrs F. Johnson, dated 8 July 1937, was included in Mrs Gibb's report from South Yorkshire and signed, 'yours fraternally' (File 459).

67 The letter from Mrs Whipp, the Secretary of the Mexborough Women's Section was dated 9 August 1937. After announcing Mrs Johnson's departure, Mrs Whipp added: 'Last year, we had three women whose husbands were communists but they got tired of trying to put their opinions and have not been this year.' (File 459.)

68 Mrs G. R. Strauss (North Lambeth, DLP), speech to the Annual Labour Party Conference, *Labour Party Report* (1937) p. 161.

69 Miss S. E. Barker (Halifax Women's Section), speech to the NCLW *Report of the NCLW* (1938) p. 42.

70 Miss Auld, *ibid.* p. 43.

71 Herbert Morrison, speech to the Annual Party Conference, *Labour Party Report* (1937) p. 162.

72 Mrs R. Morris (University Labour Federation), speech to the NCLW, *Report of the NCLW* (1938) pp. 44–5.

73 Mr Alex Gossip (Amalgamated Furnishing Trades Association), speech to the Annual Party Conference, *Labour Party Report* (1936) p. 252.

74 Miss Alexander (National Union of Shop Assistants) and Mrs Duncan (Campbell Women's Section, Barking), speeches to the NCLW, *Report of the NCLW* (1938) pp. 44–5.

75 Mr C. A. Adolphe (National Union of Distributive and Allied Workers), speech to the Annual Party Conference, *Labour Party Report* (1937) p. 160.

76 Sue Bruley, 'Women Against War and Fascism: Communism, Feminism and the People's Front' in Jim Fyrth ed., *Britain, Fascism and the Popular Front*, p. 137.

77 Labour Party, NEC Minutes (meeting held on 27 June 1934) announced the expulsion of Jessie Stephen. 'A letter was reported from the SE St Pancras DLP asking that parties should be circularised with details of the expulsion of Miss Jessie Stephen from the Party.' No reason was given but as Jessie had been in the ILP for many years, it is likely that she supported the United Front.

Wood Green DLP and the Women's Sections were threatened with expulsion but withdrew from the Unity Campaign just prior to this meeting.

78 Arthur Henderson, speech to the Annual Labour Party Conference, *Labour Party Report* (1934) p. 154.

79 Appendix on 'War and Peace' to the *Labour Party Report* (1934) p. 8, set out the results of the Peace Ballot held that year. The questions and responses on the ballot were:

   1. Should Great Britain remain a member of the League of Nations? Yes = 11,150,040; No = 357,460; Abstention etc. = 113,265

2. Are you in favour of an all round reduction in armaments by international agreement? Yes = 10,533,826; No = 867,227; Abstentions = 226,712

3. Are you in favour of all round abolition of national military and naval aircraft by international agreement? Yes = 9,592,572; No = 1,697,977

4. Are you in favour of using military measures to stop violence? Yes = 6,827,699. No = 2,346,279

80 Lucy Cox, speech to the Annual Labour Party Conference in 1935, *Labour Party Report* (1935) p. 165.

81 Councillor I. Condon (West Bermondsey Women's Section), speech to the NCLW, *Report of the NCLW* (1938) p. 36.

82 Mrs Philpot (South Ward WS, Croydon) and Miss Minnie Pallister (Bexhill WS), speeches to the NCLW, *Report of the NCLW* (1938) p. 37.

83 Mrs B. Ayrton Gould (NEC, Labour Party), speech to the NCLW, *Report of the NCLW* (1938) p. 31.

84 Quoted in the resolution on the International Situation put to the NCLW on behalf of the Labour Party NEC by Mrs Gould. *Report of the NCLW* (1938) p. 31.

85 *ibid.*

86 Mrs Brooks (Association of Women Clerks and Secretaries), Mrs Boltz (North Lambeth WS) and Mrs Audrey Hunt (London University Labour Party), speeches to the NCLW, *Report of the NCLW* (1938) pp. 34–5.

87 Labour Party Organization Sub-committee Report, 'The Women's Department', presented at a meeting held at Transport House on 20 April 1932, labelled 'Private and Confidential'.

88 Membership and section figures given in the National Organizer's Report to the Annual Labour Party Conference. (*Labour Party Report* for 1932, p. 41; 1935, p. 40; 1939, p. 77). In 1936–7, the number of sections had risen to 1,631 but membership went even higher to 189,090.

89 Organizers' Reports, Mrs Gibbs (Yorkshire) reporting on Doncaster and the Colne Valley (Labour Party Archives, File 457).

90 Minutes of the York Women's Section. Attendance figures when they are given are between five and twenty in the years, 1932 to 1937. It became impossible for York to send delegates to the NCLW because it had no funds and no prospect of raising any.

91 Minutes of the Crook Women's Section, 4 February 1931.

92 Organizers' Reports, Mrs Gibbs (Yorkshire) reporting from Bradford on February 1935 (Labour Party Archives, File 457).

93 Organizers' Reports, Annie Townley (South West), report from Melksham, Wiltshire, dated 7 July 1937 (Labour Party Archives, File 428).

94 Mary Sutherland, editorial comment in *Labour Woman* (October 1936) p. 153.

95 Organizers' Reports, Elizabeth Andrews (Wales) forwarded the letter

from Mrs A. G. Bennett from Penydarren, dated 17 October 1937 (Labour Party Archives, File 489).

96 Organizers' Reports, Mrs Elizabeth Andrews (Wales) forwarded a letter from Mrs M. Hatto (Secretary, South Ward LP, Grangetown, Cardiff) dated 11 February 1937 asking Mary Sutherland to lower the price of *Labour Woman* because her members could not afford to buy it. Mary Sutherland replied that it was not a matter of money but an 'unwillingness to read' that accounted for the lack of sales of *Labour Woman* (Labour Party Archives, File 485).

97 Mrs Margaret Mitchell, interviewed by People's History of Tottenham on 15 May 1980. Second interview, transcript p. 14.

98 From a peak of 37 endorsed women parliamentary candidates in 1928, the number fell to 17 in 1932–3. As the number of Party committees grew, it became impossible for the 5 NEC women to be on any but a few. In April 1932, there were no women on the following committees: Finance and Trade, Re-organization of Industry, Local Government and Social Services, Agricultural Policy, Land Nationalization and Joint Committee on Party Discipline. There were 26 Labour women candidates on the slate in 1935, and of these only 2, Ellen Wilkinson and Susan Lawrence, were elected.

99 The Labour League of Youth demanded the right to elect its own representative on the NEC and to place resolutions directly onto the party agenda, just as women had done in the twenties. The Party responded by lowering the age of eligibility for the League from twenty-five to twenty-one years and refusing all claims for independent power. Teresa Gorringe from Wandsworth Central DLP, explained the attitude of the Party organizers in these words: 'Go and find out what the Labour League of Youth is doing and tell them not to.' *Labour Party Report* (1937) p. 223.

100 Reports from the NCLW and the Women's Co-operative Guild Congresses commented each year on the rising numbers of women in local government. In 1933, there were 174 Guild women on municipal councils, 29 on county councils and 134 magistrates. In 1937–8, there were 244 on municipal councils, 34 on county councils and 146 JPs. Labour women's numbers would be at least double. The NCLW in 1934 noted that after the recent LCC election, 25 per cent of the elected Labour councillors were women, *Report of the NCLW* (1934) p. 22.

101 G. D. H. Cole, *History of the Labour Party*, p. 320.

102 Mrs Margaret Mitchell, second interview transcript, p. 16.

Bibliography

MANUSCRIPT COLLECTIONS

Labour Party Archives, London, England.
  National Executive Committee Minutes
  Women's Labour League
  Standing Joint Committee of Industrial Women's Organizations
  Women Organizers' Reports, 1936–7
  National Conference of Labour Women Reports
  Local Government, 1918–22
  Local Labour Parties
  Women's Section Minutes
  Dr Marion Phillips' Papers 1930–1
  War Emergency Workers National Committee
British Library of Politics, Economics and Society (BLPES), London School
    of Economics, London, England.
  Independent Labour Party Collection
  British Birth Control Ephemera
  Labour Party Conference Reports
  Margaret Llewelyn Davies' Papers
  Women's Co-operative Guild Annual Congress Reports
  Violet Markham Collection
The Fawcett Library, London, England
  National Union of Women's Suffrage Societies
  National Union of Societies for Equal Citizenship
  Open Door Council
  National Association of Women Clerks and Secretaries
University of Hull, Hull, England
  Women's Co-operative Guild Collection
Ruskin College, Oxford
  History Workshop Collection
  Jessie Stephen, Unpublished Autobiography.
University of Sussex, England
  Mass Observation Archive
Marx Memorial Library
  National Unemployed Workers Movement Annual Reports

Maud Brown Papers
Helen Crawfurd Autobiography
Women Against War and Fascism
Communist Party Archives, London, England
   Communist Party Congress Reports
Manchester City Archives
   Annot Robinson Papers
   Manchester Women's Advisory Committee Minutes
Imperial War Museum, London, England
   The Anti-War Movement, 1914–1945
The Working-Class Movement Library, Manchester
   Bilston WCG Minutes
   ILP Conference Reports
   Lily Webb Autobiography

GOVERNMENT DOCUMENTS

Public Record Office, Kew, London, England
   Ministry of Health, Public Health Survey, 1933
   Ministry of Labour Gazette
   Ministry of Labour Files (2, 5, 10 and 34)
Tottenham Urban District Council Records, Bruce Castle, Wood Green
   Minutes of the Maternal and Child Welfare Committee
Bradford City Archives, Bradford, Yorkshire, England
   Board of Guardians Minutes

NEWSPAPERS AND JOURNALS

Barking Echo, Mail and Chronicle, 1921–5
Bradford Pioneer, 1921–6, 1929–32
Bristol Forward, June 1916
Chatham Rochester and Gillingham Observer, 1920, 1923, 1926, 1931
Daily Herald, 1917–38
Daily Worker, 1930–6
Labour Woman, 1911–38
London Citizen, 1921–3
The New Leader, 1917–6
The Northern Voice, 1925–6
Tottenham and Edmonton Weekly Herald, 1924–6
Woman, 1937–9
The Woman's Dreadnought, 1914–16
The Workers' Dreadnought, 1917–19
The Woman's Leader and the Common Cause, 1925, 1932
The Woman Teacher, 1921–6
Woman Worker, 1919, 1926, 1927, 1929

BOOKS AND DISSERTATIONS

Adam, Ruth. *A Woman's Place*. London: Chatto & Windus, 1975

Andrews, Irene. *Economic Effects of the War on Women and Children in Great Britain*. 2nd edn New York: Oxford University Press, 1921

Bagwell, Phillip. *The Railwaymen: a History of the National Union of Railwaymen*. London: George, Allen and Unwin, 1963

Banks, Olive. *Faces of Feminism*. New York: St. Martins Press, 1981
 Becoming a Feminist: the Social Origins of the First Wave of Feminism. London: Wheatsheaf Books, 1986

Bealey, Frank, Blondel, J. and McCann, W. P. *Constituency Politics: A Study of Newcastle-under-Lyme*. London: Faber and Faber, 1965

Belsey, James. *The Forgotten Front: Bristol At War 1914–18*. Bristol: Redcliffe Press, 1986

Berry, David. *A Sociology of Grass Roots Politics*. London: Macmillan, 1970

Black, Naomi. *Social Feminism*. New York: Cornell University Press, 1989

Blainey, J. *The Woman Worker and Restrictive Legislation*. London: Arrowsmith, 1928

Bondfield, Margaret. *A Life's Work*. London: Hutchinson, 1948

Bornat, Joanna. 'An Examination of the General Union of Textile Workers, 1883–1922'. Ph.D. dissertation, University of Essex, 1981

Boughton, John. 'Working Class Politics in Birmingham and Sheffield 1918–1931'. Ph.D. dissertation, University of Warwick, 1985

Brailsford, H. N. *Socialism for Today*. London: ILP Publications, 1925

Branson, Noreen. *Poplarism, 1919–1925*. London: Lawrence and Wishart, 1979
 Britain in the Nineteen Twenties. Minneapolis: University of Minnesota Press, 1976

Branson, Noreen and Heinemann, Margot. *Britain in the Nineteen Thirties*. New York: Praeger, 1971

Braybon, Gail. *Women Workers in the First World War*. London: Croom Helm, 1981

Brooks, Barbara. 'Abortion in England 1919–1939', Ph.D. dissertation, Bryn Mawr College, 1981: Printed by University Microfilms International, 1987

Bruce, M. *The Coming of the Welfare State*. London: Batsford, 1961

Bruley, Susan. 'Socialism and Feminism Among Women in the Communist Party, 1920–1939'. Ph.D. dissertation, University of London: Senate House, 1980

Buhl, Mary Jo. *Women and American Socialism 1870–1920*. Illinois: University of Illinois Press, 1981

Burke, Catherine. 'Working-Class Politics in Sheffield 1900–1920 and Regional History of the Labour Party'. Ph.D. dissertation, Sheffield City Polytechnic, 1983

Bush, Julia. *Behind the Lines: East London Labour, 1914–19*. London: Merlin Press, 1984

Bussey, G. and Tims, M. *Pioneers for Peace: The Women's International League for Peace and Freedom, 1915–1965*. Oxford: Alden Press, 1980

Campbell, Beatrix. *The Iron Ladies: Why do Women Vote Tory?* London: Virago Press, 1987

Carberry, Thomas. *Consumers in Politics: A History and General Review of the Co-operative Party*. New York: Augustus M. Kelley, 1969

Chew, Doris Nield. *Ada Nield Chew: The Life and Writings of a Working Woman*. London: Virago Press, 1977

Cole, G. D. H. *The History of the Labour Party from 1914*. New York: Augustus M. Kelley, 1969

Collett, Christine. '"At Least She Was No Lady"; a Preliminary Assessment of the Feminist Contribution to Socialism and Labour Representation in Great Britain, 1890–1910'. MA thesis, Oxford: Ruskin College, 1982

Cook, Chris and Peele, Gillian. *The Politics of Reappraisal 1918–1939*. London: Macmillan Press, 1975

Cook, Chris and Stevenson, John. *The Slump, Society and Politics During the Depression*. London: Jonathan Cape, 1977

Cott, Nancy. *The Grounding of Modern Feminism*. New Haven: Yale University Press, 1987

Cronin, James E. and Schneer, Jonathan eds. *Social Conflict and the Political Order in Modern Britain*. New York: Rutgers University Press 1982

Cross, Colin. *Phillip Snowden*. London: Barrie & Rockliff, 1966

Dangerfield, G. *The Strange Death of Liberal England*. New York: Putnam, 1961

Davies, Margaret Llewelyn ed. *Life As We Have Known It*. New York: The Norton Library, 1975. First published by the Hogarth Press, 1931
Maternity: Letters from Working Women Collected by the Women's Co-operative Guild, reprinted London: Virago Press, 1979

Dowse, R. E. *Left in the Centre*. London: Routledge, Kegan & Paul, 1962

Drake, Barbara. *Women in Trade Unions*. London: Virago, 1984 (first published in 1920 by the Labour Research Department)

Englander, David. *Landlord and Tenant in Urban Britain, 1838–1918*. Oxford University Press, 1983

Ford, Isabella. *Women and Socialism*. London: Independent Labour Party Press, 1904

Fowler, Alan and Lesley. *The History of the Nelson Weavers' Association*. Manchester: Free Press, no date

Fox, R. M. *Smoky Crusade*. London: Hogarth Press, 1937

Frow, Edmund and Ruth. *To Make That Future Now: A History of the Manchester and Salford Trades Council*. Manchester: E. J. Morten, 1976
The Communist Party in Manchester 1920–1926. Manchester: North West History Group, CPGB, in conjunction with the Working-Class Movement Library, Manchester, n.d.

Fryer, Peter. *The Birth Controllers*. New York: Stein & Day, 1966

Fryth, Jim ed. *Britain, Fascism and the Popular Front*. London: Lawrence and Wishart, 1985

Gaffin, Jean and Thoms, David. *Caring and Sharing: The Centenary History of the Women's Co-operative Guild*. Manchester: Co-operative Union Limited, 1983

Gilbert, B. *British Social Policy*. London: Batsford, 1970

Glucksmann, M. *Women Assemble: Women Workers and the New Industries in Inter-war Britain*. London: Routledge, 1990

Graves, Robert and Hodge, Alan. *The Long Weekend: A Social History of Great Britain, 1918–1939*. New York: The Norton Library, 1963. First published 1940

Greenwald, Maurine. *Women, War and Work: The Impact of World War I on Women Workers in the US* Westport, Connecticut: Greenwood Press, 1980.

Greenwood, Walter. *Love on the Dole*. Harmondsworth: Penguin Books, 1976. First published 1933

Hall, Ruth, ed. *Dear Dr Stopes*. London: Penguin Books, 1981

Halsey, A. H. ed. *Trends in British Society since 1900*. London: Macmillan, 1972

Hampton, William. *Democracy and Community: A Study of Politics in Sheffield*. London: Oxford University Press, 1970

Hannington, Wal. *Ten Lean Years*. London: Victor Gollancz Ltd., 1940 *Unemployed Struggles, 1919–1936*. London: Lawrence and Wishart, 1977. First published 1936

Hardie, Kier. *The ILP After Twenty Years*. London: Independent Labour Party Press, 1912

Harrison, Brian. *Prudent Revolutionaries*. Oxford: Clarendon Press, 1987

Higonnet, Margaret R., Jenson, June, Michel, Sonya and Weitz, Margaret C. eds. *Behind the Lines: Gender and the Two World Wars*. New Haven: Yale University Press, 1987

Hinton, James. *Labour and Socialism: A History of the British Labour Movement, 1867–1972*. Brighton: Wheatsheaf Books, 1983

Hoggart, Richard. *The Uses of Literacy*. London: Pelican Books, 1958

Hogue, Richard, ed., *British Labour Speaks*. New York: Boni & Liveright, 1924

Hollis, Pat. *Ladies Elect: Women in English Local Government, 1865–1914*. Oxford: Clarendon Press, 1987

Holtby, Winifred. *Women in a Changing Civilization*. Chicago: Cassandra Editions, 1978. First published London: Bodley Head, 1934

Howell, David. *British Workers and the ILP, 1888–1906*. Manchester University Press, 1983

Hutchins, B. L. *Women in Modern Industry*. London: Bell & Sons, 1915

Hutchins, B. L. and Harrison, A. *A History of Factory Legislation*. London: King, 1926

Janosik, E. G. *Constituency Labour Parties in Britain*. New York: Praeger, 1968

Jenson, J. M. and Scharf, L. eds. *Decades of Discontent: The Women's Movement in the US 1920–40.* Westport, Connecticut: Greenwood Press, 1983

Jones, G. W. *Borough Politics: A Study of the Wolverhampton Town Council 1888–1964.* London: Macmillan & Co., 1969

Kingsford, Peter. *The Hunger Marchers in Britain, 1920–40.* London: Lawrence and Wishart, 1982

Lewenhak, Shiela. *Women and Trade Unions.* London: Ernest Benn Ltd., 1977

Lewis, Jane. *Women in England, 1870–1950.* Bloomington: Indiana University Press, 1984

  The Politics of Motherhood. London: Croom Helm, 1980

Liddington, Jill. *The Long Road to Greenham: Feminism and Anti-Militarism in Britain since 1820.* London: Virago Press, 1989

  The Life and Times of a Respectable Rebel: Selina Cooper 1864–1946. London: Virago Press, 1984

Liddington, Jill and Norris, Jill. *Ond Hand Tied Behind Us: The Rise of the Women's Suffrage Movement.* London: Virago Press, 1978

Lynch, A. J. *Autobiography.* Ann Arbor: Microfilms, 1955

Marwick, Arthur. *The Deluge: British Society and the First World War.* London: The Norton Library, 1970

McMillan, Margaret. *A Life of Rachel McMillan.* London: J. M. Dent, 1927

Middleton, Lucy. ed. *Women in the Labour Movement.* London: Croom Helm, 1977

Miliband, Ralph. *Parliamentary Socialism.* London: Merlin Press, 2nd edn, 1975

Mitchell, David. *The Fighting Pankhursts.* London: Jonathan Cape, 1967

Mitchell, Geoffrey, ed. *The Hard Way Up: The Autobiography of Hannah Mitchell, Suffragette and Rebel.* London: Virago Press, 1977

Morgan, K. O. *Labour People.* Oxford University Press, 1987

Mowat, Charles Loch. *Britain Between the Wars 1918–1940.* University of Chicago Press, 1955

Pankhurst, E. S. *The Home Front.* London: Hutchinson, 1932

  The Suffragette Movement. London: Longmans, 1931

Phillips, Marion. ed. *Women and the Labour Party.* London: Headley Bros., [1918]

Piratin, Phil. *Our Flag Stays Red.* London: Lawrence and Wishart, 2nd edn, 1980. First published 1948

Pollard, S. *A History of Labour in Sheffield.* Liverpool University Press, 1957

Pugh, Martin. *The Making of Modern British Politics, 1867–1936.* New York: St Martin's Press, 1982

  Electoral Reform in War and Peace, 1906–1918. London: Routledge and Kegan, 1978

Raeburn, A. *The Militant Suffragettes.* London: Michael Joseph, 1937

Rathbone, Eleanor. *The Disinherited Family: A Plea for the Endowment of the Family.* London: E. Arnold & Co., 1924

Rendell, Jane. ed. *Equal or Different: Women's Politics 1800–1914.* Oxford: Basil Blackwell, 1987

Rice, Margery Spring. *Working Class Wives.* London: Virago Press, 1981. First published 1939

Roberts, Elizabeth. *A Woman's Place.* New York: Basil Blackwood, 1984

Roberts, Robert. *The Classic Slum.* Manchester: Pelican Books, 1973

Rowbotham, Sheila. *A New World For Women: Stella Browne Socialist Feminist.* London: Pluto Press, 1977

Russell, Dora. *The Tamarisk Tree.* London: Virago Press, Vol. 1, 1977; Vol. 2, 1981

Scott, Joan W. *Gender and the Politics of History.* New York: Columbia University Press, 1988

Sharp, Evelyn. *Buyers and Builders: A Jubilee Sketch of the WCG, 1883–1933.* Manchester, Co-operative Union, 1935

Sheridan, Dorothy, ed. *Wartime Women: A Mass Observation Anthology.* London: Heinemann Press, 1990

Smith, Harold. ed. *British Feminism in the Twentieth Century.* London: Elgar Press, 1990

Snowden, Ethel. *The Real Women's Party.* London: Independent Labour Party Press, 1918

Sowerwine, Charles. *Sisters or Citizens? Women and Socialism in France Since 1876.* Cambridge University Press, 1982

Spender, Dale. *Time and Tide Wait For No Man.* London: Pandora Press, 1984

Strachey, Ray. *The Cause: A Short History of the Women's Movement in Great Britain.* London: Virago Press, 1978. First published 1928

Swanwick, Helena. *The War in Its Effects Upon Women.* London: 1917.

Swindells, J. and Jardine, L. *What's Left: Women in Culture and the Labour Movement.* London: Routledge, 1990

Thane, Pat. *The Foundations of the Welfare State, Social Policy in Modern Britain.* London: Longman Press, 1982

Thompson, Dorothy. *The Chartists: Popular Politics in the Industrial Revolution.* New York: Pantheon Books, 1984

Vernon, Betty D. *Ellen Wilkinson.* London: Croom Helm, 1982

Ward, Linda. 'The Right to Choose: A Study of Women's Fight for Birth Control Provisions'. Ph.D. dissertation University of Bristol, 1981

Webb, Beatrice. *Diaries.* Vols. 1–4. London: Virago Press, 1986

Weeks, Jeffrey. *Sex, Politics and Society: The Regulation of Sexuality since 1800.* London: Longman Group, 1981

Weller, Ken. *'Don't Be a Soldier!' The Radical Anti-War Movement in North London.* London and New York: Journeyman Press, London History Workshop Centre, 1985

White, C. *Women's Magazines.* London: Michael Joseph, 1970

Wilson, E. *Women and the Welfare State* London: Tavistock, 1978

Young, James D. *Women and Popular Struggle: A History of British Working Class Women, 1560–1984.* Edinburgh: Mainstream Publishing, 1985

ARTICLES

Bailey, Sarah. 'The War and Women's Suffrage'. *Fortnightly Review* Vol. 1 New Series (July 1917)

Barnes, Annie. 'The Unmarried Mother and her Child'. *Contemporary Review* 112 (July 1917)

Brookes, Barbara. 'Women and Reproduction, 1860–1939' in Lewis, Jane ed. *Labour and Love: Women's Experience of Home and Family 1850–1940*. Oxford: Basil Blackwell, 1986

Davin, Anna. 'Imperialism and Motherhood'. *History Workshop Journal* 5 (Spring 1978)

Greenwald, Maurine. 'Working-Class Feminism and the Family Wage Ideal: The Seattle Debate on Married Women's Right to Work, 1914–1920'. *The Journal of American History.* 76: 1 (June 1989)

Harrison, Brian. 'Class and Gender in Modern British Labour History'. *Past and Present*, 124 (August 1989)

Harrison, Royden. 'The War Emergency Workers National Committee, 1914–1920' in Briggs, A. and Saville, J. *Essays in Labour History 1918–1939*. London: Croom Helm, 1977

Hart, Nicki. 'Gender and the Rise and Fall of Class Politics'. *New Left Review*, 175 (September 1989)

Hart, Vivien. 'Defining the Alternatives: Class and Gender in Minimum Wage Policy'. Sixth Berkshire Conference on the History of Women. (June 1984)

Heim, Carol. 'Uneven Regional Development in Inter-war Britain'. *Journal of Economic History*, 43: 1 (March 1983)

Hunt, Karen. 'Women in the Social Democratic Federation'. *North West Labour History Bulletin*, 7 (1980–1) 54

Kent, Susan Kingsley. 'The Politics of Sexual Difference. World War I and the Demise of British Feminism'. *Journal of British Studies* 27: 3 (July 1988)

Kessler Harris. 'Problems of Coalition Building; Women and Trade Unions in the Nineteen Twenties' in Milkman, Ruth. ed. *Women, Work and Protest: A Century of US Women's Labour History*. Boston: Routledge & Kegan Paul, 1985

Lewis, Jane. 'In Search of Real Equality: Women Between the Wars' in Gloversmith, Frank. *Class, Culture and Social Change: A New View of the Nineteen Thirties*. Brighton: Harvester Press, 1980

Malos, Ellen. 'Bristol Women in Action: The Right to Vote and the Need to Earn a Living' in Bristol Broadsides ed. *Bristol's Other History*. Bristol: Bristol Broadsides Co-op. Ltd., 1984

Martin, Anna. 'The Mother and Social Reform'. *The Nineteenth Century and After.* 73 (May 1913)

Rowan, Caroline. 'Women in the Labour Party, 1906–1920'. *Feminist Review.* 12 (Spring 1982)

Pederson, Susan. 'The Failure of Feminism in the Making of the British Welfare State'. *Radical History Review*. 43 (Winter 1989) 88–98

Samuel, Raphael. 'The Middle Class Between the Wars'. *New Socialist* 10 (March/April, 1983)

Smith, Harold. 'The Issue of Equal Pay for Equal Work in Great Britain, 1914–1918'. *Societas*, 8: 1 (Winter 1978)

'Sex versus Class: British Feminists and the Labour Movement, 1919–1929'. *The Historian* 8 (December 1985)

Stacy, Enid. 'A Century of Women's Rights' in Carpenter, E. ed. *Forecasts of the Coming Century*. Manchester: The Labour Press, 1987

Index